D0964981

Holistic Guide *for a* Healthy Dog

WENDY VOLHARD

KERRY BROWN, D.V.M.

HOWELL
BOOK
HOUSE

Howell Book House
Hungry Minds, Inc.
909 Third Avenue
New York, NY 10022

Copyright © 2000 by Wendy Volhard and Kerry L. Brown

All rights reserved. No part of this book shall be reproduced or transmitted in any form or by any means, electronic, mechanical, photocopying, recording, or otherwise without written permission from the publisher. No patent liability is assumed with respect to the use of the information contained herein. Although every precaution has been taken in preparation of this book, the publisher and authors assume no responsibility for errors or omissions. Neither is any liability assumed for damages resulting from the use of the information contained herein. For information, address Hungry Minds, Inc., Howell Book House, 909 Third Avenue, New York, NY 10022.

Howell Book House is a registered trademark of Hungry Minds, Inc.

For general information on Hungry Minds books in the U.S., please call our Consumer Customer Service department at 800-762-2974. In Canada, please call (800) 667-1115. For reseller information, including discounts and premium sales, please call our Reseller Customer Service department at 800-434-3422.

ISBN 1-58245-153-2

Manufactured in the United States of America
10 9 8 7 6 5

Holistic Guide *for a* Healthy Dog

About
the Authors

WENDY VOLHARD

Wendy Volhard developed the Natural Diet in 1973 after her first Landseer Newfoundland, Heidi, was given only a few months to live at the age of 6. Once on the Natural Diet, Heidi lived to the ripe old age of 12. Since then, countless dog owners have followed Wendy's Natural Diet to enhance the health, longevity and quality of life of their dogs.

Wendy Volhard

Wendy specializes in the influence of health and nutrition on behavior and complementary sources of health care, such as acupuncture, chiropractic and homeopathy. A respected consultant to breeders, dog owners and veterinarians, she is also an internationally recognized lecturer. For the past 30 years, through her training classes, lectures, weekend seminars, five-day Holistic and Training Camps, Wendy Volhard has taught more than 20,000 dog owners how to achieve a mutually rewarding relationship with their pets. Wendy gives seminars in the United States, Canada, and the United Kingdom on behavior, instructing, training, health and nutrition and its effects on behavior, and conducts an annual five-day Holistic Camp together with Kerry Brown, D.V.M. and Sue Ann Lesser, D.V.M., as well as two five-day Training Camps. Time permitting, Wendy does a limited number of private consultations.

Wendy Volhard is a true practitioner, who has bred, raised and trained Landseer Newfoundlands for over 25 years, as well as a Briard, a German Shepherd Dog, a Labrador Retriever, Standard Wirehaired Dachshunds and

Yorkshire Terriers. Wendy shares her home in upstate New York with her husband of 35 years, six dogs and three cats. Together with her husband, Jack, Wendy has earned over 50 conformation, obedience and working titles with her dogs.

Wendy has developed the most widely used system for evaluating puppies for the right home and task, and a Personality Profile for dogs to help owners understand why their pets do what they do.

She is the co-author of four books including *The Complete Idiots Guide to a Well-Trained Dog* (Alpha Books, 1999), and co-producer of four video tapes. She is the recipient of four awards from the Dog Writers' Association of America.

. Wendy Volhard has served different dog organizations in a variety of capacities; is an honorary member of the United Kingdom Registry of Behaviour Consultants, a member of the Newfoundland Club of America, the Dachshund Club of America and other dog organizations, and a regular contributor to the *AKC Gazette*.

KERRY L. BROWN

Dr. Kerry Brown was graduated from Cornell College of Veterinary Medicine in 1973. He spent four years in a large and small animal practice before opening his own hospital, Village Veterinary Hospital, in 1977.

Dr. Brown's hospital has grown from a one-man practice to a facility with nine veterinarians, all with special interests in both large and small animals. It is one of the most highly regarded veterinary hospitals in central New York and offers clientele and patients the most up-to-date diagnostics and therapies in veterinary medicine in different fields.

Dr. Brown has developed areas of expertise in surgery (both soft tissue

Kerry L. Brown, D.V.M.

injuries and orthopedics) and internal medicine, as well as in acupuncture, nutrition and reproduction. He is a certified acupuncturist, accredited by the International Veterinary Acupuncture Society.

Kerry Brown shares his home with his wife, Nickie, their two children, Eric and Alicia, and many family pets. He loves fishing, especially on Lake Ontario, for salmon and steelhead.

Kerry has a long-standing devotion of 22 years to the Lions Club of New York State and Bermuda, working with the visually and hearing impaired, drug and alcohol abuse programs, and self-esteem youth programs.

Because of the workload at his veterinary hospital, appointments with Dr. Brown (the only holistic veterinarian on staff) have to be made several months ahead of time.

Kerry and Wendy began working together on the clinical trials of the Natural Diet in 1974. Since then, they have joined forces to investigate and search for ways to improve the health of companion animals through the use of complementary therapies. Together they conduct the Holistic Camps, which bring together experts in various fields of complementary medicine to educate veterinarians, veterinary technicians, breeders and laymen alike, in raising, training and working with dogs.

Contents

PART 1:
Your Dog's Diet & Health   1

This book is not intended as a substitute for medical advice of veterinarians. The reader should regularly consult a veterinarian in matters relating to his or her dog's health and particularly in respect of any symptoms which may require diagnosis or medical attention.

Acknowledgments

We want to thank our respective families, clients and students for their contributions and support. We are especially indebted to Diane Leadley, who helped type some of the medical text, Brigitte Volhard, for the photographs and Karen Schlipf, who has done such a wonderful job with drawings, photographs and charts. A very special note of gratitude to:

Sue Ann Lesser, D.V.M., CAC, for writing the chiropractic section.

Dr. Ron Schultz, Professor and Chair of the Pathobiological Sciences, University of Wisconsin Veterinary School, for the use of the Nomograph Charts.

Lucie Paradis, D.V.M., who supplied information on the use of homeopathics and vaccines.

I (Wendy) want to thank Scott Pollak of PHD and Robert Symons, who were instrumental in helping me develop the Natural Diet Foundation—the dehydrated version of the Natural Diet. I also want to thank Christine Duval, Roger and Joan Greenwald, and Jane Kelso who bred the dogs that I have. These dogs have been my teachers. Thanks to Andy Butler and Bill Phelps for taking such good care of my dogs while I was working on this project.

Many students and friends helped with photographs and stories of their dogs. Our thanks to Joanne Scott, Donna Kinsman, Jody Baker, Jim Chasherek, Mary Ann

Heidi, who started the journey.

Rombold, Herb Cassini, Jeanine Dunn, Pinny Wendell, Bethanne Elion, Marcia Majors and Joel Kmetz, Bill Phelps and Kathy Guerra.

Jack Volhard whipped both of us into shape, and without his help, his vision and organizational skills, this second edition would not have been presented in such a clear and concise fashion. Sincere thanks from both of us.

Finally, there is Heidi, the dog that started it all.

Preface

Our dogs are in trouble. Life spans are getting shorter and disease states are becoming more prevalent; unless something changes, the future looks bleak indeed. Four reasons contribute to this trend:

- *Breed selection* has progressed from function (the ability to perfom the job for which the dog was bred) to form (appearance) and is producing genetically weak individuals subject to debilitating diseases and a poor quality of life.

- Environmentally created *stress* on the animal's immune system, principally the result of pollution, has further reduced the dog's vital forces.

- A rising number of *vaccinations*, from two in the first 6 months of life in the early 1970s, up to as many as 45 today, has added to the attack on a puppy's immature immune system.

- *Diet* that is insufficient to meet the nutritional needs of the dog have contributed to an inability of the immune system to ward off and cope with disease. A frightening increase in autoimmune diseases and a virtual epidemic of cancer have been the result.

This book addresses what you can do about your dog's health, longevity and quality of life. In each of the three parts, we discuss different aspects of helping your dog. The material is presented in such a way so as to give you options that fit into your lifestyle and comfort zone.

Part One, "Your Dog's Diet & Health," deals with nutrition and health, and focuses on the facts that have led us to our conclusions. After years of being effectively ignored, the influence nutrition has on health and behavior is finally being recognized. Did you know that the most common causes for allergies are nutritional deficiencies? More serious and sometimes life-threatening diseases can also be caused and corrected by diet. Your pet's behavior is also affected by what you feed him. Depending on the seriousness of the condition, improvement may be achieved simply by selecting a commercial dog food that is right for *your* dog and adding a few supplements. Other options range from adding some raw ingredients to completely making your own dog food. None of the options included in this book are based on guesswork or speculation, but have undergone rigorous clinical testing for almost 30 years.

Part Two, "Medicine, Tests, Therapies & Your Dog," explores standard and complementary diagnostic and treatment modalities. We also tackle the controversial subject of vaccinations, which is finally getting the attention it deserves. For years we have maintained that more is not better, and that the onslaught of multiple vaccinations weakens rather than strengthens a puppy's immune system, and has resulted in a multiplicity of disease states. Here, too, we provide you with the information you need to make an intelligent decision about what is best for your dog and is compatible with your comfort zone.

The chapter on Thyroid and Adrenal glands, out of necessity, is admittedly technical. Thyroid disease is becoming more prevalent in dogs. Behavioral changes, such as aggression, are frequently thyroid-related. We have included this information because recognizing the symptoms is becoming increasingly important. It is estimated that the majority of dogs today show clinical signs of thyroid dysfunction, which is not picked up on routine blood tests.

Kinesiology or muscle testing, a standard technique among homeopathic veterinarians, is a diagnostic tool gaining in popularity among conventional veterinarians. We introduce you to this concept and almost anyone can learn to use it. When we teach kinesiology at our seminars and Camps, our favorite human subjects are the skeptics (the dogs never have a problem accepting it).

Homeopathy has been around for 200 years and is used extensively in Europe, by both conventional and holistic physicians. It is gaining in acceptance, and provides invaluable therapies for chronic and acute physical conditions, as well as behavioral abnormalities. We have provided you with a practical list of remedies and the conditions for which they are used.

Chiropractic adjustment of dogs has become a regular part of maintaining their good health. Although you can't do it yourself, we have included this chapter to make you aware of its benefits.

We know there are no panaceas and that no one modality will work every time. While our preference lies with a holistic approach, we are also realistic and use conventional treatments, including antibiotics and steroids when necessary—whatever works for the dog but keep in mind that all dogs are individuals.

In Part Three, "The Five-Element Theory," we introduce you to the Five-Element Theory, an integral part of traditional Chinese medicine, and a powerful diagnostic and healing concept. The Five-Element Theory divides the year into its four seasons: spring, summer, fall and winter. By looking at the calendar, you will be able to predict with uncanny accuracy your dog's behavior and his health needs.

Acupuncture is one of the mainstays of traditional Chinese medicine, but beyond the scope of this book. Even so, you can use it without the needles and we have included the acupressure points for more common ailments. While acupressure is not the same as the real thing, it is almost as effective and best of all, you can do it yourself.

Lastly, we don't want to be accused of being politically incorrect. Throughout this book we refer to the dog as "he" as a matter of convenience. The "he or she", "him or her" format is awkward and we don't like "s/he". We prefer the colloquial—dogs are "he" and cats are "she." We also refer to the dog as a "dog" and not as a "nonhuman animal companion."

Part 1

Your Dog's Diet & Health

1 Diet, Allergies & Health

FOOD—WHAT DIFFERENCE DOES IT MAKE?

Your dog's behavior, happiness, health, longevity and overall well-being are inextricably intertwined with what you feed him. Dogs, just like everyone else, have specific nutritional needs. And, to complicate matters, the needs of individual dogs vary. For example, even though your first dog may have done wonderfully well on Barfo Special Blend, it may be completely wrong for the dog you have now. We are not trying to turn you into an expert on canine nutrition, but you do need to know some basic concepts.

The most common and most visible symptoms of nutritionally caused deficiencies are allergies of one kind or another. In his best-selling book, *Pet Allergies: Remedies for an Epidemic*, Alfred Plechner, D.V.M., paints a dismal picture for the future of our pets.

> *Because many commercial foods are woefully deficient in key nutrients, the long-term effect of feeding such foods makes the dog hypersensitive to its environment. …[I]t's a dinosaur effect. Animals are being programmed for disaster, for extinction. Many of them are biochemical cripples with defective adrenal glands unable to manufacture adequate cortisol, a hormone vital for health and resistance to disease.*

Allergies can be, and often are, unrecognized deficiency diseases. Recognizing nutritional deficiencies will save you a great deal of frustration and allow you to make the necessary adjustments in your dog's diet.

The proper diet will ensure that your dog looks and feels his best.

CHOOSING THE RIGHT FOOD

Not all dog foods are alike and there are enormous quality differences. The cliché "garbage in, garbage out" applies with terrifying validity. There are so many choices available today that trying to make an informed decision can become an overwhelming task. We are going to tackle the job by the process of elimination. Three commonly used criteria immediately come to mind: advertising, ingredients and price.

- Forget about what the ad says about how good their brand of food is. You have to look at what's in it.

- Forget about price. This works both ways. Just because it costs more doesn't necessarily mean it's better than a less expensive variety.

Following is a quick checklist to determine if your dog is getting what he needs:

- He doesn't want to eat the food.

- He has large, voluminous stools that smell awful.

- He has gas.

- His teeth get dirty and brown.

- His breath smells.

- He burps a lot.

- He constantly sheds.

- He has a dull coat.

- He smells like a dog.

- He is prone to ear and skin infections.

- He has no energy or is hyperactive.

- He picks up fleas easily.

- He picks up worms easily and has to be wormed frequently.

- He frequently gets infections and his immune system becomes impaired.

All of these can happen with any dog, but only occasionally. When one or more of them occur frequently, or continuously, it's time to find out why.

A CARNIVORE NEEDS MEAT

Your dog is a carnivore, not a vegetarian. He needs meat. Unlike a human's, his teeth are made for ripping and tearing meat—they do not have flat surfaces for grinding up grains; his digestive process begins in his stomach, not in his mouth; all of the enzymes in his system are geared toward breaking down meat and raw foods. Clearly, there can be no doubt: Your dog is a carnivore.

Your dog's body is made up of cells, a lot of them. Each cell needs 45 nutrients to function properly. Cells need:

- Protein, consisting of 9 to 12 essential amino acids

- Carbohydrates

- Fat

- Vitamins

- Minerals

- Water

All of these nutrients need to be in the correct proportion for the necessary chemical reactions of digestion, absorption, transportation and elimination to occur. If the cells are going to continue to live, the exact composition of the body fluids that bathe the outside of the cells needs to be controlled from moment to moment, day to day, with no more than a few percentage points of variation. When these nutrients are not provided, cells die, and this contributes to premature aging.

These nutrients are the fuel, which converts into energy. Energy produces heat and how much heat is produced determines the ability of your dog to control his body temperature, critical to a healthy life. Everything your dog does, from running and playing, to working, and living a long and healthy life, is determined by the fuel you provide and the energy it produces.

The term *calorie* is used to indicate the amount of energy in food. The food you feed your dog must provide sufficient calories so his body can:

- Produce energy to grow correctly.

- Maintain health during adulthood.

- Reproduce.

- Live to enjoy a quality old age.

A DOG'S STAFF OF LIFE—PROTEIN

Dog food packages tell you how much protein is in the food. Protein content is important, but even more important is its source.

The manufacturer chooses the kind of protein to put into the food. Generally, the percentage of protein in the food is a combination of proteins found in less expensive plants or grains, such as corn, wheat, soy, or rice, plus a more expensive animal protein, such as chicken, beef, or lamb.

By law, the ingredient in the greatest quantity is listed first. By looking at the list of ingredients on the package, you can easily see the origin of the protein in the food. For example, if the first five ingredients consist of four grains, it tells you that the majority of the protein in that food comes from grains. The more grains in dog food, the cheaper it is to produce.

We wonder what your dog thinks of such food.

ANIMAL PROTEIN DEFICIENCIES

When your dog does not get enough animal protein as part of his diet, or there is an imbalance of his nutrients, one or more of the following may occur:

- Chronic skin and/or ear infections

- Compromised reproductive system, heart, kidney, liver, bladder, thyroid and adrenal glands

- Epilepsy or some kinds of cancers
- Spinning or tail chasing
- Aggression
- Timidity
- Lack of pigmentation
- Excessive shedding
- Crooked whiskers
- Gastrointestinal upsets, vomiting or diarrhea
- Poor appetite
- Impaired ability to heal from wounds or surgery
- Weakened immune system that cannot handle vaccines and may even contract the disease

This is only a short list of the more common symptoms associated with protein deficiency.

It has been our experience that the majority of the working breeds, sporting breeds, toys and terriers need extra animal protein in their diets. Dogs that lead a couch-potato existence can survive on food with more plant than animal protein.

AMINO ACIDS

One more thing you need to know about protein—amino acids are the building blocks of protein. When they are heated they are partially destroyed. All dry and canned commercial dog food is heated in the manufacturing process. So, commercial food contains protein that is somewhat deficient or destroyed through heating. To compensate for this loss, besides meat, you need to include an amino acid complex tablet in your dog's diet.

THE CRITICAL TIME OF GROWTH

During the first 7 months of your dog's life, he will increase his birth weight anywhere from 15 to 40 times, depending upon his breed. By 1 year of age, his birth weight will increase 60 times and his skeletal development will be almost

It is essential to feed your dog the best diet for his stage of life.

complete. For everything to go well, he needs the right food. He also needs double the amount of food as an adult dog needs while he is growing, especially during growth spurts. Nutritional deficiencies now, even for short periods, can cause problems later on.

The most critical period for a puppy is between 4 and 7 months—the time of maximum growth. His little body is being severely stressed as his baby teeth drop out and his adult teeth come in. He is growing like a weed, and at the same time his body is being assaulted with vaccines, exposure to new viruses and parasites. The right food is critical at this time to ensure that his immune system can cope with all these demands and onslaughts.

To find out how you can protect him as much as possible, you need to take a look at several different dog foods to determine which ones will best meet the criteria for your young dog's growth.

PUPPY FOODS & READING THE LABELS

Many dog food manufacturers make food for different life stages of the dog, and packages are clearly labeled. Puppy foods do contain more protein than adult or maintenance foods. Manufacturers know that puppies need more protein during growth and many of these foods provide up to 33% protein. Still, you need to know the source of the protein, that is, animal or plant.

What you are looking for is a puppy food that has two animal proteins in the first three ingredients, or better yet, one that lists animal protein as its first two ingredients. Avoid foods that do not meet these criteria.

CARBOHYDRATES—SPARINGLY, PLEASE!

Once you have selected a food on the basis of its protein percentage, your job isn't quite done. You have to check a few other items.

Your dog also needs carbohydrates. He doesn't need many carbohydrates to be healthy, but he does require some grains and vegetables for energy, proper diges-tion, stool formation and the correct functioning of the thyroid gland.

Oats, wheat, barley and brown rice are whole grains that contain a lot of vita-mins and minerals as well as protein and fat. Corn is a popular grain found in commercial dog foods primarily because of its price. Soy is another carbohydrate that is found in some foods. Soy admittedly is high in protein, but it binds up other nutrients and makes them unavailable for absorption. Stay away from dog foods that contain soy—it's best fed to those animals that have four stomachs or birds with gizzards to digest it.

Carbohydrates have to be broken down for a dog to be able to digest them. Dog food companies use a heat process to do this and therein lies the problem. The heat process destroys many of the vitamins and minerals contained in grains.

A question that comes immediately to mind is, "Where do dogs in the wild get the grains and vegetables they need?" The answer is, from the intestines of their prey, all neatly predigested, and the dog can utilize them.

A diet low in carbohydrates and high in protein is an ideal diet for your dog. Diets high in carbohydrates take a long time to digest, produce voluminous, smelly stools and gas. They also build up tartar on your dog's teeth, making his gums sore and his breath smell.

NOT ALL FATS ARE CREATED EQUAL

Fat is either saturated or polyunsaturated and your dog needs both. Together these fats supply the essential fatty acids (EFAs) necessary to maintain a dog's good health. Saturated fat comes from animal sources and is used for energy. For dogs that get a great deal of exercise or participate in competitive events, the food has to be high in animal (saturated) fat.

Dogs do not suffer from heart disease caused by higher levels of animal fat, or from fatty deposits in blood vessels. However, moderation is the key. The diet needs to have some animal fat but not too much, and anything between 15% to 18% is okay.

Not enough animal fat in the diet can create:

- Lack of energy

- Heart problems

- Growth deficits

- Dry skin

- Cell damage

Too much animal fat in the diet creates:

- Obesity

- Some kinds of cancer

Polyunsaturated fat comes from vegetable sources, such as flax seed oil, safflower oil, wheat germ oil, olive oil and corn oil. Your dog needs polyunsaturated fat for healthy skin and coat. If your dog has a dry coat, you may need to add some oil to his food.

Linoleic acid is one of the three essential fatty acids found in polyunsaturated fats that has to be provided daily in your dog's food. Cold-pressed safflower and flax seed oil provide the best source of linoleic acid and are the least allergenic. They are better than corn oil that contains only a tiny amount of linoleic acid. *Note:* Flax seed oil can be difficult for some dogs to digest.

Lack of polyunsaturated fat can cause:

- Coarse dry hair coat

- Improper growth

- Skin lesions on belly, inside the back legs, and between the shoulder blades

- Thickened areas of skin

- Horny skin growths

- Skin ulcerations and infections

- Poor blood clotting

- Extreme itching and scratching

Be aware that in the manufacturing process of most dog foods, fat is sprayed on as the last ingredient. Fat makes the food palatable, like potato chips and French fries. Look for a food that has both animal fat and vegetable oils in it. Some less expensive foods do not list individual fats and oils. They only say the percentage of fat in the food. Better foods do list them individually.

WHAT ELSE IS IN HERE?

The manufacturer chooses how to preserve the fat in dog food to prevent it from becoming rancid. He can use the chemicals BHA, BHT, ethoxyquin or propyl-gallate. If a fat is preserved with these chemicals, it will have a long shelf life and be generally unaffected by heat and light. Even so, many of us prefer not to feed these preservatives to our dogs, especially ethoxyquin.

Manufacturers can also choose natural preservatives, such as vitamins C and E. Vitamin E is usually listed as tocopherol. The down side to these preservatives is a shorter shelf life—no more than six months.

WHAT IS MISSING?

Your dog's food needs vitamins to release the nutrients and enzymes in it so his body can absorb and use them. When we were researching the first edition of this book, we called manufacturers to ask them about how they protected the vitamins from destruction during the heat process. Their responses were astonishing. They acknowledged awareness of the problem posed by the heat process and to overcome it, added more vitamins to the food to make up the difference. Of course, this is nonsense. If vitamins are destroyed by heat, it doesn't make any difference how much you put in the food—they will still be destroyed.

We also learned that the finished product was not tested by more than 99% of the manufacturers. In other words, a substantial quantity of vitamins and minerals go into the food, but what quantity actually reaches your dog seems as much a mystery to the manufacturer as it is to us.

DIFFERENT KINDS OF VITAMINS

There are two types of vitamins—water-soluble and fat-soluble. Vitamins B and C are water-soluble. Any excess is filtered through the kidneys and urinated out four to eight hours after ingestion. For this reason, they have to be present in each meal. Vitamins A, D, E and K are fat-soluble and are stored in the fatty tissues of the body and in the liver. Your dog needs both types.

Vitamins are not only lost in the manufacturing process of dog food, but begin to deteriorate as soon as you open up the dog food bag and expose the food to light and air. Particularly sensitive are vitamins B and C.

Vitamin C is needed for healthy teeth and gums. In the old days, sailors often suffered from vitamin C deficiency due to the lack of fresh fruits and vegetables while at sea. Called scurvy, this deficiency manifests itself in weakness, anemia, spongy and inflamed gums, and dirty teeth. The same thing happens to the vitamin C deficient dog.

A fairly common misconception is that dogs don't need extra vitamin C because they produce their own. While it is true that they produce their own, it is not enough to maintain good health, especially in our polluted environment.

Your dog needs sufficient vitamin C to break down the animal protein in his diet, strengthen his immune system, speed wound healing, help the function of his musculoskeletal system, and whenever he gets wormed, is given drugs of any kind or put under any kind of stress. A lack of vitamin C in the diet commonly results in urinary tract infections, cystitis and limping in the front or rear legs.

The same holds true with vitamin B, which is made up of a number of individual parts called, commonly, B complex. A fragile, water-soluble vitamin, vitamin B is needed for energy, breaking down protein and promoting biochemical reactions in the body which work with enzymes to change the carbohydrates into glucose. Since not enough of either vitamin B complex or C is contained in any processed dog food to meet our criteria for raising a puppy, you have to add both of these to his diet.

MINERALS—A LITTLE GOES A LONG WAY

Minerals make up less than 2% of any formulated diet, and yet they are the most critical of nutrients. Although a dog can manufacture some vitamins on his own, he is not able to make minerals. They are needed for:

- The correct composition of body fluids
- Proper formation of blood and bones
- Promotion of a healthy nervous system
- Co-enzyme function together with vitamins

Since 50% to 80% of minerals are lost in the manufacturing process, we recommend that you add extra minerals to your dog's food.

Stay with us—we're almost through covering the things you need to know to make intelligent decisions about what to feed your dog. We will give you some ideas of which foods to choose and what to add to them to make up for the deficiencies caused in processing. But first, one more piece of information, so everything will fall into place for you.

WATER

Your dog should have access to *fresh* water in a clean stainless-steel or glass bowl at all times. The exception would be when a puppy is being housetrained. Then you can limit his access to water after 8:00 p.m. so he will last through the night without an accident.

DIGESTION TIME

According to a Swedish study, different types of dog food require the following digestion times. Raw foods are the most easily digested by a dog. They pass through a dog's stomach and into the intestinal tract in $4\frac{1}{2}$ hours. So, after that time span, dogs are already receiving the energy from that food.

Semimoist food, the kind that is shaped like hamburgers, or rolls like sausages, and found in boxes at the supermarket, takes almost nine hours to pass through the stomach.

Dry food takes up to 16 hours. So if you choose to feed your dog any kind of dry processed dog food, it will be in his stomach morning, noon and night.

So what's the point? Well, let's take a closer look.

Enzymes & Enzyme Robbing

Enzymes make the body tick. They are either already contained in the body, or made through what we feed our dogs. When that semimoist food or dry food sits in the stomach of a dog, it does so because there are not enough enzymes in the stomach to break it down. Remember, a dog's stomach is designed to deal with raw foods. So the stomach sends a message to the brain, "Hey, brain, we need some more enzymes down here." And the brain comes back, "Okay, okay, but I need some time." It then gathers enzymes from the heart, the liver, the kidneys and other parts of the body to be transported to the stomach. In the meantime, the food sits there until enough enzymes are collected for digestion. This process is called enzyme robbing.

Robbing various organs of the body of the enzymes that they themselves need to function correctly can have a detrimental effect on those organs. This situation can give a dog a predisposition for problems in those organs, can hasten disease and reduce the life span of the dog.

HOW TO FEED YOUR DOG

Our 30 years of breeding, raising, working and living with dogs of several breeds has had a profound effect on our way of thinking. We know that a homemade diet is best. Even so, we are realists. You are a busy person and may not even cook for yourself, much less be able to prepare food for your dog (*see* Chapter 4 for a handy dehydrated version of the Natural Diet). Fortunately, using commercial dog food as your base, you can take some shortcuts to safeguard your dog's health.

HEALTHY DOG DIET FOR A 50–POUND DOG

(Adjust according to weight)

Find a dog food that has two animal proteins listed in the first three ingredients, preferably the first two, and one that is preserved naturally with vitamin C or E (*See* Appendix II, "Sources"). FEED TWICE DAILY. Follow the directions for the weight of your dog. Then add:

---

500 mg of vitamin C in the form of calcium ascorbate, twice a day

Vitamin B complex, twice a day

Amino acid complex tablet, once a day in the morning

¼ teaspoon vitamin/mineral mix, which contains digestive enzymes and probiotics once a day in the morning (see Appendix II)

Note for puppies: When your puppy is through teething and has had all his vaccinations, stop using the vitamin/mineral mix on a regular basis. Use it when your puppy is going through a growth spurt, or when your dog is experiencing stress.

The supplements replace those destroyed in the heat process. Your puppy also needs some raw foods that contain their own enzymes.

Rotate throughout one week in each meal:

> *¹/₂ cup of raw meat or 2.5 oz of raw meat and 1.5 oz of raw liver; or rotate fresh yogurt with live cultures; or cottage cheese (using either once a week)*
>
> *1 large egg cooked for five minutes, plus the shell, four times per week*
>
> The meat can be beef, chicken or fish. When using chicken or fish, pour some boiling water over it to kill any bacteria before using.

Vegetables can also be added—¹/₂ cup a day is all your dog needs. Serve them raw, but put them through a food processor and mix with the food, or slightly steam them. Since vegetables contain cellulose from the stalks of the plants and dogs can't break down cellulose, putting them through a food processor or par-boiling makes them easier for your dog to digest. Do whatever it takes for your dog to enjoy them.

Vegetables to use include: carrots, beets, sweet potatoes, green or yellow beans, broccoli, parsnips, squash, leeks, kale, collard and turnip greens, Brussels sprouts, and cauliflower. Our dogs love salad vegetables, and so they always get some lettuce, cucumbers, or whatever variety we choose when making a salad for ourselves.

Vegetables can be used for treats, and you can give carrot sticks or broccoli stalks instead of dog biscuits.

Fruit can and should be used frequently. Fruits to use are bananas, plums, prunes, raisins, apricots, apples or anything your dog begs for or craves. Dried fruits are wonderful as treats.

GIVE YOUR DOG A BONE

Once or twice a week give your dog a bone as a special treat. They love large beef bones, raw chicken necks and the tips from chicken wings. If you are not sure about how long these have been out in the supermarket case, douse with boiling water to kill any bacteria before feeding them to your dog. The side benefit of giving your dog bones is that he will have beautiful, pearly white teeth that don't need to be cleaned. Feeding him too many bones, though, will give him constipation and hard, chalky stools.

A bone or two every week will not only make your dog happy, it will also maintain clean teeth.

When you give your dog a bone, leave him alone. It is a special treat, and he should be left in a place where he can relax by himself and enjoy it. A crate or dog bed is the perfect place for him to enjoy his bone in peace and quiet.

MAKING YOUR OWN DOG FOOD

Instead of leaving it to someone else, you can make your own dog food. Many people, ourselves included, do it, and there are many recipes available. Whatever recipe you are going to use, you absolutely must follow two rules:

1. For a *benchmark*, your dog must have a blood test done which includes a complete blood count (CBC) and a chemistry screen. Your veterinarian can do these tests. After your dog has been on the diet for two months, he'll need to get another blood test to compare to the first one. Comparing the results will immediately tell you whether you are on the right track. This is a cardinal rule, and if you are not prepared to do the

testing, you should not even think about a homemade diet. Not having the blood tests done is like driving a car with a blindfold—you are bound to run off the road. We have annual blood tests done on all our dogs, so that we can make dietary adjustments, if necessary.

2.   The diet *must* contain all known required nutrients in the right proportions, that is, it must be complete and balanced. If it is not, you can cause your dog all sorts of problems, and he'd be better off with a good commercial food and some supplements. The diets discussed in Chapter 2, "The Natural Diet," and the dehydrated version of the same diet meet those requirements.

SUMMARY

- Your dog's behavior, health and overall well-being depend on what you feed him.

- Your dog is a carnivore and needs meat.

- Select a dog food that lists two animal proteins in the first three ingredients; preferably these should be the first two listed.

- Your dog needs some carbohydrates in the form of grains and vegetables.

- You need to supplement with vitamins, minerals, amino acids and fresh foods because these important nutrients are destroyed in the heat process during manufacture.

- If you make your own dog food, it must contain all known required nutrients in the right proportions, and you must get a benchmark blood test.

2 The Natural Diet

PATCH & CALI

When Herb first contacted me about his two Bull Terriers, he was a sad and frustrated man. Cali showed obsessive-compulsive behaviors, such as chasing her tail, eating sticks and chewing on rocks. She was also a very dominant dog who took great pleasure in stealing Patch's toys, usually right out of his mouth. Patch didn't take kindly to these antics and there was friction between the two.

Both dogs were in poor health. They had constant skin irritations, and Herb was reaching the end of his tether. He had visited all the veterinarians in his area, but without any lasting success. He had tried adding supplements to the dog food he was using, as well as some raw foods. He had also tried homeopathy; in fact, he had studied it intensely, but nothing he had done improved Patch and Cali's health or behavior.

I made some suggestions to Herb about the dogs' diet and training, and asked him if he would be willing to try the Natural Diet. He said he would try some of the suggestions, but was not willing to commit to the Natural Diet at that time. Some months later he called again to say that the behavior and health problems continued unabated. He was going to put Cali to sleep, as she now displayed aggression toward people. I asked Herb if he would be willing to go for one more month and try both dogs on the Natural Diet. Since there was nowhere else to go, he agreed.

The improvement was slow, but steady. As both dogs' health improved, they felt better and their behavior improved. The constant struggle for dominance ceased because they both felt well and were less irritated with life in general, and with each other. Cali, who had always been frightened of loud noises, the dark and the rain, started to calm down. Over time, she turned into a sweet and lovable dog, who can now be trusted with small children—her nemesis before the dietary change.

Cali and Patch felt and behaved better after switching to the Natural Diet.

Herb brought both dogs to my Holistic Camp some years ago, where they were models of good behavior. Not only were they calm during the lectures, lying down by Herb's side, but they also got along with the other dogs. Herb religiously exercised them early in the morning, lunch time and in the evenings to provide a healthy outlet for their energies. They were, and still are, a credit to his dedication.

WHAT IS THE NATURAL DIET?

The Natural Diet follows as closely as possible what the dog in his wild state would eat if he were eating prey. The diet takes into account the limitations of the dog's short digestive tract, his strong stomach acid and the enzymes his system produces to digest food. It consists of two meals. One is a cereal meal, plus supplements, which makes up 25% of the total diet, and the other is a raw meat meal, plus supplements, which makes up 75% of the total diet. By separating these meals—both of which are balanced—the digestive system uses enzymes already present in the stomach and intestines, plus those found in the raw food itself, to efficiently and quickly break down the food. Thus the amount of work the digestive organs have to do is decreased and they are maintained in a healthy state for a longer period of time.

Dogs are able to digest and utilize the Natural Diet well, and stool volume is less than 25% of food intake. Young dogs raised on the Natural Diet grow more slowly than dogs raised on commercial food, which means fewer musculoskeletal problems. Overall vitality and energy are unequaled and, most important of all, the dogs love it.

ADVANTAGES OF FEEDING RAW

Feeding raw is hardly a new concept. Juliette de Bairacli Levy, the great pioneer in this area, whose work preceded mine, deserves a great deal of credit for putting me on this path. My own research, which continues after 30 years, shows that dogs fed raw and natural foods live longer and healthier lives than their counterparts who are fed commercial dog food. Dogs fed naturally have stronger immune systems and are therefore better able to resist disease and parasites.

DISADVANTAGES OF FEEDING RAW

The disadvantages of making a homemade diet cannot be minimized. It takes commitment on your part. It means stocking up on ingredients, buying in bulk and finding storage space. An investment in a freezer is a must if you are feeding more than two or three dogs. While no actual cooking is involved, the diet requires boiling a pot of water, which some people find too much.

Many people don't like to handle liver or smell cod-liver oil, and may leave those ingredients out, which is not a good idea. Every ingredient in the diet is there for a reason—to meet the minimum daily nutritional requirements of your dog. A commitment to this diet requires that you use all the ingredients. You can make substitutions, of course, so long as they are equal in nutritional content to those ingredients they replace. For example, in my experience, the vast majority of dogs, when given the choice, prefer beef. At the same time, dogs who are sickly have a preference for chicken. The explanation for these preferences lies in the amino acid profile of beef, chicken, turkey or lamb. Chicken and lamb are almost twice as high in protein as beef, and as soon as a sickly dog's body rebalances itself, he will go back to beef. Balance is the key as evidenced by the blood tests you have done on your dog.

The Natural Diet makes no attempt to appeal to you, the owner of the dog. It looks and smells like raw meat, and it doesn't contain coloring agents or other visual enhancements. My advice to prospective dog food makers is, if you find you can't follow the philosophy or you don't like handling the ingredients, then making your own food is not for you. It is safer for your pet to be on either the new Natural Diet Foundation food to which you add a couple of raw ingredients, or a good quality commercial food with supplements. (*See* Appendix II for more information, and Chapter 4 for a convenient dehydrated version of the Natural Diet.)

MAKING YOUR OWN DOG FOOD

Making the transition from feeding commercial dog food to preparing your own dog food is a tremendous leap of faith. Trying something this radical tends to scare us. But it's more than that. The transition involves accepting the responsibility for your dog's well-being and health. All of a sudden, you feel vulnerable, which is uncomfortable. All I can tell you is what I have learned from my students—and that is, everyone feels this way—it's not just you. It's quite natural and normal to be a little frightened at this point.

DIFFERENT STROKES FOR DIFFERENT FOLKS

There are many recipes available on the market to make your own food. Some are good and work well, and some are not so good, and can actually be dangerous to the long-term health of your dog. Before you try one of these recipes on your dog, ask the following questions:

- Is there a guaranteed analysis?
- What is the list of ingredients?
- Does it meet the minimum daily requirements of all known nutrients?

When I started to talk about feeding dogs naturally early in the 1970s, to say I was considered eccentric would be an understatement. Yet today, nearly 30 years later, it is becoming quite common to feed dogs this way. Together with the deteriorating health of dogs in general, more and more people have realized that feeding fresh foods contributes to the health, performance and longevity of their pets. After all, this is what all dogs were fed until about 40 years ago when the dog food industry took over the total feeding of our dogs.

GETTING STARTED—STEP 1

In Chapter 1, I mentioned the importance of a benchmark blood test, which includes a complete blood count (CBC) and a chemistry screen. These procedures are important for several reasons:

- Without the benchmark test you have no clinical way of knowing whether or not the diet is improving your dog's health. Some improvements, like skin and coat, are immediately apparent, but the state of the dog's organs and other health indicators are not.

- Without a periodic blood test, and we recommend one each year, by the time you see something wrong with your dog, it may be too late. As an aside, that is usually when I am consulted, sort of as a last-ditch attempt to save the dog. A yearly blood test would have forecast most conditions before they became critical.

Hurry up, I'm hungry! This puppy looks forward to her healthful dinner.

- The blood test will also stop your veterinarian from telling you that you are killing your dog by feeding a raw diet.

- Getting the blood work and a complete physical checkup from your veterinarian once each year is one of the hallmarks of preventative medicine—and one that has proved invaluable to us and our dogs.

- Blood tests are also helpful in tailoring the Natural Diet to a chronic condition, such as Addison's disease, cancer, arthritis, or diseases of the heart, liver or kidneys.

GETTING STARTED—STEP 2

Read the entire chapter and make sure you understand why you are going to feed your dogs this way, and how you are going to do it. Give yourself time to assemble all the ingredients and decide how you are going to store them. Remember, you have to use *all* of the ingredients to supply a balanced diet for your dog, and you cannot leave out some of them because you don't understand why they are used, or because you don't like them. Every ingredient meets the needs of your dog in one way or another, and leaving something out will unbalance the diet.

To get a dog back into balance after he has been assaulted with medications, vaccinations and commercial food takes time. Following the diet exactly in the first weeks is important. Once your dog is in balance again, you can rotate foods around more, come up with shortcuts for preparation and traveling and not worry too much if you forget to defrost some meat or chicken for a meal. A healthy dog can withstand these vagaries.

DETOXIFICATION

When a dog is placed on the Natural Diet after being fed a lifetime of commercial dog food, certain changes occur. These changes are often referred to as detoxification. Body fat is reduced, and the body itself goes through a "reshaping." A dog, in an effort to flush his system, drinks a lot of water, urinates a lot and the color of the stools may change. Generally, he starts to look better than he did before.

FASTING & PHILOSOPHY

The concept of fasting to cleanse the body is older than Hippocrates, who employed fasting in his practice of medicine in Ancient Greece. Animals in the wild regularly fast because their food supply is not reliable. A wolf eats three times a week, if he is lucky. When he does, he gorges on as much food as he can, and then sleeps it off for the next three days. Animals who are sick will fast to divert the energy needed for digesting food into the healing process.

Fasting is necessary to give a dog's digestive tract a break and the kidneys a rest from dealing with the nitrogen waste from meat. This is why meat is fed only five times a week, cottage cheese is substituted on the sixth day, and the seventh day is the half-day fast.

The timing of fasting is also important. Fast your dog on a day of the week when he is not very active. For most dogs, activity level is highest on a weekend and fasting at that time is not a good idea. Fasting should be a time of rest and quiet. You don't want to fast your dog if you are going to show him or put undue stress on him when you're away from home.

Fasting consists of a half-day fast every week, and one full-day fast once a month for the healthy, adult dog. Puppies under 7 months of age and old dogs over 12 are not fasted and on the normal fast day are given two cereal meals, one of which contains an egg. Water must always be available to the dog.

Fasting is more difficult for you than it is for your dog. When you are fasting your dog, take him for a walk, play ball, or go for a drive in the car at the normal feeding time. Your dog's anxiety about not having any food at the normal time will last about fifteen minutes. Don't compare what you would feel like without food for a day, to what your dog will experience. The dog's digestive system is entirely different from yours. By fasting him you are lightening the load on all of his internal organs. In countless laboratory experiments, different species of animals that were fasted once a week lived longer and were healthier than those fed every day. *Fresh water should always be available to your dog.*

You may find it impossible to fast your dog when starting the diet. When you understand the digestive system of the dog, you will not experience these qualms. The diet is formulated to provide the dog his weekly calories in 6 ½ days, thereby maintaining him at his perfect weight.

GUARANTEED ANALYSIS

Guaranteed analysis is a breakdown of what is in the food you feed your dog. It is required by law on all commercial food packages. For comparative purposes we list below the breakdown of the Natural Diet.

Percentage is by dry weight (comparable to what you see on the back of commercial dry dog food packages).

Protein—utilizable	34.7%
Fat	17.2%
Carbohydrate (including fiber)	33.7%
Ash (mineral content)	8.6%
Linoleic acid	2.7%

Calcium	1.8%
Phosphorus	1.3%
Calories per pound	2,172

INGREDIENTS

In descending order by wet weight:

> Beef muscle meat, water, cereal grain, kefir/yogurt, cottage cheese, beef liver, egg, bone meal, apple cider vinegar, vegetable greens, herbs, molasses, wheat bran, safflower oil, fruit, honey, cod-liver oil, wheat germ, kelp, egg shell, brewer's yeast, garlic, vitamin B complex, vitamin C and vitamin E.

The Natural diet meets and exceeds the minimum daily requirement of all known nutrients. What follows are adult dog diet charts, by weight, for normal, healthy, active dogs at differing stages of life. The special needs of puppies, breeding dogs and older dogs are addressed later in this section.

TRANSFER DIET

Changing a dog's diet from one food to another has to be done slowly. The intestinal bacteria that govern absorption need time to make the adjustment to the new food. Normally this process takes 11 days, but by fasting your dog, the process is reduced to four days. If this timetable is not followed, your dog may experience an upset stomach or diarrhea. Fasting with water and honey flushes the digestive system and prepares it to accept the new food.

The following transfer diet schedule is based on the needs of a 25-pound dog who is being switched from a commercial dog food to the Natural Diet. Dogs that have been fed partially raw diets, or totally raw diets, can be transferred to the Natural Diet more quickly—starting at day four. Puppies up to 7 months of age are not fasted as long, and can start at day five. Older dogs are also not fasted as long and can start at day four. Measurements are U.S. standard.

DAY 1		No food, but fresh water available.
DAY 2	**a.m.**	No food, fresh water available.
	p.m.	½ cup of raw milk, yogurt or kefir, 1 teaspoon raw honey.

DAY 3	a.m.	¹/₂ cup raw milk, yogurt or kefir, 1 teaspoon honey.
	p.m.	¹/₂ cup raw milk, yogurt or kefir, 1 teaspoon honey, ¹/₂ teaspoon dry herbs or 2 tablespoons fresh herbs.
DAY 4	a.m.	1 cup of raw milk, yogurt or kefir, 1 teaspoon honey, ¹/₂ teaspoon of dry or 2 tablespoons of fresh herbs, ¹/₂ ounce (cooked weight) oatmeal.
	p.m.	Same as above, but use 1 ounce of cooked oatmeal, 1 garlic capsule.
DAY 5	a.m.	¹/₂ normal ration for cereal and supplements as listed on the adult dog diet charts that follow.
	p.m.	¹/₂ normal ration of meatmeal, and supplements as listed on the adult dog diet charts.
DAY 6	a.m.	Normal amount of food as listed on Day 1 of the adult dog diet charts.
	p.m.	Same as above.

Note: In England, measurements are a little different. Three teaspoons equal one tablespoon. Two teaspoons equal one dessert spoon. Four teaspoons equal one English tablespoon.

ADULT DOG DIET CHARTS

The eight adult dog diet charts that follow are arranged by weight. We've provided a blank one for you to write down what's appropriate for your dog. *Note:* Eggs should be boiled for five minutes and fed to your dog along with the shell.

Abbreviations:

oz = ounces

t = teaspoon

T = tablespoon

IU = International Units

C = cup

mg = milligrams

NATURAL DIET—5–POUND DOG

Days 1–6

Breakfast

.75	Grain mix (dry/oz)	1/4	Blackstrap molasses (t)
1/4	Safflower oil (t)	20	Vitamin E (IU)
20	Vitamin C (mg)	6	Vitamin B complex (mg)
1/4	Egg, small, 4 times a week	1	Yogurt or kefir (t)

Dinner

2	Meat (oz)—days 1–5	.45	Liver (oz)—days 1–5
2.5	Cottage cheese (oz)—day 6	20	Vitamin C (mg)
1/8	Cod-liver oil (t)	1/2	Apple cider vinegar (t)
1/16	Kelp (t)	1/8	Brewer's yeast (t)
1/2	Garlic capsule (325 mg)	2/3	Bone meal (t)
1/4	Wheat germ (t)	1	Wheat bran (t)
1/4	Dry herbs (t)	2/3	Fruit (t) on alternate days

Day 7

Half-day Fast in p.m.

Breakfast

.4	Grain mix (dry/oz)		Vitamin C (mg)
6	Vitamin B complex (mg)	1	Yogurt or kefir (t)
1/2	Honey (t)		

NATURAL DIET—10–POUND DOG

Days 1–6

Breakfast

1	Grain mix (dry/oz)	$1/2$	Blackstrap molasses (t)
$1/2$	Safflower oil (t)	40	Vitamin E (IU)
40	Vitamin C (mg)	12.5	Vitamin B complex (mg)
$1/2$	Egg, small, 4 times a week	$1/8$	Yogurt or kefir (C)

Dinner

3.7	Meat (oz)—days 1–5	.8	Liver (oz)—days 1–5
3.10	Cottage cheese (oz)—day 6	40	Vitamin C (mg)
$1/4$	Cod-liver oil (t)	1	Apple cider vinegar (t)
$1/8$	Kelp (t)	$1/4$	Brewer's yeast (t)
$1/2$	Garlic capsule (325 mg)	1.33	Bone meal (t)
$1/2$	Wheat germ (t)	2	Wheat bran (t)
$1/2$	Dry herbs (t)	1.25	Fruit (t) on alternate days

Day 7

Half-day Fast in p.m.

Breakfast

.7	Grain mix (dry/oz)	40	Vitamin C (mg)
12.5	Vitamin B complex (mg)	$1/4$	Yogurt or kefir (C)
1	Honey (t)		

NATURAL DIET—25–POUND DOG

Days 1–6

Breakfast

2	Grain mix (dry/oz)	1	Blackstrap molasses (t)
1	Safflower oil (t)	100	Vitamin E (IU)
100	Vitamin C (mg)	25	Vitamin B complex (mg)
1	Egg, small, 4 times a week	$^1/_4$	Yogurt or kefir (t)

Dinner

7	Meat (oz)—days 1–5	1.5	Liver (oz)—days 1–5
8	Cottage cheese (oz)—day 6	100	Vitamin C (mg)
$^1/_2$	Cod-liver oil (t)	1.5	Apple cider vinegar (t)
$^1/_4$	Kelp (t)	$^1/_2$	Brewer's yeast (t)
1	Garlic capsule (325 mg)	3.5	Bone meal (t)
1	Wheat germ (t)	1.5	Wheat bran (t)
1	Dry herbs (t)	1	Fruit (t) on alternate days

Day 7

Half-day Fast in p.m.

Breakfast

.8	Grain mix (dry/oz)	100	Vitamin C (mg)
25	Vitamin B complex (mg)	$^1/_2$	Yogurt or kefir (t)
2	Honey (t)		

NATURAL DIET—50–POUND DOG

Days 1–6

Breakfast

3	Grain mix (dry/oz)	2	Blackstrap molasses (t)
2	Safflower oil (t)	200	Vitamin E (IU)
200	Vitamin C (mg)	50	Vitamin B complex (mg)
1.25	Egg, small, 4 times a week	1/2	Yogurt or kefir (C)

Dinner

12	Meat (oz)—days 1–5	2.5	Liver (oz)—days 1–5
14	Cottage cheese (oz)—day 6	200	Vitamin C (mg)
1	Cod-liver oil (t)	1	Apple cider vinegar (T)
1/2	Kelp (t)	1	Brewer's yeast (t)
1.5	Garlic capsule (325 mg)	2.5	Bone meal (T)
2	Wheat germ (t)	3	Wheat bran (T)
2	Dry herbs (t)	2	Fruit (T) on alternate days

Day 7

Half-day Fast in p.m.

Breakfast

2.3	Grain mix (dry/oz)	200	Vitamin C (mg)
50	Vitamin B complex (mg)	1	Yogurt or kefir (C)
4	Honey (t)		

NATURAL DIET—75–POUND DOG

Days 1–6

Breakfast

4	Grain mix (dry/oz)	1	Blackstrap molasses (T)
1	Safflower oil (T)	300	Vitamin E (IU)
300	Vitamin C (mg)	50	Vitamin B complex (mg)
1.5	Egg, small, 4 times a week	$^1/_2$	Yogurt or kefir (C)

Dinner

15	Meat (oz)—days 1–5	3.4	Liver (oz)—days 1–5
18	Cottage cheese (oz)—day 6	300	Vitamin C (mg)
1.5	Cod-liver oil (t)	1.5	Apple cider vinegar (T)
$^3/_4$	Kelp (t)	1.5	Brewer's yeast (t)
2	Garlic capsule (325 mg)	3.5	Bone meal (T)
1.5	Wheat germ (T)	4.5	Wheat bran (T)
1	Dry herbs (T)	3	Fruit (T) on alternate days

Day 7

Half-day Fast in p.m.

Breakfast

2	Grain mix (dry/oz)	300	Vitamin C (mg)
50	Vitamin B complex (mg)	1	Yogurt or kefir (C)
2	Honey (T)		

NATURAL DIET—100–POUND DOG

Days 1–6

Breakfast

6	Grain mix (dry/oz)	4	Blackstrap molasses (t)
4	Safflower oil (t)	400	Vitamin E (IU)
400	Vitamin C (mg)	75	Vitamin B complex (mg)
2	Egg, small, 4 times a week	$3/4$	Yogurt or kefir (C)

Dinner

20	Meat (oz)—days 1–5	4.4	Liver (oz)—days 1–5
24	Cottage cheese (oz)—day 6	400	Vitamin C (mg)
2	Cod-liver oil (t)	2	Apple cider vinegar (T)
1	Kelp (t)	2	Brewer's yeast (t)
2	Garlic capsule (325 mg)	4.6	Bone meal (T)
2	Wheat germ (T)	6	Wheat bran (T)
4	Dry herbs (t)	4	Fruit (T) on alternate days

Day 7

Half-day Fast in p.m.

Breakfast

3	Grain mix (dry/oz)	400	Vitamin C (mg)
75	Vitamin B complex (mg)	1.5	Yogurt or kefir (C)
8	Honey (t)		

NATURAL DIET—125–POUND DOG

Days 1-6

Breakfast

7	Grain mix (dry/oz)	5	Blackstrap molasses (t)
1.5	Safflower oil (T)	500	Vitamin E (IU)
500	Vitamin C (mg)	75	Vitamin B complex (mg)
2	Egg, small, 4 times a week	1	Yogurt or kefir (C)

Dinner

25	Meat (oz)—days 1–5	5	Liver (oz)—days 1–5
30	Cottage cheese (oz)—day 6	500	Vitamin C (mg)
2.5	Cod-liver oil (t)	2.5	Apple cider vinegar (T)
1.25	Kelp (t)	2.5	Brewer's yeast (t)
2.5	Garlic capsule (325 mg)	6	Bone meal (T)
2.5	Wheat germ (T)	8	Wheat bran (T)
5	Dry herbs (t)	5	Fruit (T) on alternate days

Day 7

Half-Day Fast in p.m.

Breakfast

4	Grain mix (dry/oz)	500	Vitamin C (mg)
75	Vitamin B complex (mg)	1.5	Yogurt or kefir (C)
3	Honey (T)		

NATURAL DIET—150–POUND DOG

Days 1–6

Breakfast

8	Grain mix (dry/oz)	2	Blackstrap molasses (T)
2	Safflower oil (T)	600	Vitamin E (IU)
1	Vitamin C (gram)	100	Vitamin B complex (mg)
3	Egg, small, 4 times a week	1.25	Yogurt or kefir (C)

Dinner

28.8	Meat (oz)—days 1–5	5.7	Liver (oz)—days 1–5
32	Cottage cheese (oz)—day 6	1	Vitamin C (gram)
1	Cod-liver oil (T)	3	Apple cider vinegar (T)
1.5	Kelp (t)	1	Brewer's yeast (T)
3	Garlic capsule (325 mg)	6	Bone meal (T)
3	Wheat germ (T)	8	Wheat bran (T)
2	Dry herbs (T)	6	Fruit (T) on alternate days

Day 7

Half-day Fast in p.m.

Breakfast

4.5	Grain mix (dry/oz)	1	Vitamin C (gram)
100	Vitamin B complex (mg)	2	Yogurt or kefir (C)
4	Honey (T)		

NATURAL DIET FOR MY DOG

Days 1–6

Breakfast

Grain mix (dry/oz)	Blackstrap molasses (t)
Safflower oil (t)	Vitamin E (IU)
Vitamin C (mg)	Vitamin B complex (mg)
Egg, small, 4 times a week	Yogurt or kefir (t)

Dinner

Meat (oz)—days 1–5	Liver (oz)—days 1–5
Cottage cheese (oz)—day 6	Vitamin C (mg)
Cod-liver oil (t)	Apple cider vinegar (t)
Kelp (t)	Brewer's yeast (t)
Garlic capsule (325 mg)	Bone meal (t)
Wheat germ (t)	Wheat bran (t)
Dry herbs (t)	Fruit (t or T) on alternate days

Day 7

Half-day Fast in p.m.

Breakfast

Grain mix (dry/oz)	Vitamin C (mg)
Vitamin B complex (mg)	Yogurt or kefir (t)
Honey (t)	

3 Natural Diet Ingredients & Why They Work

Every ingredient in the Natural Diet is necessary to provide the nutrients your dog needs for balance at the cellular level. You can, of course, make substitutions, so long as the new ingredients provide the same nutritive value. Leaving out any of the ingredients unbalances the Natural Diet.

THE BREAKFAST MEAL

Breakfast contains cereal grains, a small amount of vegetables, oil, one egg, vitamins, molasses and kefir or yogurt, and is a completely balanced meal. Your dog needs a small amount of grains and some vegetables for energy, proper digestion, stool formation and correct functioning of the thyroid gland. Broken down rather quickly into starches and sugars, they are a quick energy food. Dogs do not need many carbohydrates to be healthy, and a diet low in carbohydrates and high in animal protein is ideal.

OATS

Seventy-five percent of the breakfast grain is made up of oats. Oats are a warming grain that calms the nervous and reproductive systems, strengthens the spleen, pancreas and immune system, as well as the heart muscle. Rich in silicon, oats help make bones strong. Acidic and not very allergenic, they are tolerated best by the largest number of dogs.

BUCKWHEAT

Twenty-five percent of the breakfast grain is made up of buckwheat, which is an alkaline grain with a sweet flavor. It cleanses the intestines and improves appetite. Buckwheat contains rutin, a bioflavonoid, which helps to strengthen

37

Raising your dog family naturally results in fantastic health and breathtaking appearance.

capillaries and blood vessels, and inhibits hemorrhaging. It, too, is tolerated well by the majority of dogs.

MILLET

Millet is a cooling, alkaline grain with a sweet and salty flavor, which can be substituted for buckwheat in the summer months or between the seasons. Millet strengthens the kidneys, because it acts like a diuretic. Good for the stomach and spleen, it can balance acidic conditions, retard bacterial growth in the mouth, and has antifungal properties. Well tolerated by dogs in the summer months.

BROWN RICE

A dog that has been sick can be fed 100% brown rice for the breakfast meal during the recovery process. It is a pH-neutral grain with a sweet flavor. Rice helps to soothe the stomach, expel toxins from the system and is high in B vitamins. Rice is not ethnic for many breeds, so not every dog can tolerate it. Rice should only be used for the time it takes to get the dog back into balance.

WHY YOUR DOG NEEDS CARBOHYDRATES

In addition to providing energy, carbohydrates maintain the health of the thyroid, liver, heart, brain, and nerve tissue. Carbohydrates regulate how much starch and fat will be broken down and utilized. Once in the digestive tract and assimilated, they are stored in the liver in the form of glycogen, which controls energy balance. The proper use and storage of glycogen prevent the channeling of protein into energy. Protein energy is needed for building tissues. Glycogen reserves regulate protein metabolism, and protect cells from incorrect functioning and injury. The heart and the thyroid gland need glycogen and some is stored in the cardiac muscle.

Not Enough Carbohydrates in Your Dog's Diet

Low carbohydrate intake may cause cardiac symptoms and angina. The central nervous system requires carbohydrates for proper functioning, as does the brain. The brain cannot store glucose and is therefore dependent on the minute-to-minute supply of glucose from the blood. With insufficient carbohydrates in the diet, protein and fat are converted to energy, weakening the immune system and preventing the body from building enough antibodies to fight disease. Poor hair growth and continuous shedding are symptoms of carbohydrate deficiency.

THYROID FUNCTION

Thyroid function is also dependent upon the correct amount of carbohydrates in your dog's diet. Vitamin B complex, found in many grains and starch producing vegetables, is needed so that the amino acids phenylalanine and tyrosine can produce T_3 (*see* Chapter 10).

GRAIN INTOLERANCE

A few dogs are actually grain intolerant, which can be a sign of pancreatic and/or adrenal gland insufficiencies. Common symptoms are chronic ear discharges and continual itching when there are no parasites on the dog's skin. Don't ignore this. Check with your veterinarian and have a blood test done. Alter the Natural Diet by substituting vegetables that have a high starch content for grains in the breakfast. These include sweet potatoes, regular peeled potatoes (with the eyes removed, because they can be toxic), all root vegetables, including beets, carrots, parsnips, and green and yellow beans. Starchy vegetables should be at least 50% of the total vegetable intake, with the remainder coming from the green leafy variety. Vegetables that produce starch, which is turned into glucose and stored in the liver, are necessary for all vital functions of the body. *Note:* For the very sick dog, the vegetables and meat should be lightly cooked and fed together with a digestive enzyme. When you see improvement, reintroduce your dog to raw food.

Some dogs, especially as they get older, and those that have been diagnosed with kidney or adrenal gland disorders, cannot tolerate grains in a boiled form. For those, I have had great success with the baked breakfast bars (*see* Chapter 4). The vitamins are fed to these dogs separately.

VITAMIN C—DIFFERENT KINDS

CALCIUM ASCORBATE

Calcium ascorbate is necessary for the breakdown of protein and seems to be accepted and utilized well by most dogs. A water-soluble vitamin, it is flushed through the body in a matter of hours, and cannot be stored. It must be fed to your dog with each meal and is easily absorbed anywhere in the intestinal tract. The ascorbate forms are thought to be the most gentle (buffered) and cause the fewest side effects, such as diarrhea or indigestion. Calcium ascorbate is a pH-neutral, slightly bitter powder. Many health practitioners are of the opinion that calcium ascorbate gives the best results in the relief of arthritic symptoms, and recent studies have shown that it helps in stress reduction.

ASCORBIC ACID

A naturally occurring vitamin C, it is tart tasting, and most commonly used in human vitamin C pills. When given in high doses, it is not efficiently absorbed by dogs and can cause diarrhea. Most dogs find powdered forms of ascorbic acid to be unpalatable due to its tartness.

ESTER-C

Like the pure forms of calcium and sodium ascorbate, Ester-C is nonacidic with a neutral pH, and does not cause gastrointestinal upset. Being a time release product, the question has come up as to its effectiveness for dogs, who, when fed properly, process their food in 8 hours. Is the Ester-C actually utilized or passed straight through the intestinal tract? One way to find out if your dog needs this expensive form of vitamin C is to use kinesiology (*see* Chapter 11).

SODIUM ASCORBATE

Sodium ascorbate is another readily available and easily absorbed source of vitamin C, pH-neutral powder, with a slightly saline taste. Shown to stay in the system twice as long as ascorbic acid, this form of vitamin C can be used in low doses in your dog's diet, especially if Addison's disease is suspected.

VITAMIN B COMPLEX

Necessary for fat and protein assimilation, vitamin B complex is made up of 17 individual parts, plus folic acid, biotin, choline, inisitol and para-aminobenzoic acid (PABA). A water-soluble vitamin, it is flushed through the body quickly and cannot be stored, and must be fed to your dog with each meal. Vitamin B helps to promote growth, deal with stress and aids in healing, especially after surgery. Necessary for vaccines to work correctly in the body, lack of vitamin B can cause vaccine reactions. Hair loss, early graying of hair coat, weakness in the back legs, loss of appetite, stool eating, attracting fleas, ticks, flies, anxiety, nervousness, edema and heart disease can all be traced to deficiencies in the B complex vitamins.

Found naturally in yogurt or kefir, molasses and eggs in the breakfast meal, vitamin B is extremely fragile. When exposed to heat, light and air, it loses its effectiveness. To make up for any potential loss, vitamin B is supplemented in the breakfast meal. Vitamin B is found in abundance in liver, yeast, wheat bran, wheat germ and kelp. More details about the individual parts of this complex vitamin can be found in Appendix III, "Vitamins and Minerals."

FOLIC ACID

Folic acid is made up of para-aminobenzoic acid (PABA) and glutamic acid. It is very fragile and destroyed by heat, light, and when left at room temperature. Needed to form red blood cells, it is also necessary for protein metabolism. Critical for the growth and division of all body cells, folic acid is needed most during pregnancy and puppy growth. Folic acid helps to build antibodies to disease, especially after vaccination, and improves lactation. Folic acid is essential for dogs suffering from Addison's Disease or epilepsy.

Deficiencies can show up as lack of pigmentation, spontaneous abortion, difficult labor, dead and deformed puppies, and watery discharge from the eyes. Folic acid is abundant in green leafy vegetables, raw liver, brewer's or nutritional yeast and some raw fruits.

VITAMIN E

A fat-soluble vitamin, which means it is stored by the body, vitamin E provides a way for oxygen to reach the tissues of the body, dilates blood vessels and improves circulation. It helps to protect the lungs and other tissues from air pollution. Vitamin E helps to retard the aging process, and is critical for the correct functioning of the reproductive organs. Used in the treatment of heart disease and arthritis in older dogs, it also promotes testicle growth in young dogs and aids in the production of sperm. Vitamin E is essential for the nuclei of cells and the utilization of sex hormones, cholesterol and vitamin D. It is fragile and is destroyed by rancid fats or sunlight.

Vitamin E comes in several forms—alpha, beta, gamma and delta tocopherols. D-Alpha is the natural form that I use in the Natural Diet. The synthetic version of vitamin E is labeled dl-alpha tocopherol.

In the breakfast meal it is supplied by the cold-pressed safflower oil, which is high in vitamin E, together with the yogurt and kefir, honey and some vegetables. Even these ingredients, however, do not meet all of a dog's needs, so it is supplemented in capsule or pill form. In the evening meal vitamin E is abundant in liver as well as raw wheat germ and therefore is not supplemented.

SAFFLOWER OIL

Safflower oil contains the correct nutritional amount of the essential fatty acids (EFAs) necessary for your dog's proper skin and coat. Safflower oil contains 95% linoleic acid to corn's 10% and is unlikely to cause an allergic reaction. Safflower oil is highly palatable and is used in its cold-pressed form (sometimes called expelled). It is readily available in supermarkets and health food stores.

OTHER OILS

There are good and bad oils. Both kinds compete for the same spot in the cell membranes. The good oils (safflower, sunflower, wheat germ, and flax) can displace other oil molecules in the cell membranes if the concentrations are high enough. The good oils seem to improve the overall health of all animals. Good oils can bring down cholesterol and triglyceride levels in the body.

Flax seed oil is a high quality and popular oil used in natural diets. Personally, I have found few dogs that can tolerate it. It causes either vomiting or diarrhea. Oils, such as cottonseed, also cannot be utilized by your dog (other "bad" oils include corn, palm, and canola).

RANCID OILS

Many oils turn rancid once they are opened. Rancidity turns oils into trans-fatty acids, which can be dangerous to your dog's health and are contributing factors to a weakened immune system, heart disease and cancer. Oils are best kept in the refrigerator after opening. Pricking a vitamin E capsule and putting the contents into the oil can keep it from turning rancid.

HONEY

Honey is used once a week in the breakfast meal. It contains protein, carbohydrates, iron, copper, manganese, silica, chlorine, calcium, potassium, sodium, phosphorus, aluminum and magnesium, plus vitamin B complex, vitamins C, D and E. It is almost a complete food. Honey should only be used in its raw form because heat processing kills the health giving enzymes it contains.

Honey is a must in dog rearing. I keep some in the refrigerator at all times. If anything untoward or traumatic happens with my dogs and one of the dogs goes into shock, I have honey in a hardened form that is easily administered to the dog. About a tablespoon brings around an 80-pound dog almost immediately and the color comes back into his gums.

Honey is a wonderful pick-me-up any time your dog gets sick, or if he doesn't want to eat for awhile. The enzymes amylase and invertase aid the digestive process, and it acts as a wonderful tonic for a stressed dog. *Hint:* Before using honey, run your spoon under hot water and the honey slides off the spoon into your dog's mouth.

BLACKSTRAP MOLASSES

I use this form of molasses in the Natural Diet primarily for its high potassium content and to balance out the rest of the minerals in the breakfast meal. Besides potassium, it contains many other trace minerals, some of the B complex vitamins, but no fat or protein. Old-time breeders used blackstrap molasses together with seaweed or kelp in their dog's diet to keep the pigmentation of the nose, eye rims and mouth dark.

KEFIR

Kefir is a grain derivative, originating in the Caucasus. Known as the "fountain of youth," kefir contains the richest known source of enzymes which spark the function of digestive enzymes. It is a lot easier to make than yogurt and is nutritionally superior because it has a very low curd tension. The curd breaks up easily into extremely small particles thereby releasing enzymes into the digestive system. The small curd size facilitates kefir's absorption into the system and provides the correct surface upon which digestive enzymes work. Kefir stimulates the flow of salivary enzymes, will increase the flow of digestive juices and enzymes in the digestive tract, and stimulates peristalsis, thus increasing the efficiency of the whole digestive system.

YOGURT

Lactobacillus acidophilus is a beneficial bacterium normally produced by the intestinal tract and is found in good quality yogurts. Acidophilus creates an environment that is undesirable for fungi and microbes to grow. It also contains a weak antibiotic substance called colicine.

The lactobacillus acidophilus in yogurt can prevent bad breath caused by food putrefaction. It aids the digestion of B complex vitamins, some amino acids, fat and milk. Yogurt offers protection against contamination of food or water supplies when traveling to different areas (use with each meal). Breeders have also successfully used acidophilus capsules with their breeding animals during gestation, lactation, and until the puppies were weaned to prevent fading puppy syndrome.

Acidophilus is killed when a dog is given antibiotics, thus leaving an environment ideal for the growth of yeast and fungi in the intestines. These latter grow and cause diarrhea, flatulence or constipation. If the lactobacillus acidophilus bacteria are not replenished by feeding your dog yogurt or acidophilus capsules, fungus can also grow in the lungs, vagina, mouth and on the front and rear paws.

EGGS

Complete in protein, they contain lecithin, choline and many of the B Complex vitamins, vitamin E, magnesium, phosphorus and selenium. Egg yolk is high in vitamin A. Lecithin and choline help to break down low–density lipoproteins— the 'bad' part of cholesterol, and help clean out the arteries. Eggs contain the sulfur amino acids cysteine, cystine and methionine, needed for cell and tissue regeneration.

The healthy dog.

Use eggs whole, including the shell, which is a pure form of calcium. Puppies going through growth spurts often need extra calcium in their diets as do some older dogs. When needed by the dog, the eggshell will be totally digested and not visible in the stool. Sometimes only part of it is needed, and you will see some particles of shell in the stool. This is normal.

Eggs should be cooked for four to five minutes in boiling water to kill any bacteria on the shell. Cooking them longer decreases protein content, and you will notice a dark ring around the yolk of the egg. The dark ring is dead protein.

Brown eggs are better than white eggs since brown shells appear to absorb less bacteria than white shells. If you have a source of organic, clean eggs, it is fine to feed them raw.

THE DINNER MEAL

The dinner meal consists of raw meat, raw liver, vitamins, minerals, oils, herbs and fruit. Supplied in their natural food states, these provide a complete and balanced meal for your dog.

APPLE CIDER VINEGAR

The old saying, "An apple a day keeps the doctor away," seems to have some validity. In their vinegar form, apples contain a large amount of potassium, phosphorus, chlorine, sodium, magnesium, calcium, sulfur, iron, fluorine, silicon, and many trace minerals. In long-term feeding studies in which apple cider vinegar (ACV) was added to the feed of cows, fewer incidences occured of mastitis, itchy skin, influenza, respiratory diseases, eclampsia and cramping after delivery, and easier freshening. Horses with ACV in their feed raced better and never came down with distemper, even when exposed. ACV is credited with killing bacteria outright, and at one time was used to prevent food poisoning.

ACV is used in the Natural Diet not only for its mineral content, but also its ability to kill bacteria in the meat, chicken or fish. It also preserves the meat meal when it is stored in the refrigerator.

NUTRITIONAL AND/OR BREWER'S YEAST

Nutritional yeast is generally grown on molasses. Brewer's yeast comes from hops. These are nonactive forms of yeast and provide extra B vitamins, protein, trace minerals and salts. Both kinds of yeast contain chromium and selenium to the diet and are crucial to its overall balance. You can use either in the diet.

Many cases of allergic reactions to brewer's yeast have been reported. My experience shows me this is true only when a dog is fed a food with insufficient animal protein. Lack of animal protein, specifically the amino acid L-Lysine produces the "allergy," which is in itself a deficiency in disguise.

KELP

Kelp provides iodine to the body for correct functioning of the thyroid gland, which influences overall health, metabolism, skin and coat. Kelp also contributes to good pigmentation. Kelp contains some protein, is rich in iodine, calcium, sulfur, magnesium, iron, copper, phosphorus, sodium and potassium as well as vitamins A, B, E and D.

Kelp also contains something called mannitol, a gentle purgative and bile stimulant, small amounts of lecithin, a phosphorus compound thought to be of great importance in the knitting of broken bones, especially in the older dog, and some carotin, a precursor to vitamin A production.

COD-LIVER OIL

Cod-liver oil contains vitamins A and D, and essential fatty acids. It is used in the dinner meal to help regulate calcium metabolism and the utilization of phosphorus. Vitamin D aids in the absorption of calcium and phosphorus, transports them to the teeth and bones and helps to keep normal blood levels of calcium.

Formerly used to cure rickets in children and young animals, cod-liver oil also aids in maintaining healthy bones, and preventing tooth and gum diseases. Cod-liver oil lowers the cholesterol and triglyceride levels in the blood—the primary causes of heart disease.

Dogs housed outside, or exposed to a lot of sunlight in the summer, don't require quite as much cod-liver oil since vitamin D is produced in the body when exposed to sunlight, and you can have too much of a good thing. So reduce by half the amount put into the dinner meal. Other dogs should stay on the amounts of cod-liver oil listed in the adult dog diet charts year-round (see Chapter 2).

BONE MEAL

Bone meal is necessary to balance the calcium, phosphorus and magnesium levels in your dog's body and it is one of the primary sources of calcium in the diet. Bone meal balances the mineral levels of both the meat and the cottage cheese, which are high in phosphorus and low in calcium. Used because of the perfect balance of these minerals, bone meal is important to the proper formation of bones and teeth, and to prevent skeletal and joint diseases.

Bone meal must be fed to your dog along with cod-liver oil, in order for the correct absorption of minerals to take place. Calcium metabolism is a complex affair involving many systems in the body. For example, calcium competes in the kidneys for storage with sodium. Too much sodium in a diet causes calcium loss and low readings in the blood work.

Buying bone meal should be done with care. The company I have used for over 20 years supplies bone meal originating in South America. It comes from ranch or range cattle not exposed to the pollutants so commonly found in cattle grazing by roadsides in the United States who show a high level of lead in their bones.

RAW WHEAT GERM

Used primarily for its vitamin E content, raw wheat germ also contains high concentrations of vitamin B and many minerals including iron, calcium, copper, magnesium, manganese, zinc, phosphorus and potassium. Used also for improvement of oxygen utilization and thereby performance, especially when under stress, wheat germ improves endurance and vitality.

WHEAT BRAN

Wheat bran provides fiber for proper stool formation and elimination of waste materials through the colon. It simulates the action of the fur or feathers of a prey animal that the wolf in your living room would be eating if he were still hunting on his own. A clean colon does not provide a suitable environment for worms. The high fiber content helps to prevent diseases of the colon such as cancer. Wheat bran contains some vitamin B and absorbs up to eleven times its own weight in water.

COTTAGE CHEESE

Cottage cheese is used on the sixth day of the Natural Diet. Meat contains a lot of nitrogen waste, which is filtered through the kidneys. Giving the kidneys a rest one day a week by using cottage cheese, and also one half-day fast, eases their workload. Cottage cheese has eight parts phosphorus to one part calcium, so for balance the correct amount of bone meal, which is listed in the diet charts, has to be used.

DIFFERENT KINDS OF MEAT

Testing thousands of dogs through kinesiology for over 20 years (*see* Chapter 11), has shown me that the majority of dogs prefer beef, some dogs prefer chicken, and some can go back and forth between the two. Some dogs test periodically for lamb, turkey and fish. Chicken, lamb, turkey, fish and venison all contain higher amounts of amino acids than beef so have a higher protein content. A healthy dog does not need the higher amount of protein, but prefers to be maintained on beef.

Keep in mind that your adorable pet needs foods to complement the needs of his body—he is, after all, the "wolf in your living room."

During certain seasons where individual weakness in a system may appear, chicken may be needed to bring the dog back into balance. I prefer not to use turkey on a regular basis, since it is high in tryptophan, which acts as a depressant.

RAW OR COOKED

One thing all of the preceding proteins have in common is that they need to be fed to your dog raw. Stories abound in the dog world about parasites that are contained in raw meat, and that feeding a dog raw meat makes him vicious. Like other old wives tales, there is little truth to this one either. Raw meat may have a high bacterial count on the outside of it, and chicken may have salmonella. A healthy dog can cope with both. If you feel nervous about this issue, clean your meat using the Parcell system of cleaning food (*see* below). Remember that apple cider vinegar also kills bacteria.

RAW MEAT & SICK DOGS

If you have to use cooked meat because your dog has been sick and cannot yet tolerate raw meat, you need to add digestive enzymes to help break it down. Use either Hydrozyme or Unleash (*see* Appendix II). When your dog is feeling better and on the road to recovery, reintroduce raw meat.

WATER

Your dog should have access to fresh water in a clean stainless-steel or glass bowl at all times. For the puppy that is being housetrained, pick up the dish at 8:00 p.m.

Your dog uses water for absorption of nutrients, as well as maintenance of body temperature. It helps to detoxify the body and transport toxic substances out of the body through the eliminative organs. Water is also used to keep the acid levels of the blood constant.

The kind of food you feed your dog will determine how much water your dog will drink. Dry food contains very little moisture, about 10%, and your dog needs

Fresh water should always be readily available to both puppies and older dogs.

to drink around a quart of water for every pound of dry food consumed. A dog that is fed canned food, which contains up to 78% moisture, will drink much less. A dog fed the Natural Diet will drink little water, since the raw foods contains a large amount of moisture. If your dog is drinking more water than usual, this can be the first sign of kidney or bladder problems, and a visit to your veterinarian is in order.

WILLARD WATER XXX

Dr. Willard, Professor Emeritus of Chemistry at the South Dakota School of Mines and Technology, discovered a unique catalyst that alters the molecular structure of ordinary water. In his product, Willard Water XXX, one of the ingredients is fossilized organics from refined lignite. The lignite, which is rich in carbon, is added to "reactivate" the catalyst-altered water (CAW). Lignite is a source of trace minerals, nutrients, amino acids, humic acids, carbon and natural ingredients that act as growth accelerators in plants. Researchers have also found traces of antibiotics that naturally occur in lignite.

Farmers have used Willard Water XXX to improve crops and cattle ranchers have used it in their cattle's drinking water to keep them healthy. Farmers who soaked their seeds in it found that it produces better crops, even withstanding droughts. It's been used on third-degree burns that healed with healthy, pink, unscarred skin.

A kennel that specialized in racing Greyhounds reported that Willard Water XXX was able to get rid of a stubborn virus. Other dog owners describe aggressive dogs becoming mellow after using Willard Water XXX in their drinking water. A tablespoon can be added to your dog's meat meal to kill bacteria.

Willard Water XXX works topically as a treatment for many skin disorders, especially hot spots. It acts as an eyewash, and can be used to clean ears. When you are traveling with your dog, add it to the drinking water to keep his stress levels under control and to counteract polluted water supplies. I have used Willard Water XXX for many years. I use it on hot spots and it dries up the inflamed areas over night. I spray it on cuts to stop the bleeding, and insect bites to reduce the swelling and irritation.

There are two kinds of Willard Water XXX, clear and dark. Both are available in a concentrated form, and you add one ounce of the clear and two ounces of the dark to a gallon of distilled water.

DR. PARCELL'S SYSTEM OF CLEANSING FOOD

Hazel Parcell, Ph.D., D.C., N.D., developed a system of cleansing food of pesticides, fungi, parasites, bacteria and heavy metals using bleach.

Add a small amount of Clorox to a large amount of water, and soak raw foods in this mixture. The bleach acts like a magnet to toxins and pulls them out of the produce. Most of the toxins used in the production of food are removed. Apples and grapes, for example, are sprayed at least 15 times before they reach the marketplace. Dr. Parcell maintains that there are many other advantages to using this system of cleansing. Fruits and vegetables last much longer, their flavor is enhanced, and wilted vegetables return to their normal crispness. Grapefruit seed extract can be used in place of Clorox.

Sort your vegetables and fruits into different piles. Eggs and meat should be separated. Use ½ teaspoon of Clorox to 1 gallon of water. Fruits and vegetables are soaked for 10 minutes, then rinsed. Fill up the sink and soak them again in fresh water for 10 minutes. Drain, dry and store.

Eggs are soaked in the Clorox bath for 30 minutes and then rinsed as above. Meat can be placed into a colander and is soaked from 10 to 15 minutes, then rinsed as above.

4 Preparation of the Natural Diet

Any new endeavor looks daunting at the beginning, like learning a new computer program, or trying to make heads or tails out of the instructions for programming your new VCR. The Natural Diet is no different, but after you have gone through the preparation process for the first time, and with a few repetitions, it soon becomes second nature.

THE CEREAL MEAL

Flaked oats make up 75% of the cereal meal, and 25% comes from other grains, such as buckwheat groats, a combination of which seems to agree with most dogs. If your dog refuses to eat this combination, or it is expelled undigested, go to a different combination. You can substitute either barley grits or cracked wheat for the oats, and millet for the buckwheat. If those still pass through undigested, go to brown rice. The cereal meal produces a stool that is less formed than that of the meat meal and is relatively pale in color. This is normal.

Oats, barley and wheat are acid-based grains, buckwheat and millet are alkaline grains, and brown rice is a neutral grain. Your dog needs the combination of both acid and alkaline grains. Some dogs like their grains changed throughout the course of the year. If your dog starts to leave his breakfast, you might try feeding him barley grits or wheat instead of oatmeal, and substitute millet or brown rice for the buckwheat. Rye is a grain that few dogs can digest, so we generally avoid it. Organically grown grains are best, but are also more expensive.

How to Make the Cereal Meal

The weights in the charts are dry weights. For easy use, weigh the grain on a scale and establish a cup measure. Use three times the amount of water to one part grain.

Take a large saucepan and bring the water and vegetables (one-half cup for a 50-pound dog) to a boil. Stir in the grain. Mix well, bring back to a boil and turn off the heat. Leave for at least two hours, or preferably overnight before using. Some grains take longer to cook than others and leaving them overnight will cook all the grains and make them digestible for your dog. The finished product should be runny rather than sticky, which makes it easier to handle. Place the cereal into a glass or high quality stainless-steel bowl and add the appropriate supplements. Mix well, add yogurt, kefir or raw milk, and feed at room temperature.

VEGETABLES TO USE IN THE CEREAL MEAL

While vegetables are not a crucial part of the Natural Diet since all nutrients are found in the other ingredients, they provide an additional rich source of vitamins and minerals and dogs love them. Use a variety of vegetables each week. Fresh vegetables are preferred, but frozen vegetables can be substituted when necessary. Fresh locally grown vegetables are best, especially if organic. Using vegetables that are in season helps to support the function of various organs in the dog's body and is generally cheaper. Before using any vegetables, make sure they are washed thoroughly.

When you use vegetables, put them through a food processor, or lightly steam them, it doesn't matter to your dog. I put the vegetables into the cereal water as it is coming to a boil, so they flavor the cereal.

WINTER TO EARLY SPRING

Use root vegetables such as carrots, parsnips, leeks and beets, as well as celery and cucumbers; green leafy vegetables (not spinach or beet tops too often, because they leach out calcium from the body); escarole or endive; pumpkin; sweet potatoes; garlic and any variety of squash and asparagus when in season. Broccoli, Brussels sprouts, cauliflower and cabbage can be used once a week, but are more difficult to digest for some dogs, and frequently cause gas. Lettuces, radishes and garlic can be used year-round.

LATE SPRING, SUMMER AND EARLY FALL

Use green leafy vegetables such as collard greens, kale, mustard greens, and any variety of squashes, green or yellow beans, garlic and radishes. Avoid peas, collard, mustard, and turnip greens, if your dog is on thyroid medication.

THE MEAT MEAL

Feed your dog meat and liver raw, five times a week. Put all the supplements into your dog's bowl, add a little hot water to break down the cellulose in the herbs, and make into a sticky paste. Then add the meat and liver, mix well and serve. On the sixth day the cottage cheese is substituted for the meat, and on the seventh day the dog is fasted in the afternoon.

The meat to use is beef muscle meat. This is labeled rump roast, sirloin, filet, or chuck in your supermarket. You can also use heart or ground versions of the above. Avoid meat that is too fatty. Deboned chicken can be used for those dogs that cannot tolerate beef, and should be used in the same way.

The stool produced from the meat meal is small, dark and well-formed.

USING HERBS

Herbs bridge the gap between nutrition and physical well-being. While the diet provides all known nutrients, there are times when something is missing. It could be caused by the season, the source of the ingredients, or the environment. Herbs fill that gap. Full of vitamins, minerals, protein, carbohydrates and fat, herbs play an important part in the dog's diet.

Still present in many of our domesticated dogs today is the instinctive ability to select grasses and weeds that balance their systems. At different times of the year, they will eat different grasses, because they know they are good for them. They don't go around talking to each other or you, saying "Hum, it's spring and I need to eat some milk thistle to strengthen my liver," they just know that at that time of the year, milk thistle is what they need.

Herbs work together with a good quality diet, and many of them can be used for medicinal purposes. When you are starting out on the Natural Diet, choose for your meat meal those that you can use all year. As you progress and feel more confident in what you are doing, you can then start using herbs to stimulate certain systems of your dog's body, from season to season.

You can buy herbs from your supermarket, health food store, or in bulk from catalogs. At first, buy small amounts and freeze or store them in a dark, cool place. Exposing them to the air or heat diminishes their nutritional value.

HERBS TO USE THROUGHOUT THE YEAR

Alfalfa, garlic, comfrey leaf, watercress, goldenrod, dandelion and rosemary can be used in all seasons. Available in dried form at most health food stores and some supermarkets, buy around ¼ pound of each. At different times of the year, most of these are also available fresh in your supermarket. Fresh or dried, they both work. Mix together and use three or four of the herbs listed at the beginning of this section. If you use fresh herbs, use double the amount of dry. The first week, use the appropriate amount listed on the correct weight chart for your dog. The following week, use the herbs you didn't use the first week. The following weeks you can mix and match the herbs. If you use the same combination over and over, they lose their nutritional effectiveness. To get the same benefit, you would have to feed larger quantities of the herbs. Rotating the herbs takes care of this. Do not isolate herbs and use them by themselves except for medicinal purposes.

Fall and Winter Herbs

Herbs for fall and winter are: mullein leaves, angelica root, marshmallow root, parsley, nettles, comfrey root or leaf, corn silk, burdock root, ginger root, goldenrod, raspberry leaves, watercress, rosemary, sage, cayenne pepper, dandelion root and alfalfa. These are used on a rotational basis. Mix three or four together into several combinations and use them for one week at a time. Use cayenne, which together with ginger root stimulates the circulation and digestive tract, in tiny amounts. Add a pinch to each herbal mix.

Spring and Summer Herbs

For spring and summer make up several combinations using dandelion leaves and flowers, borage, peppermint leaves, sorrel, goldenrod leaves, golden seal, licorice root, rosemary, watercress, comfrey leaves, alfalfa and milk thistle.

MEDICINAL HERBS

When used for medicinal purposes, fresh herbs are best because their potency is so high, but you may have to settle for dried. Herbs also come in capsules, tablets, liquids and infusions. Medicinal herbs are wonderful for dogs, but are beyond the scope of this book. Many good books have been written on the subject and my favorites are listed in Appendix II.

CAUTION

Comfrey is a herb that contains ingredients which can interfere with the kidneys when they are not functioning correctly. It should not be used when kidney disease has been diagnosed.

FRUITS

Apples, apricots, bananas, dried unsulfured raisins, prunes and dates are some of the fruits you can feed your dog. Use fresh fruits that are in season in the area or country in which you live. In general, dogs do not like citrus fruits, but during spring and early summer they may have a craving for oranges or lemons. Make sure they are thoroughly washed before giving them to your dog.

BONES

Once or twice a week your dog can have a bone. The kind of bone is important. The large femurs or leg bones from a cow are safe, as well as large knuckle bones. These do not splinter. You can also use chicken neck bones and wing tips a couple of times a week. Bones should be fed to your dog as a dessert, after the dog has eaten a regular meal. All bones should be fed raw. *Note:* Never feed a fresh bone to your dog on an empty stomach.

Dogs love bones and large beef bones keep them happy for hours at a time. Giving your dog bones to chew has the added advantage of keeping his teeth spotlessly clean. Bones are invaluable in raising puppies. Bones satisfy the craving to chew, which is especially strong in young dogs. Puppies that have bones to gnaw on, particularly during the teething process, are less likely to chew furniture or clothing. This directed chewing also furthers the development of their jaws, cheek muscles and head formation. Cabbage stumps and carrots provide an alternative to fresh bones.

BONE CONTAMINATION

A healthy dog can withstand the bacterial contamination that comes from the bones lying around or being buried, dug up again and eaten with renewed relish later. However, if your dog is recovering from an illness, or is being switched over

Not only is exercise fun, it is absolutely necessary for a healthy dog.

from a commercial food to the Natural Diet, you will need to reduce the bacterial count. For the first month of the diet, scald the bones in boiling water to reduce their bacteria count. Place them into a sieve or colander in the sink and pour boiling water over them, and cool before feeding them to your dog. Do not use cooked bones—they splinter!

EXERCISE

For the Natural Diet to work correctly, it presupposes a certain amount of daily exercise. This is a program for health; and no diet, however superior, will provide the kind of health necessary to live a long life without adequate daily exercise. Take your dog for regular walks, which not only improves his health, but yours too. Aim for exercising up to two hours daily, depending on the needs of your breed. You don't have to do it all at once. But, letting your dog out into the yard to exercise himself is just not good enough.

TOO FAT OR TOO THIN

Your dog will get fat on the amount of food listed on the charts, unless you regularly exercise him. For the relatively inactive dog, you may have to cut the cereal and meat meals by as much as 30%, but keep the supplements the same. There are some dogs that simply get fat no matter what. The important thing to remember is that you need to keep the supplements at the ideal weight for your dog, and cut back as you need to on the cereal and meat meals.

In the morning meal you cut back on the amount of cereal you feed, but keep everything else the same. In the evening meal, you reduce the amount of beef, liver and bone meal, keeping all the other supplements the same for the weight of your dog.

Conversely, there are true working dogs, and they may require up to double the amounts listed on the charts. These dogs work for a living, putting in their 8 hours, and using an enormous amount of energy. It takes more food for them to maintain their weight. If you have a dog like this, just increase their food by adding the amount for the 10-pound dog as described in Chapter 2 to the amount you are already feeding. When you get to the next weight on the chart, use that. For example, my 58-pound labrador retriever, Annabel, is extremely energetic. She gets the 100-pound dog diet that my more laid-back newfy gets. She needs this amount of food and supplements to maintain her weight.

This dog is working for a living—he needs the proper diet to fuel his busy lifestyle.

RECIPES

HOMEMADE DOG BISCUITS

>   8 cups whole-wheat flour
>
>   2 tablespoons molasses (optional)
>
>   2 tablespoons honey
>
>   ½ cup mixed dried herbs (optional)
>
>   2½ cups or so of warm water
>
>   2 tablespoons safflower oil

Turn the oven to 375°F, and warm the flour in the oven for a few minutes. When it is warmed through, make a well in the center of the flour. Pour in the molasses, honey and water, and mix to a sticky dough. Cover and leave for 15 minutes.

Make a well in the center of the dough and add the oil and dried herbs. Mix the dough thoroughly. Shape dough into small balls, flatten them to about ¼-inch thick, and put onto a baking sheet which has been sprinkled with whole-wheat flour. Bake at 375°F for about 40 minutes until evenly browned. Cool and refrigerate. These last about seven days in the refrigerator, unless your dog gets to them first.

For extra hard and crunchy biscuits, flatten them more, brush with egg white before putting them in the oven, and after they have cooked, turn off the heat, and leave in the oven two more hours or overnight to dry out. A great snack for you as well.

CARROT STICKS

Scrub carrots thoroughly and rinse under cold water. Cut into strips and put into a plastic bag in refrigerator. Use these as treats when traveling or at shows. They are refreshing to both dog and handler. Can be used instead of dog biscuits at night.

LIVER TREATS

Wash liver, then place in a saucepan with water to cover. Bring to a boil and cook for four minutes. Drain, cool and cut into small bite-sized pieces. Put them on a lined baking sheet and place in a 300°F oven for around two hours, or until dried out. These are wonderful training treats and are not messy to carry around in your pocket. If you keep them in a covered container in the refrigerator, they last several months.

For a change, liberally sprinkle garlic powder over the liver before it is baked.

HOMEMADE COTTAGE CHEESE

2 gallons of milk that has high fat content

³/₄–1 cup of lemon juice or vinegar (the preference is vinegar)

1 old clean pillow case

large pan, not aluminum

colander

slotted spoon

thermometer

Heat the milk to 180°F (that's just after it scums on the top). Remove from the stove and cool down to about 100°F. Set pan in sink with ice cubes and cold water. Remove, add vinegar and stir gently. The fat will separate from the whey. It takes about 10 minutes.

Place opened pillow case in colander and pour curds and whey into pillow case. Lift out of colander and allow to drain. The longer you let it drain, the dryer it will become. To make it a more creamy cottage cheese, add some fresh cream to get the consistency you like.

If you add chives and garlic to the curds and whey after it has finished draining, then chill for a couple of hours, you have a nice farmer's cheese, which you can enjoy with your dog.

This recipe comes from Kathy Allen, Huzar Farms in Ohio. Kathy raises Briards, sheep and goats.

OTHER TREATS

Any vegetables or fruit, fresh or dried, can be used as treats. My dogs love lettuce, so when I have salad I save the outer leaves for them. They also like cucumbers and radishes. Radishes are particularly popular in the winter in my dog family, and I have to be careful that they don't eat too many. Use treats in moderation. In training I find raisins to be ideal. They are the right size and they don't take a long time to chew, although the liver treats are the favorites.

My dogs have a passion for sourdough bread, and so once in a while they get a small piece as a treat. Other breads do not seem to have the same appeal.

KENNEL MIXES & LABOR-SAVING IDEAS

Making up each individual meal is a tedious job, even for one dog, much less six, which is how many I have. To save time, I prepare the meals ahead of time.

For the breakfast meal, I make enough cereal for three days by multiplying the ingredients by three. After the grain/vegetable mixture has cooled, I add the remaining ingredients and mix, except the eggs and the yogurt or kefir. This mixture will keep for three days refrigerated if kept tightly closed in a container. After that it turns sour. Now breakfast is reduced to mixing the grain mixture with the yogurt or kefir and adding an egg every other day.

When I need to make larger amounts for a longer period, I multiply the ingredients by the number of days and freeze what will not be used in three days. The mixture can be stored as individual meals, or in bulk.

For the evening meal, I make enough for five days. I mix the meat/liver and remaining ingredients. This mixture will keep for five days in the refrigerator (the ACV acts as a preservative). The cottage cheese meal I still make up individually, or I use the Natural Diet Foundation P.M. Crumble (*see* below).

MULTIPLE DOG HOUSEHOLDS

I have a multiple dog household with two dogs just over 100 pounds, one 65-pound dog, one 58-pound dog and two 25-pound dogs. I make up food for a 100-pound dog in bulk. I then feed my 100-pound dogs what is listed on the charts; the 65-pound dog and the 25-pound dogs get that much less. For my dogs it works out like this: 100-pound dog = 4 $\frac{1}{2}$ cups, 65-pound dog = 3 cups, and 25-pound dog = 1 cup. As mentioned above, the 58-pound Labrador gets the same as the larger dogs. This is the dry mix, meat and liver combined. Being concerned that everyone was getting what they needed, I followed up this mixing concept with blood work to make sure I had it right. It works for me. The amount you need to feed your dog also depends on his metabolism. With different activity levels, you adjust according to appearance and weight. The only dogs I have to watch carefully are the Dachshunds who gain weight at the drop of a hat. If they appear too fat, and this depends on the time of the year and their exercise levels, I drop their meat meal down to ³/₄ cup until they are a good weight again.

TRAVELING WITH THE NATURAL DIET

I have traveled with several dogs for up to 10 days with the Natural Diet. That is, traveling by car and staying in hotels. When I stay in hotels, I make sure that the cooler in which the food is stored is kept cold. I put in fresh ice in the morning and in the evening when I return to the room. As long as the meat is kept cold, it will last.

TRAVEL PREPARATION

There are several ways to prepare the meals for traveling, and with experience, you'll find the one best suited to you.

The individual cereal meals can be prepared ahead of time and frozen. The supplements can be added separately. I have successfully traveled with the whole meal, supplements and all, mixed together in a Ziploc™ bag, frozen and then defrosted.

The breakfast bars from the recipe given below are a good alternative. You will have to add your supplements separately, but you can do that by putting them into some fresh yogurt. If you make the breakfast bars, your dog will be thirsty, because by baking them, the moisture is removed and he is not receiving the same amount of water he is used to getting.

To determine how much to feed your dog, weigh an individual breakfast bar and compare it to the dry weight of grains on the appropriate chart. You can then calculate how many breakfast bars to feed him. Vitamin C, B complex and E are fed to your dog separately, usually in a little yogurt. I do travel with some cans of natural cat food for those dogs that stress when traveling. I place the supplements into the cat food and feed them on a spoon to the dogs.

BREAKFAST BARS

> 4 cups oats
>
> 1 cup buckwheat or millet, or wheat, or barley
>
> 1 cup of whole-wheat flour
>
> 1 cup boiling water
>
> 8 tablespoons cold-pressed safflower oil
>
> 8 tablespoons blackstrap molasses
>
> 2 tablespoons raw honey
>
> 4 medium eggs with shells
>
> 1 cup of raisins (optional)

Set oven for 350°F. Put all the ingredients into a large bowl. Mix with about 1 cup of boiling water. Make a sticky dough. Place on a well-greased baking pan and cook at 350°F for 45 minutes. Take out and score into squares. Turn out onto a wire rack to cool. If your dog prefers his breakfast bars on the crispy side, put back into the oven when you turn it off and leave overnight to dry out more.

THE NATURAL DIET FOUNDATION—
THE DEHYDRATED VERSION

When we wrote the first edition of this book, a dehydrated version of the Natural Diet was just an idea. Having worked several years on the concept, I have finally found a way to make it possible.

I was able to find a reliable manufacturer to help me. No compromises in selecting the ingredients have been made—all are human grade. The breakfast meal called NDF Porridge, excluding the vegetables and yogurt, is dehydrated. For breakfast, all you have to do is add fresh vegetables, water and yogurt, and you have a complete meal.

The evening meal called NDF Crumble is even easier. All the ingredients, except the meat but including the liver, are dehydrated into a crumble. Add the appropriate amount of raw meat, a little water for the crumble to stick to the meat, and voilà—a complete meal.

For those of you with busy lifestyles, you can now use this form of the Natural Diet on a regular basis. No more excuses this time. It also makes traveling with the diet a cinch.

CLINICAL TESTING

Before making the dehydrated version available, it was tested to make sure it did not compromise the raw Natural Diet. Dogs of all breeds, ages, lifestyles, and from different climates and environments were tested. The results were fantastic: Dogs and owners loved it, especially the convenience.

WATER SUPPLY

Taking your own supply of drinking water is preferable, but if that is not possible, use what is available on your trip, and add 2 tablespoons of Willard Water XXX to each bowl, so that your dog is not affected by the change.

TIMING OF MEALS

For best results, feed at approximately the same time of the day. Dogs have an extremely accurate biological clock, and they will be hungry at feeding time, whether or not it is convenient for you. They do best on a regular schedule. The same rule applies when you are traveling. That is why I like to pre-package the meals in their entirety, to make it easy for me to feed them on time.

Feeling good at the show.

Many dogs get nervous and suffer from stress when they are traveling and do better when the meat meal is fed in the morning. I like to start off days when I am exhibiting my dogs in shows with dogs that have eaten well and are well balanced; thus, they are able to fight off any viruses that may be present on the show grounds. I then feed them breakfast when we return to the hotel room in the afternoon and after they have had time to rest.

CRAVINGS

Dogs that show a marked preference for certain foods probably need that food to balance their diet. I had a dog that craved eggs and cabbage. Two years after these cravings surfaced, she was diagnosed with a rare blood disorder—her blood would not clot properly. Vitamin K, which is specific for blood clotting, is abundant in eggs and cabbage. She knew what she needed long before I knew of her disorder. By observing and listening to our dogs, we learn their needs.

Bull Terriers need a special diet.

BREED SPECIFICS

We have referred to the special needs of certain breeds of dogs. German Shepherds, Labrador Retrievers, Boxers, Bull Terriers, Newfoundlands and many of the working and herding dogs require a diet that is more acid based. For those dogs, add an amino acid complex tablet to the morning meal, except when feeding eggs. There may be other breeds or individuals that need a similar adjustment to their diet. One indication of a need for this adjustment is a dog that has dark-brown to black discharge in his ears, cystitis or urinary tract infections, poor pigmentation, hair coat and skin eruptions and an alkaline reading of his urine. To determine this, get some pH strips and test your dog's urine *first thing in the morning*. It should read between 6.2 to 6.5. If it is a number greater than 7, then add the amino acid complex.

Dalmatians, West Highland White Terriers and some Bedlington Terriers represent a special challenge. Since they are unable to deal with the nitrogen waste associated with high amounts of animal protein in their diets, or cannot eliminate some metals from their systems which are present in food, a diet higher and more carefully balanced is probably the best. These breeds do not tolerate beef or beef liver, which have a high nitrogen waste; so, you should rotate animal proteins that have a low nitrogen waste such as chicken, fish, yogurt, cottage cheese and eggs. I have been successful with these breeds by adding the amino acid complex tablet in their morning meal, vitamin B complex two times a day

Newfoundlands need a special diet, too.

and some extra vitamin C, so they can utilize the protein being fed to them. Many of these breeds do well on the Recover Formula (*see* Appendix II) used a couple of times a week, when they are under stress. These breeds need careful and continual monitoring by blood work to check protein levels and kidney function.

GRAIN INTOLERANCE

A few dogs are actually grain intolerant, which can be a sign of pancreatic and/or adrenal gland insufficiencies. Common symptoms are chronic ear discharges and continual itching when there are no parasites on the dog's skin. Don't ignore this. Check with your veterinarian and have a blood test done. Alter the Natural Diet by substituting vegetables that have a high starch content for grains in the breakfast. These include sweet potatoes, regular potatoes (peeled and the eyes removed—they can be toxic), all root vegetables, including beets, carrots, parsnips, and green and yellow beans. Starchy vegetables should comprise at least 50% of the total vegetable intake, with the remainder coming from green leafy vegetables. Vegetables that produce starch, which is turned into glucose and stored in the liver, are necessary for all vital functions of a dog's body, especially the thyroid gland.

Some dogs, as they age, and dogs that have been diagnosed with kidney or adrenal gland disorders, cannot tolerate grains in a boiled form. For those, I have had great success with the baked breakfast bars. Feed the vitamins separately.

GENERAL INFORMATION

Feeding your dog the Natural Diet is no more expensive than feeding a good quality, dry commercial dog food with supplements. You can save money by joining food cooperatives in your area where organic grains can be obtained. Raw honey, blackstrap molasses, wheat germ and herbs, as well as meat, can often be bought through cooperatives.

Blackstrap molasses and wheat bran can also be bought inexpensively from feed stores. These items are used in other animal feeds. Raw cow's milk is hard to find, and in many states it is against the law for farmers to sell unpasteurized milk. Call your local 4-H group to find someone who sells raw goat's milk, which is excellent for dogs, indispensable when raising puppies, and great for older dogs. You can also successfully freeze it.

SUBSTITUTIONS TO THE NATURAL DIET

The suppliers listed in Appendix II, are those that I have used for years. Their products have been tested for many years through blood work, and their quality has remained consistent. Will using different suppliers make a difference? Only a blood test will tell.

WHAT HAPPENS IF?...

It will happen to you, just like it happens to everyone else—you'll run out of food or you'll forget to defrost your meat, or you'll run out of cereal. It doesn't really matter, and your dog won't keel over and die! Give him whatever you are eating and for future reference, keep some extra meals in the freezer. Follow the Boy Scout motto—be prepared!

What you don't want to do is suddenly substitute commercial dog food for the raw food in the Natural Diet, because that will certainly upset your dog's stomach, sometimes with unpleasant results.

5 Special Supplements

In putting together this list, it was difficult to know where to stop. There are so many supplements available that it is virtually impossible to evaluate them all. The ones listed here are those that I use most frequently with my own or clients' dogs and have found to be effective. They have personally been researched by me, used on my own dogs and clinically tested using blood work.

As your dog's life progresses, you will occasionally have to add special supplements to his food to put his body in balance. Those with which I have had a great deal of success and have used with my own and clients' dogs, and have clinically tested are listed below. I do recognize that there are hundreds of supplements to choose from, and there is no one way to do things. *See* Appendix II, "Sources of Ingredients & Products" for information about where to obtain these products.

VITAMIN & MINERAL MIXES

Vitamin and mineral mixes are used to supplement diets that are deficient in vitamins and minerals. There are hundreds of mixes out there all containing various igredients. A word of caution—a poor quality or an unbalanced vitamin/mineral mix will cause more problems than it will cure, while a good vitamin/mineral mix can do wonders for a dog suffering from deficiency diseases. Use kinesiology (*see* Chapter 11) to see:

- If your dog needs a vitamin/mineral mix.

- How much to give.

- When to give the mix.

Retest on a regular basis. Overuse of vitamin/mineral mixes can create musculoskeletal dysfunctions in puppies and the overproduction of red blood cells in older dogs.

Pay special attention to the health of puppies. Since they grow so fast, it is essential that they receive excellent nutrition.

If you cannot use kinesiology, the rule of thumb is to use the mix for three weeks to one month, then reevaluate. I prefer to use these products only for a short time until the dog is once again in balance. Then I use them when he is subjected to any kind of stress. The time of the year has a great influence on how much your dog will need. The one we recommend, "Wellness," produced by PHD Products, contains herbs, enzymes, chelated vitamins, minerals and probiotics.

COPING WITH STRESS

Puppies going through growth stages, older dogs, and those dogs who have undergone surgery have special needs to counteract stress. The product I prefer contains vitamins and minerals from herbs, additional herbs that target and support each organ system in the body plus probiotics, enzymes, amino acids and fatty acids. Called "Recover," and put out by PHD Products, it also contains a small amount of colostrum. Colostrum is dried mother's milk and is a total food containing ingredients that help to boost the immune system of the weakened animal. Used for a short period of time, your dog will tell you when he has had enough. Colostrum will build the immune system to a point of saturation at which time your dog will start to scratch. This is the time to stop using the product. It can be used intermittently any time your dog is severely stressed.

COLOSTRUM

Colostrum can be bought as a separate product and used for other situations. It can be used to boost immune-deficient dogs. It supports normal cell growth, tissue repair and healing from trauma. Colostrum also helps to rejuvenate older animals. Wonderful for recovery from dog bites and in accident cases. Use for only a short time, as the saturation point is reached quickly.

COAT ADDITIVES

There are many coat additives on the market, and it is hard to know which is best. The beauty of using the Natural Diet is that you don't need any of them. Perfectly formulated to meet your dog's needs, the diet itself provides your pet with the most glorious coat he has ever had.

In making the transition from commercial food to a natural diet, or when a dog has been severely stessed, there will be times when a well-balanced coat additive can be utilized. I chose "Radiance" put out by PHD Products because most of the ingredients come from herbs. It also contains essential fatty acids.

AMINO ACID SUPPLEMENTS

Amino acids are necessary for almost every physical process within your dog's body. His energy production, muscle growth and repair, hormone production, the correct working of the endocrine gland system and the nervous system, which includes his brain activity, are all reliant upon amino acids.

Amino acids combine with vitamins and minerals in the body to produce the raw materials from which the body manufactures enzymes and hormones. They not

A naturally raised dog rarely needs coat supplements, as you can see from this dog's lustrous coat.

only act as catalysts for enzyme reactions, but can make up the enzymes themselves. They actually help run your dog's body.

THE KIND OF AMINO ACID SUPPLEMENT TO USE

After working with these supplements, I have reduced the number I actually use down to two products. One is a complex, meaning that all the amino acids are arranged in a natural way and come from a casein or milk base. I use Nature's Most product on a regular basis to supplement older dogs, or dogs on the Natural

Diet who require extra protein in their breakfast meal on the day the egg is not used.

The other supplement comes from a whitefish base and is actually predigested for easy absorption. Called Seacure, and available from Moss Nutrition, it is used in specific cases of illness and recovery. It is extremely effective with dogs undergoing cancer treatment, preventing nausea and loss of appetite. I have also used it effectively for puppies who show side effects from vaccines, for dogs recovering from surgery and for older dogs needing a boost in energy.

DIGESTIVE ENZYMES

Named after the food substances they digest and ending in '–ase,' there are many different kinds of enzymes. Pancreatic enzymes are protease, which help to digest protein, amylase, which helps to digests starch and lipase, which helps to digest fat. Enzymes that digest sugar are called sucrase; those that digest phosphorus are called phosphatase, etc. The Natural Diet is abundant in enzymes, but there are dogs who, because of illness or genetically acquired diseases, are deficient and need to be supplemented. Older dogs benefit greatly from the addition of enzymes. As their digestive tract ages, they become less efficient in digesting their food. Enzymes are put into the food directly before serving. They come in capsule, pill or powder form. "Unleash," put out by PHD Products, comes in both powder and pill form and is unique in terms of products available. It aids digestion through the entire digestive tract, starting in the stomach. Most products target the small intestine or just the pancreas. "Hydrozyme," available through Moss Nutrition, is used in cases where the stomach is unable to break down the food before passing into the small intestine. It is a little stronger than Unleash when targeting the stomach, although there are cases where these products can be used together.

WHY USE ENZYMES?

Found in all cells and fluids in the body, enzymes are specialized protein substances that speed up and create chemical reactions. They control, promote and guide all of life's vital processes, including the action of the muscles, storage of energy, breathing, digestion, reproduction and more. Enzymes are necessary for all digestion to take place, and particularly for the correct functioning of the stomach and the pancreas. Pepsin is the stomach's protein-splitting enzyme and rennin, only present in puppies, causes milk to coagulate changing its protein casein into a usable form. Killed at temperatures above 118° to 170°F, enzymes are not available in commercial dog foods.

Enzymes are catalysts, which means they cause an internal action without themselves being destroyed or changed in the process. Each enzyme acts on a specific food and one cannot be substituted for another. Enzyme deficiencies often mean the difference between health and sickness.

Degenerative diseases and cancer in particular, have been linked to enzyme deficiencies by researchers from the Universities of London, Wales, Wisconsin, Loyola and Yale Medical School. Cooked food is almost completely deficient in enzymes which are destroyed during the cooking process. The pancreas of rats increased in weight by 20% to 30% when fed cooked food. Cooked food makes the pancreas work harder because it passes through the digestive tract more slowly than raw food, tends to ferment, throws poisons back into the body causing gas, heartburn, headaches, eye troubles and more serious illnesses. Toxins begin to collect on the walls of the large intestine which causes putrefaction and auto-intoxication. Cooked foods also rob the stomach, salivary glands and intestines of enzymes. There seems to be a finite reservoir of enzymes in the body. If various organs and glands are continually robbed of their own enzymes, which must be utilized to digest food, then eventually the body breaks down. Studies from the Center for the Advancement of Cancer Education have shown that pancreatic enzymes selectively destroy cancer cells. If the pancreas is provided with the correct enzymes through feeding your dog the correct diet, then those enzymes can protect the body against cancer.

One third of the body's energy is required in the process of digestion. By supplementing with enzymes, the amount of time needed for digestion is reduced. Raw foods contain enzymes and do not rob the enzyme excreting organs in order to break down food reaching the stomach. Aging is directly related to enzyme robbing.

DIFFERENT KINDS OF ENZYMES

Bromelain from pineapple and Papain from papayas are different from other enzymes. They are digestive aids which selectively digest tissue that is dead. Both are helpful to the structural system of the body and in the reduction of scar tissue. Use when taking your dog for chiropractic adjustments—they will help your dog to hold the adjustment longer.

Papaya and vitamin B_6 used together, will help dogs overcome stool eating, which can be a sign of an enzyme deficiency, as well as becoming a nasty habit.

WHEN TO USE ENZYMES

If you have a breed that is predisposed to bloat or cancer, or that has difficulty maintaining weight, you will need to use digestive enzymes. Production of too much gas in the intestines, poor skin and hair coat, reproductive difficulties, changes in vision, fatigue, depression, muscle pains, cramps in chest and back, changes in the texture of the hair, brittle nails and all early cancer signs show a need for enzymes.

MELATONIN

Melatonin is a hormone that is produced by the pineal gland located near the center of the brain. Said to reduce stress, boost immunity, prevent insomnia and jet lag, it also promotes longevity. Melatonin can, in certain instances, be a valuable tool.

Used when epilepsy is first diagnosed, melatonin can be successful in eradicating seizures. Taken before bedtime, use a 3 mg tablet which comes with added vitamin B_6. Melatonin is available in most good health food stores. However, when a dog is continually having frequent grand mal seizures and is on medication, melatonin has had limited results.

A more holistic approach to reducing stress in the body and giving some of the same effects as melatonin, is a diet rich in foods which increase the body's ability to produce melatonin on its own. These are complex carbohydrates which maximize the amino acid tryptophan, one of the precursors to seratonin, which is then used to manufacture melatonin. Many of these foods are found in the Natural Diet, and include dairy products, chicken and turkey. Oats and bananas actually contain melatonin. All of these foods have a calming effect on the brain.

Some dog owners have been successful in using melatonin to control separation anxiety, fear of loud noises and thunderstorms, especially in the older dog. In some dogs lick dermatitis and flank sucking have responded to melatonin. Lick dermatitis is not a habit but signs of a diseased state. Dog people would not call flank sucking a habit, more a genetic fault since it is limited to one or two breeds. *Note:* Do not use melatonin with pregnant or lactating females.

DHA

Referred to in the section on Cancer in Chapter 7, DHA is short for docosa-hexaenoic acid. It is an omega-3 long-chain polyunsaturated fatty acid that is the primary building block of the brain and retina of the eye. The brain is 60% fat, and DHA is the most abundant fat in the brain and retina. DHA is abundant in eggs, red meat, fish and organ meats such as liver and kidney. Helpful in the treatment of cancer, eye diseases and senility in older dogs. One capsule a day in the evening meal would be enough for a medium size dog. The product we have used is called "Neuromins" and is available through Moss Nutrition.

DHEA

DHEA, or to give the chemical name, dehydroepiandrostrone, is the most abundant, naturally occurring hormone in the dog's body. It is produced by the adrenal glands and it has been called the mother of all hormones. The body uses it to produce both male and female hormones. While the fetus is still developing, DHEA levels are high and get even higher as the young dog grows to adulthood. Then production slows down dramatically and trickles almost to a stop as the dog ages.

The reduction in levels of DHEA are associated with aging diseases and impaired function of the immune system. At proper levels DHEA helps to lower cholesterol, reduce the incidence of cancer, diseases of the arteries, and brittle bones, all associated with the aging process. It helps to stabilize blood sugar while improving liver function. But the great news is that it protects the brain from senility, as well as increasing memory and retention of learning. This means that indeed we can teach an old dog new tricks.

Since DHEA is a precursor to hormones naturally found in the body of your dog, use it for three weeks at a time, with a one-week break, or alternatively every other day. I have found that it keeps my old dogs young for a longer period of time and that their working ability and retention of those things they have been taught over their lifetimes are maintained until they leave us.

Researchers found that giving DHEA to elderly mice when vaccinated makes them produce antibodies to the diseases as fast as, and equivalent to, those of young mice.

Available from many sources, the one that tested the best for the largest number of dogs comes from Nature's Most and is simply called DHEA.

CM—CETYL MYRISTOLEATE

As I mentioned in the story about Katharina and her arthritis, a product comes along once in awhile that actually lives up to its claims. Such is the product named CM for short. Experiments on this totally natural product were started in 1982, but it has only become popular in the last year or so, mainly because of its price reduction. It is unique in that it is only used in dogs for a short period of time—up to three weeks. It either works or it doesn't. CM is a medium-chained fatty acid, which is one of the major components of the membranes that surround the cells of the body. They are necessary for the building and maintainence of healthy cartilage.

Agility Labs.

CM is what is known as an immunomodulator. It acts to regulate the immune system. In its own way, it seems to reset the clock of some T-modulated memory cells. In the case of arthritis, these cells have been programmed to attack cartilage, causing inflammation, allowing the gel-like synovial fluid between the affected joints to become watery in substance, thereby allowing bone to hit bone causing the pain of arthritis. Once these memory cells are reprogrammed, inflammation ceases, the synovial fluid thickens and goes back to its gel-like consistency and therefore the joint is cushioned.

While the claims made for this product for humans cover many inflammatory diseases including arthritis, TMJ, sciatica, diabetes, Crohn's disease and many skin problems such as leg ulcers, lupus and psoriasis, more research needs to be done in dogs. Still, it is worth trying. Use it if you have a dog, old or young, with recurring limps, a weak rear end, a fused spine, arthritis of any description, or other diseases that may be T-cell related.

This product comes in two bottles. One contains the medium chained fatty acid, and the other contains supplements with which it acts in synchrony. If you can use kinesiology (*see* Chapter 11), test to see whether your dog needs a short course of CM.

Available through EHP Products, it is called Miristin (the fatty acid itself) which works together with Miristaid, a capsule that contains many nutrients that make the fatty acid work better.

GLANDULARS

Another word for glandulars is cell therapy. It is defined as either injection of, or oral administration of healthy cells into a body to promote physical regeneration of organs and tissue. For example, liver glandulars given to a dog with liver disease will help that dog make more healthy liver tissue. Glandulars have been used successfully on more than 30,000 human patients. Glandulars can come from dead, but healthy adult animals or neonates. I prefer the neonatal product available from Moss Nutrition.

When cells from a specific organ or gland are introduced into another species, they recognize their own kind. A liver cell recognizes a liver cell, a heart cell recognizes a heart cell, and so on. Therefore it is possible to treat not only the major organs of the body, but also the brain, ovaries and testes, the endocrine gland system, respiratory system, etc.

I have found these products to be a very powerful tool in the healing process. By using glandulars in dealing with kidney or liver disease, for example, the healing process is considerably shortened. They are rarely used more than three to four weeks at a time.

GLUCOSAMINE SULFATE

This is an amino sugar formed from glucose needed by the body tissues, especially the synovial fluid in the joints, to function correctly. Deficiencies can show up in tendons, ligaments, cartilage, synovial fluid, mucus membranes, parts of the eye, blood vessels and heart valves. Many studies have been done show-ing its efficacy when used for inflammation in tissues, ligaments, and muscles, disc and sciatic nerve functions, inflamed joints associated with aging and the elasticity of spinal discs.

Good results have been obtained in arthritis cases, as well as weak rear ends, and spinal fusion when glucosamine sulfate is used in dogs either by itself, or together with chondroitin sulfate. Products containing chrondroitin are very expensive. It is my experience that the majority of dogs do not need it, and that glucosamine works well by itself. Use kinesiology to see what is appropriate for your dog (*see* Chapter 11).

With the advent of the product CM, which includes glucosamine, I have found a short course of CM to be more beneficial for most dogs rather than using glucosamine sulfate daily.

PARA-YEAST

This product is fast becoming one of the staples to use when rehabilitating a dog with an overgrowth of yeast or parasitic infestation. The environment in which many dogs live is saturated with yeasts, molds, fungus and parasites. These growths are found in city parks, the woods, under the trees and in the ground, and are likely to be present in your dog's body, too. When your dog's body is under stress—surgery, vaccines, medication—these parasites and yeasts multiply. A natural wormer, Para-Yeast contains a mixture of cleansing herbs. Use Para-Yeast if your dog has:

- Been treated regularly for worms
- Recurring ear infections
- Eye irritations, swelling of eyelids or dry eye
- Sore throats
- Respiratory difficulties
- Thyroid disease
- Swollen joints
- Ongoing skin rashes, or is constantly washing his feet or genital areas
- Hair loss or brittle nails

Para-Yeast is available through PHD Products.

SKIN PRODUCTS

The Neem tree is called the village pharmacy in its native India. The entire tree, from its bark to its leaves, is used to make remedies. These remedies are used to cleanse the body of internal and external parasites.

Neem comes in a powder form, used to make a tea for internal use; and creams, oil, lotions and sprays for external use. The Neem leaves, made into a strong tea, and put into a spray attached to your hose, can be used in your kennel to disinfect it, and in your garden to rid the ground of parasites. I use an outdoor Neem spray to protect my dogs against ticks and the Lyme disease they carry. A few drops of the concentrated oil, in a mild herbal shampoo, will get rid of fleas. It is also effective for skin conditions, including hot spots, eczema and minor cases of mange and fungus.

Elbow calluses can be softened with the lotion and the skin rejuvenated.

Neem is available only through Naturamix.

6 Breeding Your Dog & Raising Puppies

Before breeding your dog, you will need to make some adjustments to the Natural Diet.

THE MALE

Two weeks prior to breeding, double the amount of vitamin E in his diet. Continue to use this amount during the time he is servicing the female. Feed him eggs five times a week. Egg yolk contains selenium, which together with vitamin E, helps to increase the sperm count.

THE FEMALE

Your female will be pregnant for nine weeks. For the first six weeks, keep her on a maintenance diet for her normal weight. For the remaining three weeks, gradually increase her food until it is 25% more than her maintenance diet at the time of whelping.

At about 28 days into her pregnancy, she will not be hungry. This is normal, as the growing puppies push up against the bottom of the stomach, giving her a feeling of being full. This lasts about two to three days and then her appetite returns to normal. At the end of her pregnancy, she again may not want to eat. Just feeding a meal of goat's milk and honey is enough during this time.

RASPBERRY LEAF TEA

Four weeks before your female's due date or halfway through the pregnancy, add raspberry leaf tea to each meal. This tea helps to tone up the uterus making whelping easier. Take two tablespoons of dried raspberry leaves and put them into two cups of water. Bring to a boil and simmer for a few minutes. Remove from the heat and leave overnight. Strain out the leaves, and put the tea into the refrigerator. Use one tablespoon per meal for a 50-pound dog. After the puppies are delivered, halve the amount of raspberry leaf tea, and feed it to the female in each meal for the first week. This helps to clean the uterus of any fluids, tissues, and waste that may be left from the pregnancy.

EXERCISE

To keep her muscles toned for the job of whelping, your female should be well exercised during her pregnancy. For the last two weeks, however, do not make the exercise too vigorous or take her to places where she could be exposed to infections from other dogs.

AFTER WHELPING

For 48 hours after delivery, the new mother will be reluctant to leave her puppies. If she has eaten some of the placentas, she won't be very hungry. Her first meal needs to be a liquid one. Offer some raw goat's milk and raw honey, or yogurt or kefir and raw honey to boost her energy. The next meal can be her regular cereal meal and followed by her regular meat meal. For the first week after whelping, keep to the 25% increase in her diet. As the puppies grow, their demands for milk from her will increase, until she reaches maximum capacity during the third and fourth week. During this time you have to increase her diet up to four times her normal amount. Remember to add the raspberry leaf tea to her meals.

Few females can eat enough at two meals a day to produce enough milk to support a litter of fast-growing puppies. My Newfoundlands required four to five feedings a day to keep up the milk supply, and the Wirehaired Dachshunds needed six meals daily to keep up with the milk production. The mother dog should maintain her own weight, plus produce sufficient milk for her litter without the need of supplementation.

If the stress on the female feeding puppies is too great and she has a large litter to feed, the weaning process may have to start at 21 days instead of the normal 28 days.

WEANING PUPPIES

Puppies from 0–28 days are fed entirely by their mothers. After 28 days the weaning process can begin. When weaning, I've found it easier to take the entire weight of the litter and use it as a guide for determining the litter's diet. For example, if you have six 5-pound puppies at around 28 days, the weight of the litter is 30 pounds. Use the Weaning Diet for 10-pound Puppies chart that follows and multiply it by three to equal 30 pounds. If the litter weighs 24 pounds, multiply the 10-pound diet by 2.4, etc. Make up the food for the entire litter, divide it and then feed each puppy individually in a separate bowl so that all the puppies have a chance to eat the same amount of food. Some puppies eat very quickly, and some more slowly.

Before feeding the puppies, take the mother dog away from the litter and let her out to play. Let the puppies eat, bring the mother back and let the puppies nurse. Allow the mother to finish whatever food the puppies leave uneaten.

Puppies need to nurse from their mother as long as is possible. Remember, mother's milk is the perfect food for them and provides protection from disease. A well-fed mother can supply milk to her puppies at least up until they're seven weeks of age and sometimes longer. As time goes on, her milk supply will start to dry up naturally. She will rarely spend more than a few minutes in the whelping box allowing the puppies to nurse and then she'll jump out. I like my females to feed the puppies up to the point they leave for their new homes at 49 days.

Feeding pups individually eliminates the competitive frenzy of dinnertime.

Females who feed their puppies for the entire seven weeks, and who are carefully supplemented, should show no sign of having whelped a litter at the end of the lactation period. Puppies suckling on the mammary glands helps them to contract and return to normal. Your female will return to her sylph-like figure. If, however, you take the puppies away at the peak of feeding, the mammary glands do not have a chance to contract and return to normal and she will look "baggy" ever after.

MOTHERS WHO RUN OUT OF MILK

When an older female is bred, she may have difficulty in making enough milk to supply a large litter. The weaning process may have to start at 21 days. Use the charts that follow for feeding the puppies. If the mother is not feeding her puppies and weaning has to start at 21 days, it is okay to decrease her diet to 10% over maintenance during this time. After the pups have left at seven weeks, reduce the mother's diet back to normal. Increase her amount of exercise and she will regain her figure in no time.

MOTHERS WHO MAKE TOO MUCH MILK

Some females make too much milk for their puppies or they have too much milk for the number of puppies they have had. If the milk is not equally suckled from each of the mammary glands, the mother dog can get mastitis which is a hardening of the mammary glands. These get hot and hard and she may run a temperature. You need to apply hot packs and express the milk yourself for a while until the glands soften up. The homeopathic remedies, Apis, Belladonna, Bryonia, Phytolacca and Urtica Urens are helpful. If this goes on for more than a few hours, a visit to the veterinarian is in order. You do not want her to get an infection. She may have to go onto a course of antibiotics anyway. Keep the pups away from nursing on the affected gland—which is painful, until it is soft and pliable again.

Antibiotics in the milk can cause the puppies to have runny stools. Add some slippery elm powder to the mother's food, plus some acidophilus tablets or capsules to replenish the natural intestinal bacteria which are swept out with the use of antibiotics. This will bring her stools back to normal, as well as those of the pups. If the pups have persistent runny stools, make up some peppermint tea and, using an eyedropper, put some into their mouths. The homeopathic Carbo Veg.

is also good for upset stomachs (*see* Chapter 12 for aid in dosage amounts). Having the pups miss one meal may also help. There is a liquid homeopathic remedy just for diarrhea called Diarrhea Relief, which is easy to use with puppies.

HOW TO START WEANING PUPPIES

Some puppies are more active than others, and you may have to double the amounts below. Your puppies should be satisfied after eating and not whine or cry. You want the puppies to be slim so that you can feel their ribs, but not so thin that the ribs can be seen. A covering over the ribs is just right.

- Separate the mother dog from the litter.
- Mix up the entire amount of food and then divide, feeding each puppy in an individual bowl.
- Have fresh water available.

After feeding the pups, bring back the mother, allow the pups to nurse, and then put them outside into fresh air and sunshine if the weather allows.

This puppy wants to make sure there is nothing left!

WEANING DIET FOR 10–POUND PUPPIES

28–35 Days

8 a.m.   Feed at room temperature.

½ cup of raw milk, or goat's milk

½ teaspoon raw honey

¼ teaspoon slippery elm powder

Put into a blender and mix. Feed puppies in individual bowls. Then allow the mother to nurse her puppies.

Noon

1 ounce dry-weight baby cereal, consisting of oats and barley mixed and cooked

½ cup raw milk

50 mg. vitamin C

Mix up in a blender and serve in individual bowls. Now allow the mother dog to nurse her puppies.

4 p.m.   Same as 8.00 a.m. feeding.

8 p.m.   Same as noon feeding, but add ¼ teaspoon cod-liver oil.

Before going to bed, allow the mother to nurse her puppies. If raw cow's or goat's milk is not available, use an active, naturally cultured yogurt diluted with water, ⅓ water to ⅔ yogurt.

36–42 Days

Quantities represent 10 pounds of litter weight, and the increase of solid food. The mother's diet is decreased by 25%. If you have had to start the weaning process earlier than normal, the amounts below may not be enough. Use common sense here.

8 a.m.

²/₃ cup raw milk

¹/₃ teaspoon raw honey

¹/₄ teaspoon slippery elm powder

1.2 ounces dry-weight cereal (oats and barley)

50 mg vitamin C

¹/₈ teaspoon Recover Formula (use in one meal only)

Cook cereal, cool and mix with other ingredients. Feed puppies individually, then allow mother dog to nurse pups.

Noon   Same as 8 a.m. without Recover Formula.

4 p.m.

1 teaspoon of fresh, ground raw meat, increasing to 3.5 ounces over 8 to 12 days. This represents an increase of around 1 tablespoon each day. Add:

¹/₈ teaspoon nutritional yeast

¹/₄ teaspoon bone meal, increasing to ²/₃ teaspoon

¹/₂ teaspoon herbs or finely chopped vegetable greens

¹/₁₆ teaspoon kelp

¹/₄ teaspoon wheat germ

¹/₂ teaspoon wheat bran

¹/₈ teaspoon cod-liver oil

Mix all together, and divide into individual dishes. When pups have finished, allow the mother to nurse the puppies.

8 p.m.   Same as above, but add ¹/₃ capsule of garlic.

43–49 days

The puppies now can have all the rest of the ingredients mixed into their diet, so that by the time they are 6½ weeks of age, they will be on the complete Natural Diet.

Take the weight of the entire litter and double it. Go to the appropriate adult dog diet chart (*see* Chapter 2). Divide the amount into individual bowls. Feed to the puppies four times a day. Allow the mother dog in to nurse her puppies after they have eaten.

At 49 days they will be placed into their new homes. This "double quantity" feeding should continue until the puppy is 7 months old, regardless of whether the pups continue to eat the Natural Diet or are put on commercial dog food.

ANGIE, THE BULLMASTIFF

When Jim obtained his new Bullmastiff puppy, Angie, he decided to raise her on the Natural Diet right from the start. I first met Jim a number of years ago, when he had a very sick dog, Buster, on his hands. As Jim explained:

> *Buster was hypothyroid, had skin problems and was on a constant roller coaster of steroids and antibiotics to control his various symptoms. He never seemed to do well on dog food for more than a month or two.*
>
> *Quite by chance, I picked up your book and decided to further explore the idea of natural feeding. Buster, in just three months on the Natural Diet, was able to cut his thyroid medication in half and went from an exercise intolerant dog, to being very athletic. He looked better, he felt better and acted much better. Having seen what a powerful medicine the Natural Diet could be, there was no doubt in my mind that any dog I owned in the future would be raised this way.*

Angie, at 7 weeks, took to the diet like a fish to water. It has been an absolute pleasure to watch her develop. Angie has grown well, been very balanced, and has never been "up in the front" or "down in the rear." She has boundless energy, teething has been uneventful and her disposition is wonderful. Her attention span has been quite remarkable. Her coat is beautiful, as if each hair has been individually polished and groomed.

The Natural diet helps Angie reach her genetic potential.

I am convinced that the Natural Diet is the best thing anyone can do to ensure that their dog reaches its full genetic potential.

RAISING PUPPIES FROM SEVEN WEEKS

Growing to almost 70% of their adult weight during this time, puppies need to eat double the amount of food for their weight until they are 7 months old. For the 5-pound puppy, you feed the 10-pound adult dog diet, which provides the correct number of calories. Because rates of growth vary between breeds, it is difficult to establish exact amounts. The rule of thumb is that a lean puppy is healthier than a fat puppy. Heavy puppies put too much stress on growing bones. Puppies up until four to seven months should be fed four times a day. Keeping the ratios of 75% raw meat to 25% cereal is crucial. Some high activity pups may need even more. For the very active puppy, you can feed a banana or any fruits and vegetables he will eat to fill him up for that extra meal, without unbalancing the diet.

Once teething is complete, gradually decrease the quantities fed until the puppy is on the same amount of food as the adult dog, and reduce the meals to three times a day. In a short time, the puppy will start to leave the third meal, at which time you can go to two feedings a day. During the first 18 months, your puppy will go through growth spurts, and you may have to increase its food. For the hungry young dog, increase his food until he no longer licks his dish clean.

FEEDING SCHEDULE

SEVEN WEEKS TO SEVEN MONTHS

Mix up the cereal and supplements and divide into two equal parts. Mix up the meat meal and divide into two equal parts.

- 8:00 a.m.   Feed half the cereal and supplements.
- Noon   Feed half the cereal and supplements.
- 4:00 p.m.   Feed half the meat meal.
- 8:00 p.m.   Feed half the meat meal.

If the puppy is hungry before bedtime, he can have some fruit, or some yogurt, honey and a little cereal. Puppies are not fasted until they are through teething, or 7 months of age.

EXERCISE

Exercise is as important for puppies as it is for adult dogs. A nice morning and evening walk is good for both of you.

ANNA BELLE

While writing this chapter, I have been fortunate to be raising a puppy of my own. Little Anna Belle is a wonderful Labrador Retriever puppy bred by the famous field-trial trainer, Jane Kelso. She has a high activity level and has been eating a huge amount of food. So I have had to feed her more than any other puppy I have raised.

Instead of feeding her just four times a day, which would have left her unsatisfied, I increased her meals to five times a day. If she was still hungry, which she was during periods of extreme growth, I gave her a banana, a pear, an apple, or some cantaloupe as a snack to keep her happy until the next meal.

My guideline was her weight. If she looked skinny and I could see her ribs, I added an extra meal. If she looked round and in good weight, I didn't.

Except for some common sense, there are no hard-and-fast rules to raising puppies. I find that as the generations of Natural Diet dogs progress, the puppies get more and more active, and therefore their dietary needs increase. Joanne Scott, of Scottsbrae English Cocker Spaniels (she owns the cocker spaniel puppies in the sec-

Anna Belle getting educated.

tion on weaning puppies), told me that on her fourth generation of Natural Diet puppies, she had to quadruple the above amounts. Not only were they the best-quality litter she has had, they were also the most lively.

7 The Older Dog— Dietary & Emotional Needs

Used extensively in TV and print commercials, a walk-on part in a popular · movie, and a therapy dog visiting local nursing homes to cheer up the patients, Breaker was a star. Now Breaker was getting older and Pinny, his owner, wanted to make his senior years as comfortable as possible. He wasn't as nimble as he used to be and getting in and out of the van was getting difficult, as was climbing stairs. Always happy and bright, Breaker needed some help.

To help improve the quality of Breaker's old age, Pinny:

- Got a small ramp so he could get in and out of the van more easily.
- Added some supplements to his diet to keep his rear end stable.
- Maintained all regularly scheduled chiropractic and acupuncture treatments.
- Elevated his food and water dishes.

All of these things made his last years just a little bit better for her aging friend.

WHAT IS OLD?

Age is relative; but according to a recent study, 80% of dogs are classified as geriatric at age 5 due to tissue and organ degeneration. In human terms they are only 35! Dogs should have only just fully matured at this age. For those of us whose dogs live to 12 years old and even longer, this is a dreadful statistic. It's as though we have lost sight of the normal life expectancy of dogs. Or, have we become brainwashed to accept that giant breeds have short life spans, medium-sized dogs can live until 10, and that small dogs have a chance of reaching their teens?

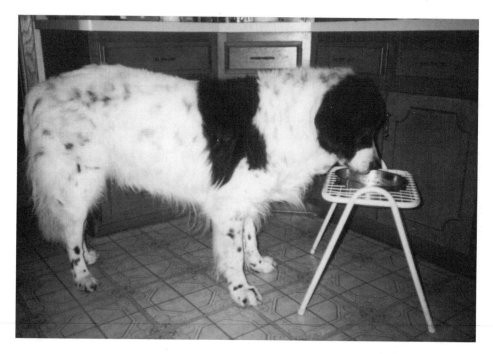

Elevating the food dish of an older dog makes him more comfortable while eating.

When I first visited the kennels in Germany, from which I bought my original Newfoundlands, I saw dogs walking around in good shape that were 15 to 17 years old, and I thought that was the norm. Of course, that was in the 60s, and the breeders were still feeding a homemade diet, similar to the Natural Diet, and using vaccines sparingly. All of which made the difference between living to 7 years or 14 years.

DIETARY RESTRICTIONS

Studies on laboratory animals have shown that slightly underfeeding an older animal brings back many of its youthful behaviors, and results in a substantially longer life than that of siblings given more to eat. Similarly, a study of the lifestyle and habits of centenarians found one common denominator—they were all slightly underweight. Moral of the story: Skinny is better.

Applying that moral, cut down on the amount you feed your dog. For the 75-pound dog keep him on exactly the same supplements for his weight, but reduce the grain and meat meals to the 50-pound dog diet (*see* Chapter 2 for directions). Limit treats to dried fruits or fresh vegetables. You want to be able to easily feel his ribs. Regular exercise and keeping the weight off those old bones helps to keep him mobile.

CATO

Cato was a male Landseer Newfoundland male from my third litter. Perfectly marked, with terrific structure, Cato turned out to be a top obedience dog and was shown both in this country and Canada.

By the time he was five, he had his Utility Title and Newfoundland Club of America Water Dog Rescue titles. He was in his prime and looking for new challenges. And then disaster struck. Within a three-month period, his mother, father and sister died, sending all of us into a deep depression. Our close-knit

family had been torn apart. I didn't feel much like training and Cato got so depressed that he didn't even want to go for his daily walks. He just moped around the house.

To get him out of his depression, the only thing I could think of was to go back to what he really enjoyed——training and going to dog shows. So, that is what I did and Cato snapped out of his depression. It was the best thing I could have done for him. At the age of 7 Cato entered his first Canadian show and two years later had obtained his Canadian Obedience Trial Champion title. I particularly remember one incident when he was 10 and after he had turned in a particularly spectacular perform-

Cato is another beautiful, naturally raised dog. We kept him healthy by adjusting his diet to his stage of life.

ance, I came out of the ring and the judge asked me, "How old is that dog?" I answered, "He is 10." The judge replied, "My, what a precocious puppy."

Although Cato was officially retired at age 10, I continued to work him because I knew he needed the exercise and especially the mental stimulation. Cato lived to be 14, feeling useful and needed.

DIETARY CHANGES

I raised Cato on the Natural Diet as listed in the adult dog diet charts. When he got to be around 12, I added digestive enzymes to his food so his aging system could break down and better utilize the nutrients in his food. I cut back slightly on the amounts of grains, meat, bone meal, liver and cottage cheese. I increased his vitamin E to 600 IUs in his breakfast meal, together with the addition of 25 micrograms (mcg) of selenium. The combination of vitamin E and selenium helps to keep the musculoskeletal system functioning. They especially help those dogs whose rear ends become wobbly and stiff. I also increased his vitamins C and B complex as well.

KATHARINA

Katharina, my 12-year-old German Shepherd, is a true working dog and nothing gives her so much pleasure as doing her obedience routines. She had just started agility and loved it. Then one day during our daily morning walk through the woods, Katharina, who was in front of me, got hurt by my Newfoundland youngster, Evo, and my Briard, DJ, who came thundering up from behind, picking up Katharina between their bodies and carrying her along for a few steps, and then they dropped her. Poor Katharina, who was 10 at the time, fell with both back

This healthy dog is ready and raring to go.

legs landing up behind her. She screamed. Scared to death, I massaged her and kept her quiet for several minutes until she caught her breath. When she tried to get up, her right back leg gave out. She had torn a cruciate ligament.

Normally, this kind of an injury requires surgery, but at her age, I was reluctant to pursue that option. But even with regular acupuncture treatments, chiropractic adjustments to keep her body straight, plus regular veterinary care and the use of homeopathy, she refused to put weight on that leg. With the help of the homeopathic remedies and acuncture treatments, the tendon itself was healing, but the muscles in that leg atrophied, and the other ligaments and tendons started to shorten. By now she could barely complete her walks and became quite depressed.

ARTHRITIS & WEAK REAR ENDS

When Kerry, my co-author and veterinarian, examined Katharina during one of her physicals, he remarked that her hip joint had so much arthritis in it, that there was little hope that the ball would ever go back into the socket. That was when I was introduced to Cetyl Myristylate (CM) and it turned out to be the most effective natural product I have found for arthritis, rheumatism, and general aging of the musculoskeletal system. After one week using the specified dosages I thought I saw some shrinking of the swelling in the joint, and after 10 days there was a noticeable difference. At the end of the treatment, which lasted 19 days, the femoral head slipped back into the socket, the synovial fluid which had been reduced to a watery substance because of the inflammation from the arthritis, came back to its gel-like consistency, allowing normal cushioning of that joint. Katharina now placed weight on the leg and was using it daily. And, in a very short period of time, the muscles had rebuilt.

I took Katharina back into Agility class, and lowered all the equipment. Much to my amazement, and her delight, she was able to take the course, slowly but surely. She has never looked back and the leg—while not as strong as her other back leg—is nearly normal in function.

Katharina still receives regular chiropractic care, which is so essential for the older dog, as well as acupuncture and massage to keep her whole body in balance. At 12 years old, she is in excellent shape, looks like she's 5 years old, and is full of vim and vigor.

Glucosamine sulfate and chrondroitin sulfate are other products to help our aging pets deal with arthritis and rheumatism. They can be used singly or in combination. Many dogs respond just to glucosamine, but some need the combination. Try the glucosamine first, and if it doesn't work after a month, add chrondroitin sulfate, which is available through your veterinarian. For dosage, consult the labels on the products or your veterinarian.

TEETH

On the Natural Diet, your dog requires very little tooth maintenance. The correct acid/alkaline balance of the diet does not provide a good environment for tartar. Eating bones on a regular basis also prevents tartar buildup. Another tartar fighter is a homeopathic remedy called Frageria, used in a 30x potency (*see* Chapter 12 for more information).

Still, some dogs have poor teeth to start with, either from poor nutrition, vaccinations, or genetic factors. Toy breeds, for example, are notorious for having too many teeth in their tiny mouths, causing overcrowding, bacteria buildup, gingivitis, abscesses and other gum diseases. The bacteria that build up by draining into the system can cause serious heart disease. Some dogs get split teeth or cavities and you need to have these taken care of by your veterinarian. Having your dog's teeth cleaned on a regular basis, and changing to the correct diet, helps to minimize teeth and mouth diseases.

RESPIRATORY SYSTEM

Older dogs often develop shortness of breath upon exertion, especially during hot and humid weather. They gasp for air, their gums turn white and they have to lie down and rest to catch their breath. The homeopathic Antimonium Tart is an effective treatment for respiratory deficiencies (*see* Chapter 12 for dosage recommendation).

INCONTINENCE

Perhaps the number one reason for taking the dog for his last visit to the veterinarian is incontinence. It is difficult to put up with, but it can be controlled with chiropractic adjustments, and acupuncture or acupressure (*see* Chapter 13). The point behind the stifle joint in the back legs (BL40) helps to strengthen the sphincter muscle, and another point just above the rectum of the dog (GV1), helps control fecal incontinence. Homeopathic remedies also strengthen the liver which controls muscles. There are also homeopathic remedies that can support both the kidneys and bladder, and the use of glandulars is often successful. Using the product Recover, which contains colostrum, in conjunction with the above therapies, has also helped many older dogs. In some cases, incontinent older dogs can undergo a hormone therapy to alleviate their symptoms. Hormones often have unwanted side effects, but a course of PPA (phenylpropanolamine) which has few side effects, given to your dog up to three times a day, may be an alternative treatment that you need to discuss with your veterinarian. Don't give up on an older dog because of incontinence.

FAILING KIDNEYS

The kidneys are made up of tiny structures, called nephrons,that filter blood and waste from the body. Either through the aging process, or trauma of some kind, nephrons cease to work, and they cannot be fixed.

The signs of kidney failure are increased intake of water, excessive urination, and retention of fluids giving the dog the appearance of being overweight. Waste is no longer being filtered through the kidneys and finds its way into the blood stream. A blood test will show an elevated blood, urea and nitrogen (BUN) count. Creatinine will also rise, as will phosphorus.

THE KIDNEY DIET

Feeding the Natural Diet allows you to tailor the ingredients and their proportions to your dog. For dogs suffering from kidney failure, recent research has shown that a moderate restriction of protein is more effective than a low protein diet, as formerly thought. The meat should be changed to a more fatty variety. Use fatty beef, chicken with skin, and occasionally fatty lamb. Substitute calcium carbonate for bone meal, which reduces the phosphorus levels in the diet. Keep your dog lean—remember, skinny is better. Glandulars are also helpful. For more details on the proportions and supplements needed to treat failing kidneys, *see* Chapter 16.

FOOD REFUSAL

If your older dog refuses to eat, which will happen at different times of the year, pay attention to him. It may be a signal to change your grains from acid to alkaline, the meat from chicken to beef, or vice versa. Gocelyn, one of my Newfoundlands, was a great teacher. When she turned ten, she refused to eat her regular meals of oats and beef around the beginning of March. She simply stopped eating and looked at me. It took me a while before I figured out that she needed a change in grains and meat. After switching her to millet and chicken, she ate as heartily as ever. Then a few months later, at the end of the summer, she stopped eating again and looked at me, as if to say, "It's time to switch back to oats and beef." By keeping notes, I could see her pattern emerging, and this eating pattern continued until the day that she left us at age 14. Gocelyn knew what she needed.

HOW TO ENTICE YOUR DOG TO EAT

If your dog absolutely refuses to eat anything, don't panic. Going without food for a few days helps to cleanse his system, and diverts the energy of his body to healing itself, rather than using the energy for digestion. The most essential thing is to make sure your dog is drinking enough water during this time.

One recipe I have used over the years to coax sick dogs back into eating is the following:

---

¹/₂ pound of beef or chicken liver

2 cups of Willard or spring water

Put ingredients into a saucepan and bring everything to a boil. Stir the liver until cooked through, about four minutes. Take off the stove and cool. Put through a blender or food processor until it is a soupy mixture. If not soupy enough, just add more water.

Suck some of this mixture into a turkey baster. With your dog at your side, head parallel to the ground (elevating his head will cause gagging), gently squeeze a small amount of the mixture into the side of his mouth. Go slowly, and he will swallow. For a medium sized dog about ¹/₂ cup of this mixture two to three times a day is sufficient. Liver is full of vitamins, minerals and amino acids, which help the healing process.

Instead of the liver mixture you can give your dog two Seacure capsules three times a day (*see* Appendix II). Once you start the eating behavior, most dogs will start to eat on their own. In the transition period, use the liver mixture poured over his food.

THE DIGESTIVE TRACT

As a dog ages his digestive tract doesn't work quite as efficiently as it used to. So the food you are feeding him is not broken down as well and absorbed. The thyroid gland, which has a great influence over the digestive tract, ceases to function as efficiently and supplementation or medication is often necessary as your dog gets older.

Older dogs may lose their ability to break down boiled grains, but can handle the breakfast bars (*see* Chapter 4). He may start eating more weeds and grass than usual, which tells you that digestive enzymes are needed. Digestive enzymes help your dog absorb the nutrients in his food better (Chapter 5 supplies more information on digestive enzymes; also *see* Appendix II for recommendations).

OLD AGE & BEHAVIOR

You'll start to notice subtle behavioral changes as your dog gets older. He will become more dependent on you. You may find that he has become a bit crotchety, and prefers not to be around young children. He may feel threatened because his mobility is not what it once was, and he may experience aches and pains.

Give your dog a place where he can retreat and be undisturbed. Old dogs sleep a lot and they don't take kindly to being woken up suddenly. Not hearing or seeing as well as they once did, they can become quite snappy if suddenly startled. Providing them with a safe environment is the best thing you can do.

SENILITY

Dogs are no different from people—senility is a reality in old age. Now being called "cognitive dysfunction," research is finding that this senility is quite similar to Alzheimer's disease in people. Again, there is hope. Anapryl, recently approved for veterinary use, is proving to be very effective in making the "old mind" young again. Talk with your veterinarian about this new medication. There are several natural alternatives to Anapryl, one of which is DHEA (*see* Chapter 5).

CANCER

It is inevitable, either through genetics or through the environment, that some dogs will get cancer. In the past, this diagnosis was the "kiss of death" for most dogs. But much progress has been made over the years, and treatments have improved considerably.

One of the most notable changes has been the use of the diet as a form of therapy. While conventional chemotherapy, radiation and steroids are still used; they are used together with a high fat diet. Tumors need carbohydrates for energy, and a diet high in fat and protein and low in carbohydrates makes tumors energy-deficient and can literally starve them. This combination of treatments has been successful in many cancer cases.

The noted veterinary cancer specialist, Dr. Gregory K. Ogilvie of Colorado State University's Department of Clinical Sciences, suggests following the percentages listed below for making a cancer diet for your dog.

- 37% animal protein
- 32% fat—mostly from animal sources
- 21.6% carbohydrates
- 3.5% Omega-3 fatty acids
- 2.5% DHA (fatty acids)
- 3.4 % Arginine (amino acid)

This diet provides adequate protein for the dog to heal during the process of treatment and not enough carbohydrates to sustain the tumors.

CRYSTAL— THE BOUNCY NEWFOUNDLAND

Kinesiology helped determine the treatment for Crystal's cancer.

When Crystal was first diagnosed with Lymphosarcoma, her owner Pinny was very depressed and she called me not knowing quite what to do. I assured her that strides in cancer treatment had been made in the last few years and that we should try together to support Crystal and give her the best quality of life we could. She agreed to try. Using kinesiology (*see* Chapter 11), we determined that the best course of treatment for Crystal would be a combination of traditional therapies including chemotherapy, plus dietary and supplement support.

The first thing that happened after Crystal's chemotherapy started was that she got very sick, lost weight and refused to eat. Pinny had to be very creative. Because I insisted that she keep accurate notes while she was going through this ordeal, we discovered a pattern. For two days after treatment, Crystal didn't want to eat, then she slowly started to feel better and began to eat again.

The following diet used for Crystal can be adapted to any cancer case, with the understanding that not every dog needs all the supplements. Crystal looked wonderful throughout her treatment and she enjoyed a great quality of life. All the supplements listed below, can be found in Appendix II and are also described in Chapter 4.

CRYSTAL'S CANCER DIET

Supplements:

- 2 capsules of Seacure three times a day to counteract nausea from chemotherapy
- 400 IUs vitamin E, each meal
- ¼ teaspoon Unleash (digestive enzyme) with each meal
- 1 tablespoon of nutritional yeast in evening meal
- ½ teaspoon of fresh chopped garlic in each meal
- 1 capsule DHA daily
- 1 teaspoon cold-pressed safflower oil once a day
- 2 vitamin B complex each meal
- 1 gram of vitamin C (calcium ascorbate) each meal
- 2 capsules of Essiac Tea (called E-Tea) each meal
- 1 tablet of Germanium in each meal—short-term
- 25 mg DHEA
- 1 capful of the homeopathic product called Detoxification in the morning before breakfast—short-term
- 1 capful of the homeopathic product called Lymphatic Drainage in the morning before breakfast—short-term

BREAKFAST

- 1 cup of cooked oatmeal

- 1 egg with shell with any of the following: ¹/₂ cup of sour cream, heavy cream, butter, cheese or chicken fat

- appropriate supplements tested with kinesiology daily

Pinny found that Crystal sometimes did not want oatmeal, so she substituted either white or red potatoes with the skin, sweet potatoes or yams, green beans, broccoli, carrots. Since Pinny can use kinesiology, it was an easy matter for her to find out what Crystal would eat each day.

DINNER

Crystal would only eat cooked chicken during her treatment. Pinny fed it to her with skin and fat. Crystal got chicken livers slightly steamed and tuna in oil was a once-a-week favorite. She would eat raw beef, with at least 25% fat in it, when she was feeling good. Remember, beef is lower in protein than chicken, and more protein is needed for healing.

Immediately after her chemotherapy treatment, Crystal would not eat at all and looked like she was at death's door. Her white cell count was low and she looked as if she didn't want to live. First, Pinny gave her two capsules of Seacure to counteract nausea. Then, she would lightly cook some chicken and beef livers together, put them through the food processor, mixing them with lots of chicken broth to make a very soupy mixture, which she fed with a turkey baster, ¹/₂ cup, several times a day. With all the nutrients in the liver, together with the use of Seacure, Crystal would be up and moving again in just two days.

Pinny learned several valuable lessons during Crystal's treatment. The first one was to keep an accurate weight record. Chemotherapy is given by weight, and when a dog is going through the treatment, it will lose weight. Therefore, the chemotherapy has to be adjusted with each treatment. Pinny made sure that with each treatment the veterinarian adjusted Crystal's dosage taking into account her loss in weight.

The second lesson was, don't give up. Dogs can look like they're at death's door one moment, then bounce back in no time. Giving Crystal the liquid liver was just what she needed.

Crystal received massage and Reiki treatments on a regular basis, acupuncture for her back legs, which got very weak from lack of use, and halfway through the treatment, CM (*see* Chapter 5) was used. This strengthened her immune system and helped to get her back on her feet.

Crystal begged for vanilla ice cream occasionally, and of course this craving was indulged!

Crystal went into remission several months after the chemotherapy treatments began. She was rested for three weeks, undergoing no chemotherapy. When she was stronger, had gained her weight back, and had had lots of exercise, she was returned to the normal program of treatment which in total lasts around one to two years depending on the type of cancer being treated.

All through the treatments, Crystal's eyes were clear and she was full of life, her coat was beautifully shiny, and she didn't shed a hair. She demanded to be worked, and at 11 years of age, she looked years younger.

INTRODUCING A PUPPY

Bringing up a young dog and teaching him life's lessons goes a long way in keeping your old dog young. Puppies brought up with elderly dogs are easy to train because the older dog will take much of the burden off you. Don't wait too long to introduce a new puppy to your old friend. Bring in the pup when your older dog is young enough to enjoy him. Anna Belle, my Labrador puppy, was brought in when Katharina, who has raised all my puppies, was 11. Katharina enjoys teaching puppies everything she knows. She gets more exercise trying to keep up with the puppy and looks years younger than her chronological age.

CONCLUSION

Old dogs are wonderful to have around. They have known us for so long, shared so many memories, been there for us through our good times and bad, and know our every move. They are a very precious resource and loving family member. They deserve the best we can give them.

Part 2

Medicines, Tests, Therapies & Your Dog

8 Vaccinations, Heartworm & Common Medical Procedures

No one topic has created as much controversy as vaccinations, and rightly so. Over the last 20 years there has been an explosion in:

- The number of vaccinations given at the same time

- The frequency of vaccinations

- The types of vaccines used

All of this is causing growing concerns about the immediate and long-term effects vaccines have on our pets.

Our purpose in presenting the following information is to make you aware of the important questions that are being asked about vaccination protocols and to provide you with the available options.

THE LATEST FINDINGS

Many veterinarians, veterinary colleges and renowned research veterinarians such as Dr. Ronald D. Schultz, University of Wisconsin, and Dr. Leland Carmichael of Cornell University, are asking how often do we really need to vaccinate and do we need to vaccinate for all the diseases for which we are currently vaccinating? Are too many vaccines being given at one time? Do they do more harm than good? What are the options?

Over the next five years, many changes will occur to prevent serious diseases from affecting our pets. Your veterinarian should be up to date on these changes and be able to help you make the right decision on how you approach vaccines, always keeping in mind that your pet is an individual and that no one program is right for every dog.

AGAINST WHAT & WHY TO VACCINATE

The sole reason for vaccinating your pet is to protect him or her from the life-threatening diseases of:

- **Distemper**—A highly contagious viral disease that affects both the respiratory and the nervous systems. Initially, its symptoms start with a high fever of 103° to 105°F, thick, greenish yellow nasal and eye discharge, and coughing. The owner can mistake these symptoms for a "cold," but dogs don't get colds like people do. Severe, and often fatal, pneumonia follows. The virus is most severe in puppies and young dogs. If the dog survives the initial respiratory phase, a neurologic syndrome often follows as the virus affects the nervous system. Survivors can be left with a multiplicity of clinical signs, such as epileptic seizures, head tilts, loss of muscular coordination, and rhythmic jerking of single or groups of muscles.

- **Parvo**—Another highly contagious viral disease, which principally affects the gastrointestinal system. Initially its symptoms are a high fever, lethargy and loss of appetite. Vomiting and bloody diarrhea soon develop. Parvo can be, and often is, fatal in puppies and geriatric dogs.

- **Infectious Canine Hepatitis**—Caused by an adenovirus, it most commonly affects puppies, but dogs of any age can be infected. Within hours of the infection, the virus can result in death. The more common syndrome symptoms are fever, vomiting, diarrhea, depression, loss of appetite and small hemorrhages on the mucous membranes of the skin. Pneumonia and diseases of the eyes (corneal edema) may follow the acute signs.

- **Rabies**—One of the world's most publicized and feared viral diseases. This virus, transmitted by the saliva of an infected animal, affects the nervous system and results in death. It can incubate as long as six months in the infected dog before clinical signs and death occur. Clinical signs appear in stages. During the first stage, only subtle behavioral changes are seen. The second stage shows increased irritability, aggression, possibly seizures, loss of muscular coordination such as staggering, and sensitivity to light. The third and final stage begins with severe weakness and paralysis of the limbs, a change in the bowels, drooling and an inability to swallow, severe depression and death. Since this virus can be transmitted to people, it is a very serious human health concern.

Vaccinations against these viruses are called the core vaccinations and with the proper protocol, immunity can be accomplished safely and effectively, and with a minimum of side effects. But, when giving any kind of vaccine, consideration must be given to how much stress the dog's immune systems can take, and the negative affects improper and over-vaccination can have.

Unfortunately, some dogs may experience allergic reactions to these vaccines, ranging from mild hives to much more severe reactions, such as anaphylaxis and auto immune diseases. According to published reports, serious adverse reactions occur in approximately 1 in 15,000 cases, but we suspect that due to undiagnosed, misdiagnosed and unreported cases, the actual number is much higher.

Less severe reactions, such as vomiting and diarrhea, lethargy and malaise, can be attributed to too many vaccines being given at one time, unnecessary vaccines being used, the wrong type of vaccines being used and vaccines being given too often.

Vaccines such as leptospirosis, lyme and microsporum, are noted for causing many more reactions than the basic core vaccines. Vaccines that use adjuvants (aluminum or formaldehyde) to make them more "stimulating" are known for causing a higher frequency of reactions.

HOW OFTEN TO VACCINATE

The purpose of vaccinations is to stimulate the immune system to set up a defense against the disease. Once this has been accomplished, do we need to revaccinate and if so, how often?

Research is now finding that lymphocyte memory cells are most responsible for long term protection. Drs. Schultz and Carmichael, through challenge studies, have shown that distemper vaccine provides protection for five to seven years. The current yearly booster protocols are based on the USDA requirement that vaccine producers prove a duration of immunity (DOI) of one year, and rabies three years.

Up to now, no one has tested to see how long the immunity truly lasts, and only challenge studies can tell us that. Research is also showing that the lymphocyte memory cell protection may actually prevent yearly booster vaccinations from producing any "noticeable response" by the immune system. Nevertheless, your dog is fully protected.

NUMBER OF VACCINES

For many years we have been concerned with the number of vaccines being given. One protocol uses 62 vaccines by the time the puppy is six months old. The immune system cannot handle this kind of abuse. Too many vaccines at one time do not allow the immune system to respond fully and efficiently. Aside from being ineffective, so many vaccines may cause severe adverse reactions.

Research indicates that the body also needs at least two, and preferably three, weeks between vaccine challenges to recover and be ready to mount a response to the next vaccine. To limit the numbers of vaccines, Dr. Schulz recommends giving only the core vaccines, as well as those your individual location or situation mandates. All others are noncore vaccines and should only be given because individual conditions require it. Lyme vaccine has absolutely no medically acceptable rationale for use in nonendemic locales, according to Dr. Alice M. Wolf of Texas A & M College of Veterinary Medicine. It has resulted in many adverse reactions and produces a questionable duration of immunity. If you have to use it, the vaccine produced by Merial appears to be the best available at the present time. Request it from your veterinarian.

Leptospirosis is another questionable vaccine. It can be immunosuppressive to puppies less than 16 weeks of age and is often the most reactive agent in the distemper, lepto, hepatitis series. Unless this disease is widespread in your locality, there is no indication for its use.

Vaccines for Contagious Respiratory Disease Complex (CCRD), Bordatella (kennel cough) and Parainfluenza, need only be used in dogs that are boarded frequently or exposed to a congregation of dogs. Corona vaccine is used to prevent a disease that causes short term vomiting and diarrhea, which a healthy dog should be able to handle without this vaccine.

TYPES OF VACCINES

The next question and controversy concerns the types of vaccines used:

- Modified Live Vaccines (MLV)—In modified live vaccines the viruses are altered to decrease their virulence or ability to produce disease and yet retain their ability to stimulate the immune system. In order to produce enough antigen to cause immunity, the MLV must replicate after your dog is vaccinated. The time it takes an MLV to produce immunity—the window of vulnerability—is short, from a few days to two weeks. MLVs are stressful and may result in an unusual return to a more active form and can cause a vaccine-induced disease. But, the duration of immunity appears to be long, perhaps the lifetime of the animal, with the better vaccines.

- Killed vaccines cannot replicate and as a result are much safer. But, their window of vulnerability is much longer, sometimes up to two months to produce immunity. Killed vaccines also use adjuvants to improve the response, which can and often do cause adverse reactions.

- Recently, recombinant vaccines by Merial have been approved. The DNA structure of the virus is changed, making the virus "inactive," yet safe and effective in stimulating immunity. It appears to be an ideal vaccine, and the direction vaccines will probably take in the future.

REDUCING THE NUMBER OF VACCINES

Where does this new information lead us? For the present you want to:

1. Decrease the frequency of vaccinations. Initial vaccinations should be three weeks apart. After initial boosters, consider vaccinating every three years (titering is an option, *see* below).

2. Separate vaccines and give only one vaccine at a time.

3. Give only the core vaccines, and noncore vaccines only if absolutely indicated for your area.

VACCINATION SCHEDULE

Following is a proposed vaccination schedule from puppyhood throughout life.

AGE	VACCINE
6 weeks	Parvo (CPV)
9 weeks	Canine Distemper (CDV)
12 weeks	CPV

AGE	VACCINE
15 weeks	CDV
18 weeks	CPV
6 months	Rabies (no choice)
16 months	give booster, but separate out CDV, CPV (consider titers instead)
18 months	Rabies (no choice)
2 years	follow-up booster—CPV (titers?)
3 years	follow-up booster—CDV (titers?)
4 years	Rabies (no choice)

It is important to follow some basic rules with this vaccine protocol:

- Do not vaccinate when your pet is stressed or traumatized.

- Do not vaccinate when your female is in heat (estrous).

- Do not vaccinate, if your dog is sick or undergoing surgery. Wait until he is fully recovered.

- *Always* discuss your vaccination program with your veterinarian. Every dog is an individual!

Rabies vaccines are required by law and each state has different requirements. Check with your veterinarian about how often your dog needs to have a rabies vaccine.

VACCINE REACTIONS

If your dog has had an adverse response to vaccines (vaccinosis), a homeopathic remedy called Thuja, can negate that reaction. Use in the 30c potency, with the following schedule:

- One vaccine, 1 dose of Thuja

- Three in one vaccine, 1 dose of Thuja once a day for three days, preferably in the p.m.

- Five in one vaccine, 1 dose of Thuja, once a day for five days

To prevent an adverse reaction from vaccination (except rabies) for a dog who has shown previous reactions, use Thuja as follows:

Dose 1—p.m. before vaccination

Dose 2—a.m. of the vaccination

Dose 3—immediately after vaccination

Dose 4—a.m. of the following day

Dose 5—p.m. of following day

TITERS

Titers are a way to check the immunity level of your dog to a particular disease. It is an option for those who don't want to vaccinate. Cornell Diagnostic Laboratory's vaccine titer panel will tell you the immunity levels for both distemper and parvo. Knowing the titer value will help you determine if a booster vaccination is necessary for your dog. Titers do not however indicate the level of memory cell protection.

Titers are tricky to interpret. A low titer can mean:

- That your dog has not been recently challenged by the disease for which he is being tested, but that memory cells are still in place and can activate when the dog is being challenged.

- That the dog is not protected.

I have an 11-year-old German Shepherd, Katharina, who has not been vaccinated, except for rabies. In the winter, when she was at home and not exposed to other dogs, her titers were extremely low. In April, she came with us to our training camp, as she has done ever since she was a puppy. Titers done for the distemper and parvo viruses after Camp were so high that the laboratory report came back saying that "This dog has just been vaccinated."

Only you can decide what you think is best for your dog. I choose not to vaccinate my dogs, except for rabies, which is required by law. They outlive their counterparts by many years and have healthy and happy lives. But then, my dogs are on the Natural Diet, and get plenty of fresh air and exercise in a country setting. You have to do what you think is best for your dog.

VACCINE ALTERNATIVES

NOMOGRAPHS

Dr. Ron Schultz has recommended the use of the nomograph as an alternative to decreasing the number of vaccines a puppy receives. By means of a blood test taken from the pregnant female two weeks prior to whelping, or at whelping or directly after, the nomograph determines how long the puppies are protected by the maternal antibodies. Once this time frame has been established, one distemper and one parvo vaccine should produce protective levels of antibodies. He also advises that the puppies should be titered one month after the last vaccine to check levels of antibodies. If they do, they may be protected for life. He goes on to say that if you feel nervous about this, titer again or booster at one year of age.

One problem exists with this alternative—it depends on every puppy receiving a good volume of colostrum within the first 24 hours of life. A puppy that nurses poorly will not receive the maternal antibody protection that a well-nursed littermate will.

NOSODES—AN ALTERNATIVE TO VACCINES?

Nosodes are homeopathic remedies made from the diseases themselves. They come in liquid or pellet form like other remedies. While there is insufficient data on the efficacy of nosodes to prevent disease, anecdotal data suggest they may be beneficial and many homeopathic veterinarians recommend them.

Like vaccines, nosodes sensitize the body to a particular virus so that the immune system can react quickly to natural exposure. Nosodes are safe to give your dog, and no side effects have been reported. They can even be safely given to very young puppies or to the mother dog before she is bred.

There are three ways to use nosodes:

1. Dose a puppy twice daily for a few days, and thereafter monthly, continuing until 6 months of age. After that, nosodes are given twice annually for the rest of their lives. This is a general schedule used by homeopathic veterinarians. Each has his or her own preferred schedule.

2. When your dog contracts a disease. If the dog has already received the nosodes as a young dog, he may indeed contract the disease later on, but

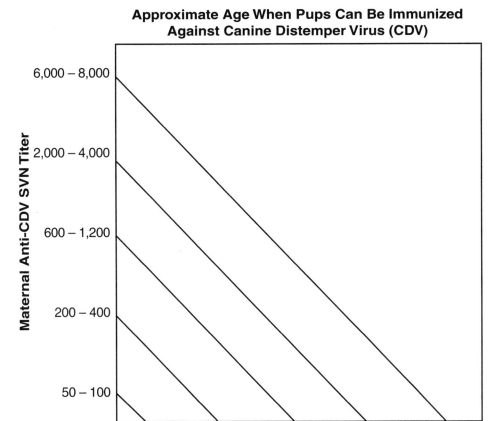

Approximate Age When Pups Can Be Immunized Against Canine Distemper Virus (CDV)

Dr. R. D. Schultz, Professor and Chairman, Dept. Pathobiological Sciences, School of Veterinary Medicine, University of Wisconsin, Madison, WI 53706

Nomograph—CDV.

it will be in a mild form, and recovery, using more nosodes, should be rapid.

3. To "clear" any long-term, adverse reactions to vaccines, commonly called vaccinosis. If your dog has had any of the core vaccines, and has had an immediate reaction to any of them, or hasn't been well since, you can use the nosode specific to the disease to safely clear these reactions.

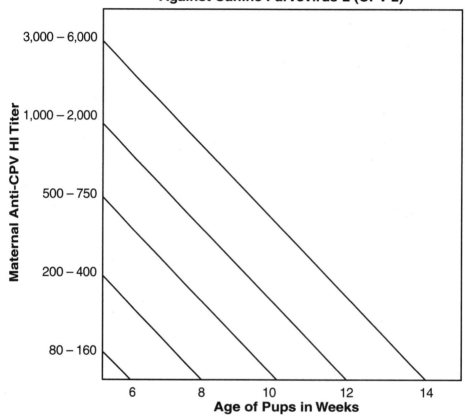

Dr. R. D. Schultz, Professor and Chairman, Dept. Pathobiological Sciences,
School of Veterinary Medicine, University of Wisconsin, Madison, WI 53706

Nomograph—CPV-2.

ANOTHER ALTERNATIVE

One more alternative to the vaccine issue is to combine both nosodes and vaccines. Give the very young puppy nosodes for parvo and distemper around 6 and
8 weeks and then at 10 weeks and 13 weeks or 11 and 14 weeks, depending on
the titer of the mother dog at whelping shown on the nomograph charts, give
the parvo and distemper vaccines singly, separated out by 3 weeks. One month
after the last vaccine, titer the puppy to see levels of antibodies.

NOT A SOLUTION!

A final option is not to vaccinate, titer or use nosodes. You need to remember that the core diseases are very serious, if not deadly. We still see and diagnose them far too often and feel that this is not an option that should be considered by anyone.

HEARTWORM DISEASE

The heartworm is an insidious parasite that moves about and spreads without you realizing its presence. Mosquitoes spread the disease by feeding on an infected canine (dog, coyote, fox, etc.), ingesting the circulating young larva of the heartworm (microfilaria), then passing them on while feeding on an uninfected animal.

Before it can infect a new victim, the microfiliaria must incubate and develop in the mosquito for two weeks. Once injected into its new host, the microfiliaria migrate through body tissue to reach the right ventricle of the heart and become adults. These reproduce worms six months later. The newly infected dog will show no clinical signs for three to four years. In the meantime, the adult heartworms are reproducing, putting thousands of microfiliaria into circulation, waiting for the next mosquito to come along and transport it to a new victim.

It is a simple procedure to monitor your dog and keep him free of heartworms. The first step is testing to evaluate your dog's heartworm status. We recommend testing once a year, at the time of your dog's yearly physical. If you have a large number of dogs and cannot afford to test all of them each year, test half of them one year and the other half the next year. The minimum they should be tested is once every two years.

When your dog is tested for heartworm, ask what type of test is being used. Four types of tests are available.

- A direct smear of several drops of fresh blood, which is checked under a microscope. The microfiliaria can be seen on the slide.

- The Knotts test, in which a fresh blood sample is mixed with a special solution that lyses (use of a compound that disintegrates the cell) the red blood cells. This mixture is passed through a special filter and the sample stained and observed under the microscope. Again, the actual microfilaria can be seen. Both of these tests can give false negatives. I have had several cases that showed large numbers of microfilaria in an evening blood sample, but which were negative in a morning sample. There is evidence that the numbers of circulating microfilaria is greatest at the peak mosquito hours.

- A much more reliable test checks specifically for the antigen produced by the adult heartworm. The "in-house" concentrated immunoab- sorbent technology (CITE) test is very accurate and can be done in less than 10 minutes at the hospital.

- Large testing labs have another form of test available. Many practices use this test because it is a little less expensive, but it does take 24 to 48 hours to get your results back.

Prevention is the next step. Again, multiple preventative treatments are available.

- Diethylcarbamazine is a tablet that must be given daily. It acts at the time of the mosquito bite and a missed day can result in infection.

- Heart Guard (Ivermectin) by Merck and Interceptor (Milbergci) by Novartis, are medications that are given once a month. They act by treating any exposure that has occurred 30 days prior to the day of treat- ment. Some dogs will show reactions to the once-a-month medication, such as diarrhea or vomiting within 24 hours of giving the medications. Observe your dog closely for any sign of side effects.

The majority of dogs have no trouble with these medications, but again, every dog is an individual.

How long you give the preventatives is determined by how long you have mosquitoes present that can spread the microfilaria. In our area we recommend April through December. Remember that the monthly preventative works by treating the 30 *previous* days of exposure.

A POSITIVE TEST FOR HEARTWORM

All is not lost. Heartworm can be treated effectively and safely. Where we have difficulty is when the infection has been present for three to four years and has started taking its toll on the heart, liver and kidneys.

A new drug, Immiticide, is now being used to kill the adult heartworm. It does not have the toxic affect on the liver that previous treatments did. The dead adult worms are carried to the lungs in the bloodstream where they are encapsulated and walled off. Over a period of time, they are broken down by white blood cells and expelled from the body. Six weeks later, Ivermectin is given to eliminate the circulating microfilaria. An antigen test four months later is run to be sure that all of the worms have been eliminated.

SPAYING & NEUTERING

We are often asked why and when should a dog be spayed or neutered. If you don't have any plans for breeding, we strongly recommend either *overiohysterectomy* (spaying) of females, or *castration* (neutering) of males. Females should be spayed after 6 months of age, and preferably before their first estrous cycle because with each ensuing estrous that occurs, the risk of mammary tumor development in later life increases dramatically. Spaying can also reduce:

- False pregnancies
- Reproductive hormone imbalances
- The inevitable pyometras (uterine infections) that develop in later years

The one disadvantage that occurs with approximately 5% of the spayed females is urinary incontinence in later geriatric years. Incontinence is caused by the lack of hormone control of the urethral sphincter muscles. Its symptoms are urine leaking from the bladder while your dog is sleeping. If a diagnosis of urinary incontinence is confirmed, it can be treated effectively in a number of ways. Estrogen supplement and phenolpropanalomine are oral medications that increase the tone of the urethral sphincter. Equisetum 6c, a homeopathic remedy and acupuncture are also effective alternative therapies.

Males should also be neutered at 6 months of age or soon after. The longer a male remains intact, the more male habits become ingrained—urination marking, riding of legs, breeding pillows, and all the wonderful things that males do to embarrass their owners. Neutering is most beneficial in preventing males from searching out females that are in heat, and preventing male dominance and aggression. The longer a male is left intact, the less effective neutering will be. Male dogs that have one or both testicles retained and not descended into the scrotum should be neutered to prevent problems due to testicular torsion (twisting) and testicular tumors.

THE BEHAVIORAL VIEWPOINT

Although there are compelling medical reasons for early neutering, there are equally good reasons from a behavioral perspective to wait until your dog is 1 to 2 years of age.

Spaying or neutering your pet during the juvenile period (5 to 9 months) means that his or her behavior remains more juvenile. So if you want a dog that retains puppy-like characteristics for the rest of his life, then spay or neuter your dog at around 6 to 9 months of age. This can be advantageous if there are young children in the family.

If you want your dog to show more adult behaviors and take more responsibility, like being a protector or guard dog, training for competitive events, or working for a living, then you should think about not spaying and neutering until later.

A male that has not been neutered until after 1 year of age, or a female that has gone through two seasons, is generally easier to train for competitive events such as obedience or agility trials. They have become fully grown by that time, are emotionally mature, have learned more adult behaviors and can accept more responsibility.

For those who blame obesity on neutering or spaying, the simple facts are:

- Metabolism is altered and as a result fewer calories will cause weight increase.

- Proper and careful nutrition controls obesity.

- Activity and personalities do not change unless we allow them to change.

SUMMARY

- A thorough, annual checkup is important, as well as annual chemistry profiles, fecals, titers, heartworm tests and urinalysis.

- Choose your veterinarian with care. You need to be able to communicate with him or her, express your ideas and discuss these current issues. If you feel uncomfortable, or you receive only criticism, consider looking for a new veterinarian.

- If you choose to vaccinate, separate out your individual vaccines by three weeks, and only give those that are core vaccines or necessary against infections in your area.

- If you are not going to breed your dog, neutering or spaying is your best decision.

- There are no real benefits to keeping a nonbreeding dog intact.

- The benefits and advantages to your pet of neutering and spaying far outweigh the few disadvantages.

- Before you neuter, consider what behaviors you expect from your dog as an adult.

Laboratory Tests— What Do They Tell Us?

Every dog needs a thorough yearly veterinary examination. Establishing yearly physical and blood chemistry exams as part of the routine health care you provide for your dog will give you invaluable information for the future. These tests establish normal levels for *your* dog. If there is a deviation in those levels, your veterinarian would be alerted that trouble is brewing. A good habit to form with your dog, this annual check up will provide the following information.

PHYSICAL EXAMINATION

A complete and thorough physical examination will consist of evaluating the dog's general attitude and appearance. His eyes, nose, ears, mouth and skin will all be checked, as will the musculoskeletal, respiratory, nervous, digestive, genitourinary and circulatory systems. Your dog's temperature will also let your veterinarian know if his health is within normal parameters. During this physical examination, your veterinarian will probably also ask you for more details on your dog's history. If any abnormalities are found during the examination, your veterinarian will explain them to you. He may suggest doing blood work on your dog—these are divided into separate tests and listed below. In addition, your veterinarian will examine a sample of your dog's urine and feces. All of these tests help your veterinarian to make a proper diagnosis.

COMPLETE BLOOD COUNT

A complete blood count, or CBC, is a routine profile of tests used to indicate the quantity and quality of the cells in the blood.

SERUM CHEMISTRY PROFILE OR CHEMISTRY SCREEN

A serum chemistry profile, sometimes called a chem screen or chem scan, is an extensive battery of tests that provides a broad database to evaluate your dog's general health. These tests confirm the results of the physical examination and provide early warnings of unsuspected problems. They are needed to establish a "norm" for your dog or a base line. To ensure accuracy with these tests, the dog should be fasted for 12 hours prior to blood being drawn.

URINALYSIS

This test examines the urine of your dog, which not only reveals the health of the genitourinary system, but also reflects a variety of disease processes that involve other organs in the body.

FECAL ANALYSIS

The feces, or stool, of your dog can reveal not only the presence of parasites but also undigested food particles which would indicate that your dog is not able to break down and digest his food properly.

BLOOD TESTS & RESULTS

Every laboratory doing blood work establishes its own level of what they consider normal. These values vary depending on the particular laboratory equipment being used. Normal readings are established by taking a certain number of dogs—many laboratories use 29 dogs—analyzing their blood and then averaging it out. Check out how the norms are established for the laboratory you are using.

If you are using blood chemistry to work out a diagnosis, you need to stay with one laboratory for consistent results. Ask if the laboratory being used is for veterinary or human purposes. Human laboratories often perform tests that are less expensive than a veterinary laboratory but they can be inaccurate because the instruments are not calibrated for animal blood and may provide inaccurate results.

By working with your veterinarian on a yearly basis, you can establish the normal levels of blood chemistry for your dog. It may be that you have an individual, or a breed that falls outside of the established norm, for example, sight hounds and some working breeds. Establishing norms prior to any health problem is good preventative medicine. This is clearly evident in the taking of a temperature. Most dogs are in the 101.5° range. It is reasonable to assume that if your dog's temperature goes above 103°, you would need to get that dog to the veterinarian immediately. But if your dog's normal temperature was 102.5°, a rise of one half a degree need not signify an emergency. Establish a norm for *your* dog while he is in a state of good health.

NORMAL COMPLETE BLOOD COUNT VALUES

Test	Reference	Range
RBC count	MILL/CMM	4.8–9.3
PCV (Hematocrit)	%	36.8–54%
Hemoglobin (Hb)	G/DL	12–18
Reticulocyte count	%	0–1.5%
MCV		60–77
MCH		19–28
MCHC		30–38
Platelet count	10^5/CMM	$2.0–6.0 \times 10.5$
WBC count	10^3/CMM	4.0–15.5
Neutrophils (seg)		3,000–11,400
Neutrophil Bands		0–300
Lymphocytes		690–4,500
Eosinophil		0–1,200
Monocytes		0–840
Basophils		0–150

There may be a variation in the "norm" depending on the laboratory used.

EXPLANATION OF CBC VALUES
RBC—RED BLOOD CELL COUNT

The function of red blood cells is to transport oxygen and carbon dioxide between the lungs and body tissues. Red blood cells are produced in the bone marrow and are under the control of chemicals that are secreted by the kidneys. What follows is a discussion of the various component parts of red blood cells called Hematocrit or PCV, Hemoglobin, Reticulocytes, Platelets and the Erythrocyte Indices or MCV, MCH and MCHC.

PCV—Pack Cell Volume

Pack cell volume (hematocrit) is the most commonly used expression of red cell numbers and is measured as a percentage of blood composed of red blood cells.

Decreased levels of RBC or PCV, commonly termed anemia, have three basic causes:

- Reduced bone marrow production that can be from an iron deficiency, a vitamin B_{12} deficiency, or chronic kidney or liver disease.

- Loss of blood from the body such as external or internal hemorrhage, or parasites.

- Destruction within the body called hemolytic anemia (breaking down of red blood cells).

Increased levels of RBC or PCV are most often the result of dehydration. It can also be the result of the bone marrow over-producing red blood cells, but this is rare. Over-use of vitamin/mineral products can also cause increases in hematocrit levels.

Hemoglobin (Hb)

Hemoglobin is the essential oxygen carrier of the blood. It is found within the red blood cells and is responsible for the red color of the blood. It is essentially equivalent to the PCV.

Decreased hemoglobin levels indicate the presence of hemorrhage and anemia.

Increased hemogloblin levels indicate a higher than normal concentration of red blood cells.

Reticulocytes

Reticulocytes are immature red blood cells that have been released from the bone marrow prematurely.

Decreased reticulocyte count, if associated with chronic anemia, indicates a lowered red blood cell production by the bone marrow.

Increased reticulocyte count is associated with chronic hemorrhage or hemolytic anemia (destruction of RBCs).

MCV, MCH, MCHC

MCV, MCH and MCHC levels together are called *Erythrocyte Indices*. This count includes the total of the mean corpuscular volume (MCV), mean corpuscular hemogloblin (MCH), and mean corpuscular hemoglobin concentration (MCHV). They are calculated by using the RBC count, the PCV count and the Hemoglobin concentration. These indices are used to classify the different kinds of anemia and their response to therapies.

Platelet Count

Also called thrombocytes, platelets are derived from the bone marrow and play an important part in blood clotting. This test indicates the blood clotting ability of the dog.

Decrease in the number of platelets occurs in bone marrow depression, autoimmune hemolytic anemia, systemic lupus (a blood clotting disorder), severe hemorrhage or intravascular coagulation.

Increase in the number of platelets occurs sometimes when there is a fracture, a blood vessel injury or if the bone marrow is overproducing (cancer).

WBC

WBC is the total number of white blood cells. WBC's are often called leucocytes. There are different kinds of white blood cells and the figure shown on the chart is reached by combining the total of these various kinds of white blood cells together. The different kinds of cells are called neutrophils, neutrophil bands, lymphocytes, eosinophils, monocytes and basophils.

Decreased levels of WBCs may indicate developmental or metabolic disorders, an overwhelming infection, especially from viruses, or drug and chemical poisoning.

Increased WBC levels can be seen in infections, especially bacterial, as well as emotional upsets and blood disorders.

Neutrophils

Neutrophils are the white blood cells that function primarily in the face of inflammation. They act by consuming foreign material and destroying bacteria.

Decreased number of neutrophils would indicate viral infection, starvation, certain drug reactions, or overwhelming bacterial infection.

Increased levels would indicate local bacterial infections and inflammation, stress, tissue destruction such as abscesses or tumors, or the use of steroid drugs.

Neutrophil Bands

Neutrophil bands are immature neutrophils which are released prematurely from the bone marrow when there is an immediate need for them, such as at the site of inflammation.

Increased number of neutrophil bands together with mature neutrophils would indicate that the bone marrow has the infection or inflammation under control. If the band cells are greater than 10% of the mature neutrophils, and the total WBC is normal or low, then it would show that the bone marrow is losing the battle.

Lymphocytes

Lymphocytes function primarily with the immune system. They recognize antigens (enzymes, toxins or foreign substances) and produce antibodies (protein substances) which fight the antigens.

Decreased numbers are seen from stress, treatment with steroids or cancer chemotherapy drugs.

Increased numbers result from a strong stimulus to the immune system such as chronic inflammation, recovery from acute infections and underactive adrenal glands (Addison's disease).

Eosinophils

Eosinophils are the primary detoxifiers of histamine, a substance released by the body whenever tissue is damaged.

Decreased numbers occur with stress, the use of steroids, or an overactive adrenal gland (Cushing's disease).

Increased numbers occur when a dog is showing an allergic reaction to something in his environment, or when he has parasites in his system or when he has an underactive adrenal gland (Addison's disease).

Monocytes

Monocytes are single cells which are immature forms of macrophages. Macrophages are those cells which "eat" foreign bodies and cellular debris.

Decreased numbers are not considered important.

Increased numbers occur with chronic fungus infections, dying tissue, chronic inflammatory and immune diseases, as well as a stress reaction from using steroid medications and Cushing's disease.

Basophils

Basophils contain both histamine and heparin which is a blood clotting *inhibitor*. These cells start the inflammatory response after the body is injured. Basophils are rarely found on the blood smears of dogs.

Decreased number of basophils can be an indicator of an underactive thyroid.

Increased number of these cells are associated with high fat levels in the blood, heartworm disease, Cushing's disease, thrombus formation (blood clot within the blood vessels) and ulcerative colitis.

SERUM CHEMISTRY PROFILE

The blood chemistry profile is a panel of tests that provides a broad database to evaluate your dog's general health. The results not only confirm abnormalities found on the physical examination, but also highlight unsuspected problems. The most accurate results are obtained if a 12-hour fast precedes the drawing of the blood sample.

What appears on the following chart is what you would normally receive from the laboratory. Some laboratories include other chemicals on their list. There are numerous tests that can be requested if you are looking for a specific disease, some of which are shown at the end of the chart.

These results are those norms used by Antech Diagnostics, Farmingdale, NY, which is the lab most often used by veterinary offices nationwide.

CALCIUM

Blood calcium levels are influenced by diet, hormone levels and blood protein levels. Calcium readings represent a balance between bone formation and bone reabsorption and is regulated by the hormone parathormone. Calcium is needed for blood clotting and keeping cell membranes intact.

SERUM CHEMISTRY PROFILE

Test	Reference	Range
Calcium	MG/DL	8.9–11.4
Phosphorus	MG/DL	2.5–6.0
Sodium	MEQ/L	139–154
Potassium	MEQ/L	3.6–5.5
Chloride	MG/DL	102–120
Cholesterol	MG/DL	92–324
Triglycerides	MG/DL	29–291
LDH	U/L	20–250
AST (SGOT)	U/L	15–66
Bilirubin, Total	MG/DL	0.1–0.3
Gamma Glutamyltranspeptidase (GGT)	U/L	1–12
ALT (SGPT)	U/L	12–118
Alkaline Phosphatase (SAP)	U/L	5–131
Total Protein	G/DL	5.0–7.4
Globulin, Total	G/DL	1.6–3.6
Albumin	G/DL	2.7–4.4
A/G Ratio	G/DL	0.50–1.68
BUN	MG/DL	6–25
Creatinine, Kidney	MG/DL	0.5–1.6
BUN/Creatinine Ratio	RATIO	4–27
Uric Acid	MG/DL	0.0–1.0
Glucose, Serum	MG/DL	70–138
Amylase, Serum	U/L	400–2000

Sometimes listed:

CPK		59–895
Lipase		77–695
Magnesium		1.2–1.9

Decreased levels indicate acute damage to the pancreas or an under-active parathyroid gland. The parathyroid is a small endocrine gland attached to the thyroid that secretes the hormone *parathormone* which regulates the calcium/phosphorus metabolism in the body.

Increased levels may indicate the presence of certain cancers, an overactive thyroid gland, too much protein in the blood or too much Vitamin D in the system.

PHOSPHORUS

Blood phosophorus levels are affected by carbohydrate metabolism, diet, parathormone levels and kidney function.

Decreased levels show an overactive parathyroid gland and malignancies caus-ing the appearance of an overactive parathyroid gland, malnutrition, and mal-absorption.

Increased levels develop with an under-active parathyroid gland and kidney failure.

SODIUM

Sodium is found in both bone and the body fluids outside of individual cells. The concentration of sodium is controlled by a naturally occurring steroid produced by the adrenal glands. This steroid (aldosterone) promotes excretion of sodium by the kidneys.

Decreased levels can be caused by lack of sodium in the food, diarrhea, vom-iting, kidney disease and diabetes mellitus as well as an under-active adrenal gland (hypoadrenocorticism).

Increased levels are rare but can occur with salt poisoning and dehydration.

POTASSIUM

Potassium is found in the fluid that is inside cells. It is excreted by the kidneys, influenced by the adrenal gland steroid, aldosterone.

Decreased levels of potassium are the result of prolonged vomiting or diarrhea, an overactive adrenal gland (hyperadrenocorticism) and an increased alkaline pH level in the blood. Irregular heart beat.

Increased levels can be caused by kidney disease, blockage of the urethra, dehydration and under-active adrenal glands. If pH acid levels are too high (acidosis) the death of large amounts of tissue will result and cardiac arrest may result.

CHLORIDE

These levels are measured to ascertain the acid-base balance of the body, as well as the water balance.

Decreased levels of chloride often result from vomiting with a loss of gastric juices and with hypoadrenocorticism.

Increased levels would result from dehydration and the body being too acid (acidosis).

CHOLESTEROL

Produced by the liver, cholesterol is excreted in the bile. *Blood cholesterol levels tend to be inversely related to thyroid function.*

Decreased levels are found in an overactive thyroid gland.

Increased levels can occur when there is obstruction in the bile duct, kidney disease, dietary intake, diabetes mellitus, an overactive adrenal gland and an under-active thyroid gland.

TRIGLYCERIDES

Triglycerides show the levels of fat in the blood. High levels will be found in the blood four to six hours after eating, regardless of diet. 12-hour fasting is needed to produce accurate test results.

Decreased levels appear not to be a problem.

Increased levels may indicate diabetes mellitus, starvation, under-active thyroid and acute (sudden onset) of pancreatitis.

LDH

Lactic dehydrogenase is an enzyme found in many body tissues. It is not a reliable test to pinpoint specific disease states. Heat stable lactic dehydrongenase (HLDH) is a test that is used to aid in the diagnosis of heart disease (myocardial infarction), but is used in conjunction with other tests.

Increased levels may be present in some malignancies (up to three times normal).

THE LIVER

AST (SGOT)

Aspartate aminotransferase is an enzyme present in high concentration in liver, heart and skeletal muscle. It is not as specific to liver injury as in an increase of ALT.

Decreased levels are considered insignificant.

Increased levels are seen in liver damage, heart problems (myocardial infarction), inflammation of skeletal muscle, tissue damage and rupture of red blood cells. More tests should be considered when diagnosing liver disease.

Bilirubin

This is the orange or yellow colored bile pigment that comes from the breakdown of hemoglobin from old or damaged red blood cells. It is chemically changed in the liver, secreted into the bile and delivered to the small intestine. As it passes through the intestines it is converted by bacterial enzymes into a waste product excreted mostly through the feces and is responsible for their brown color. Some bile is secreted into the circulating blood and excreted through the urine. Bilirubin is measured as both *direct* (the changed form) and *total* bilirubin. No significance should be placed on direct bilirubin levels unless the total bilirubin levels are increased. As the total levels increase, yellow membranes (icterus) occur.

By comparing the direct bilirubin levels to the total bilirubin levels we can localize where the problem is occurring if:

- *Total* bilirubin is three times normal and *direct* is less than half of the total, the changes are due to destruction of red blood cells.

- *Total* is two times normal and *direct* is much greater than half the total then the changes are due to obstruction.

- *Total* bilirubin is elevated less than two times and *direct* is greater than half the total, then obstruction is caused by damage within the liver.

Decrease in direct—not significant.
Increase in direct—bile duct obstruction or liver disease.
Decrease in total—not significant.
Increase in total—disease in the liver, bile duct obstruction, destruction of red blood cells.

Gamma-glutamyltranspeptidase

GGT is a protein enzyme produced by the liver and circulated in the blood. The body's resistance to disease is related to the concentration of these proteins in the blood.

Increased levels indicate pancreatitis, blockage of bile excretion.

ALT (SGPT)

Alanine aminotransferase is an enzyme present in large quantities in liver cells. This enzyme is very specific for liver disease and increases of three times or more indicates cell damage in the liver. Increases do not necessarily correlate, however, with the *seriousness* of the disease as the ALT enzyme persists for two to five days before it begins to break down.

Decreased levels are usually not significant.

Increased levels may indicate circulatory problems in the liver, trauma to the liver, active liver disease, degeneration of the liver (cirrhosis), obstruction to the bile duct, death of liver tissue, liver cancer and acute pancreatitis.

Alkaline Phosphatase

SAP is an enzyme found in high concentration in the liver and bone. Levels will be higher in young growing dogs. SAP of bone origin is normally elevated in puppies of less than eight months of age. In adult dogs a steady increase in the levels may indicate cancer.

Decreased levels not considered significant.

Increased levels indicate obstruction or congestive liver disease, overactive adrenal glands and drug treatments including steroids, anticonvulsants and barbiturates. New bone growth from breaks or fractures and rheumatoid arthritis.

Total Protein

This is the combination of various proteins produced by the liver and lymphoid organs.

Decreased levels occur with kidney disease, liver disease, starvation and malabsorption syndromes.

Increased levels occur with severe dehydration, cancer of the lymph nodes (lymphosarcoma) and bone marrow tumors (myeloma).

Globulins

These come in three types. Alpha globulins which transport fats, beta globulins transport iron and gamma globulins, sometimes called immunoglobulins, function as antibodies. Globulins total on the chem scan measures a *combination* of all three globulins.

Decreased levels indicate deficiencies in the immune system.

Increased levels can be due to infections involving the whole body (systemic), cancer of the lymph nodes, bone cancer, parasites in the system and liver disease.

Albumin

This blood protein which transports fatty acids, affects the pressure of the fluid in the cells (osmotic pressure).

Decreased levels indicate low production of blood protein associated with chronic liver or pancreatic disease, malabsorption, hemorrhage, burns and kidney disease.

Increased levels are the result of dehydration.

KIDNEY

BUN (Blood Urea Nitrogen)

Urea is an end product of protein breakdown. It contains large amounts of nitrogen found mostly in the urine, as well as in the blood and lymphs. It is formed in the liver from ammonia derived from amino acid breakdown. The amount of urea excreted through urine is less when your dog is on a low protein diet. Expect low readings from dogs being fed special diets, or dogs that are being fed the "lite" foods.

Decreased levels are seen with low protein diets, liver insufficiency and with the use of anabolic steroid drugs.

Increased levels (azotemia) occur from any condition that reduces the ability of the kidney to filter fluids in the body or interferes with protein breakdown. Before kidney problems arise, diseases such as renal azotemia can be seen. Heart disease, low adrenal gland function and shock can create azotemia. If more than 75% of the kidney tissues become non-functional through aging or kidney disease, the BUN will increase. Post renal problems such as obstruction of the ureters (small tube-like ducts connecting the kidney to the bladder), injury to the bladder or urethra (tube that carries urine out of the body), will cause an elevated BUN. As the urea nitrogen cannot be eliminated, it builds up in the body. This extremely dangerous condition can kill your dog if not taken care of *immediately*.

Creatinine

Creatinine is a nonprotein nitrogen waste product of muscle metabolism.

Decreased levels are not significant and rarely seen.

Increased levels would indicate poor kidney filtration. This poor filtration results from the same prerenal and postrenal causes that produce an increased BUN. An increased BUN and normal creatinine would suggest an early or mild prerenal problem. A severe prerenal azotemia would cause both the creatinine and BUN to be high. An increased creatinine and increased BUN with elevated phosphorus would indicate a long-standing, severe kidney disease (kidney failure).

Uric Acid

Uric Acid is the end product of purines which are the other end product of proteins. Purines mainly come from the nuclei of cells.

Decreased levels not considered important.

Increased levels show marked cellular destruction in such diseases as leukemia, pneumonia and toxic states often associated with pregnancy. Severe kidney disease would elevate the levels of uric acid, but should not be taken alone as an indicator.

Glucose

The metabolism and concentration of blood glucose is affected by many disease states. It is greatly influenced by diet, the ability of liver to handle the diet and the rate at which glucose is excreted.

Decreased levels can result from an overdose of insulin, tumors or abnormal growths on the pancreas. Low levels may also come from a liver that is malfunctioning, under-active adrenal glands, excessive exercise and long-term starvation.

Increased levels can be caused by diabetes mellitus, recent feeding, an excess of the hormone progesterone, over-active adrenal glands and stress.

Amylase

Amylase is a pancreatic enzyme that is released into the small intestine which allows starch to be converted to sugar.

Decreased levels of amylase are not considered important.

Increased levels show up in certain types of pancreatic disease or pancreatic duct obstruction. Both conditions cause the release of amylase into the surrounding tissue creating tremendous tissue damage that produces severe pain and inflammation. Severe or acute pancreatic damage should cause a three- to fourfold increase in the serum amylase. Sometimes stomach problems, poor or incorrect diet, obstruction in the intestines or diseases of the salivary glands can create elevated levels.

OTHER TESTS THAT CAN BE SHOWN ON LABORATORY REPORTS:

Lipase

This is a pancreatic enzyme that chemically changes fatty acids in the body. It is used most often to confirm acute pancreatic disease.

Decreased levels not significant.

Increased levels indicate acute pancreatitis, kidney disease (decreased excretions), and upper intestinal inflammation.

CPK

Creatine phosphokinase is an enzyme that is found both in heart and skeletal muscle. Levels are normally lower in females.

Decreased levels not significant.

Increased levels are caused by heart muscle damage (myocardial infarction), or death of skeletal muscle tissue.

Carbon Dioxide

Used to measure blood levels of bicarbonate that plays a major role in maintaining the body's acid-alkaline balance and changes in cases of respiratory insufficiency.

Decreased levels occur when the body pH is low (metabolic acidosis) and kidney failure. This is often the result of shock, severe diabetes, diarrhea and underactive adrenal glands. The rise in body pH often results in low potassium and low chloride levels.

Increased levels are seen when there have been severe bouts of vomiting.

URINALYSIS

The examination of the urine is an absolute necessity in the evaluation of your dog's health. It is not just a measure of kidney and lower urinary tract problems, but also reflects a variety of disease processes that involve several other organs. A urinalysis consists of the physical characteristics of the urine, as well as the chemical and sediment present.

PHYSICAL CHARACTERISTICS

Color :   Normal urine is yellow to amber

Abnormal color can be caused by:

blood=red

bilirubin=dark yellow to brown with yellow foam

hemoglobin/myoglobin=reddish brown

Transparency: Normal urine is clear

Abnormal urine is cloudy which can be caused by:

crystals, cells, blood, mucous, bacteria or cast

Volume: Normal 12 to 20 ml of urine per pound of body weight in 24 hours.

Increased volume (polyuria) comes from an increase in water intake and may indicate acute (sudden) kidney disease, long-term kidney disease, diabetes mellitus, liver failure, over-active adrenal glands, too much calcium in body, diabetes associated with kidney dysfunction, diabetes associated with pituitary gland dysfunction, excessive thirst or uterine infections (pyometra).

Decreased volume of urine output indicates dehydration, which in turn may point to a sudden onset of kidney disease, shock, end stage of kidney disease and urinary tract obstruction.

SPECIFIC GRAVITY

This is an indicator of how well the kidneys are able to concentrate or dilute urine. Normal levels should be greater than 1.030.

Decreased levels 1.007–1.029 occur with diabetes insipidus, over-active adrenals, excessive thirst (polydipsia) and pyometra.

Increased levels greater than 1.040 are associated with high fever, dehydration, diabetes mellitus, vomiting, diarrhea and severe hemorrhage.

pH LEVELS (HYDROGEN-ION CONCENTRATION)

A dog's diet should be on the acidic side making the pH of the urine 6.2–6.5. If the diet is too alkaline, the urine pH may be greater than 7.0 which is the neutral point. A fresh urine sample is needed to obtain an accurate pH as urine becomes more alkaline the longer it stands. Urine pH alone should not be used to determine the acid/alkaline status of the body. The pH of urine has a major effect on the formation of crystals and the types of crystals that form.

CHEMICAL CHARACTERISTICS OF URINE

Protein

The level of protein is tested by using a test strip which has a scale of 0–4+. Normal urine=0–1+ protein level.

Increased levels of protein are 2–4+. A *temporary increase* (false positive) may result from very alkaline pH urine (more than 7.5), muscular exertion, being in season (vaginal bleeding) or excessive protein intake.

True increases are associated with chronic kidney disease, infection, inflammation or tumors in the urinary tract.

Glucose

This sugar is not normally found in the urine.

Increased levels may be temporarily seen when the dog is stressed or on cortisone therapy as well as hyperglycemia caused by diabetes mellitus, over-active adrenal glands and acute inflammation of the kidneys.

Ketones

These acids represent the end product of fat metabolism and have a scale of 0–3+. Normal is 0.

Increased levels indicate excessive fat in the body and occur when fat provides the bulk of energy in the diet. It is highly suggestive of diabetic problems. Starvation diets will also increase urine ketones especially in young, immature dogs.

Bilirubin

Reagent strips are used to detect direct bilirubin. Range falls between 0–3+. Trace quantities 0–1+ are considered normal.

Increased levels or high normal levels 2+–3+ would indicate the obstruction of bile flow and the reflux of direct bilirubin. *Severe liver disease is often present before elevated bilirubin in urine is detected.*

Urobilinogen

Urobilinogen is formed in the intestines from the bilirubin excreted by the liver. Range = 0–4+. This test must be performed on fresh urine.

Absence indicates complete bile duct blockage.

Presence indicates the bile duct is open 2+–4+. This occurs in diseases that result in the destruction of red blood cells (hemolytic diseases).

Occult Blood

Red blood cells apparent in the urine give it a red, cloudy appearance. In the absence of anemia or muscle disease, it is evidence of urinary tract disease. If the urine is reddish brown with no red blood cells present, it would indicate loss of hemoglobin from the blood vessels causing anemia. Brownish urine with an absence of red blood cells in the sediment indicates muscle damage.

Sediment

The evaluation of the sediment in the urine must be interpreted with consideration of the specific gravity and how the sample is collected. Samples collected by the owner from the dog may yield cells and bacteria from the urethra and genital tracts as well as the bladder, ureter or kidneys.

RBCs—Presence of red blood cells result from inflammation or trauma to the urogenital tract.

WBCs—White blood cells are few in number in normal urine. Large numbers in collected samples indicate inflammation of the urinary or urogenital tract and possible kidney infections.

Epithelial Cells—Originating in the ureters, bladder wall and urethra, epithelial cells are increased in numbers with inflammation and tumors.

Crystals—These are formed by precipitation of minerals present in the urine. The pH of the urine will determine the kind of crystals formed. Crystals may indicate the presence of stones (calculae) in the bladder.

FECAL ANALYSIS

To check for intestinal *parasites*, a fecal analysis should be run at least twice a year. Internal parasite eggs that can be detected under a microscope are *round-worms* (ascarids), *hook* and *whip* worms. *Tapeworms* are noted on the surface of the stool, or around the anus as small flat ¼ inch white segments which may stretch to a full inch in length. These segments are filled with eggs. *Coccidia* and *giardia* are simple, single celled parasites (protozoa) that can be detected in the stool. *Undigested food material*, muscle, fat and starch granules may indicate that the food is passing through the digestive tract too quickly, or that there is a pancreatic enzyme deficiency which results in malabsorption syndrome. *Occult blood* (microscopic blood) indicates hemorrhage into the gastrointestinal tract. *Gross blood* which can be seen by the naked eye, looks like a dark, tarry stool when it comes from bleeding in the upper gastrointestinal tract (mouth to the small intestine). Bleeding in the colon (large bowel) and rectum looks like bright red blood in the stool.

SUMMARY OF BLOOD WORK

- Your veterinarian is one of the most important people involved in your dog's life. Just as you select your own doctor by reputation, evaluating the quality of service and your interaction with him or her, so you should choose your veterinarian. He or she should have a good reputation and you and your dog should feel at ease with him or her. You need to feel that you can trust him or her, especially in an emergency situation.

- Be sure that you have stated your own goals, your intentions with your dog, so that your veterinarian can know what you are expecting. You need to be able to work together; your dog's health depends upon this.

- When you have a puppy, you will be visiting your veterinarian several times in the first year. After that first year, establish a routine by visiting every six months for fecal and physical examinations and once a year for a complete work-up including blood work. Use this as a preventative measure. Your dog cannot tell you "where it hurts" or if he is not feeling very well. Preventative medicine can put years on your dog's life.

- When your dog is going to have blood work done, make sure he is fasted at least 12 hours before the test is run.

- Blood work and urinalysis need to be handled very carefully and in some of the tests, there is a time factor involved. If you have a large number of dogs, having your veterinarian visit to take samples will only work if he can be back in the office within the time limit.

- There are some differences in clinical chemistries between the breeds. German Shepherds tend to be lower than other breeds in Glucose, LDH, Alkaline Phosphatase, BUN and Uric Acid. Their amylase and transaminase may be higher. Phosphorus and SGPT are higher in Beagles and Labrador Retrievers.

- Your best gauge is the comparison of your own dog's test results. Establish what is normal for him and be sure that the tests are always run using the same laboratory.

- If you have made the decision to change your diet from commercial dog food to the Natural Diet, have blood drawn before you change. You should have a CBC, a chemistry screen or profile, and also a fecal analysis. One month after putting your dog onto the new diet, have the same tests run. This will give you a basis for comparison. Changing to the Natural Diet often puts a dog who had health problems back into balance.

LIST OF TERMS FOR LABORATORY PROFILES

The following is a glossary of terms that are helpful for you to know. These are terms that you will see and hear frequently. Knowing them will help you to understand and better communicate with your veterinarian.

Acidosis:	A physiological state in which the body's pH becomes too low (acid range).
Alkalosis:	A physiological state in which the body's pH becomes too high (alkaline range).
Cardiac:	Refers to the heart.
Hepatic:	Refers to the liver.
Hyperadrenocorticism:	The state of an over-active adrenal gland (Cushing's disease).
Hypoadrenocorticism:	The state of an under-active adrenal gland (Addison's disease).
Hypoglycemia:	Low blood sugar levels.
Hyperthyroid:	An over-active thyroid gland.
Hypothyroid:	An under-active thyroid gland.
Necrosis/Necrotic:	Dying or dead tissue.
Pyometra:	An infection of the uterus.
Polyuria:	Increased urination.
Polydipsia:	Increased thirst.
Renal:	Refers to the kidneys.

10 Thyroid & Adrenal Glands

The thyroid and adrenal glands are two of the most significant endocrine glands in the body. Both are regulated by the pituitary gland. When functioning normally, they are the major controllers of metabolism—keeping the body systems flowing smoothly. When there are abnormalities, major metabolic dysfunction occurs.

More and more dogs are being diagnosed with thyroid and adrenal problems and the purpose of including relevant material in this chapter is to help you understand what the test values mean so you can work more closely with your veterinarian.

THE THYROID GLAND

The thyroid gland is a bi-lobed endocrine gland located on either side of the trachea, just below the larynx. The hormone thyroxine (T_4) is produced by the thyroid and is responsible for maintaining optimal levels of metabolism of all cellular functions. The thyroid gland, under the control of thyroid stimulating hormone (TSH) produced by the pituitary gland, produces all of the T_4 in the body. T_4 is converted to tri-iodothyronine (T_3) in the liver and peripheral tissues. T_3 is the metabolically active form, which can enter the cells and be used in cell metabolism.

A very important aspect of the routine physical examination and chemistry profiles is to evaluate thyroid function. We use the premium thyroid panel performed by Michigan State University to do our routine baseline thyroid screens, and the follow-up "life-stage" rechecks. This profile reports:

- Total T_4 (TT_4)

- Free T_4 by equilibrium dialysis (FT_4)

- Total T_3 (TT_3)

147

- Free T_3 (FT_3)

- Circulating T_3 and T_4 autoantibodies

- TSH levels

The most important factors are the TT_4, FT_4, and the TSH levels. It is important to remember that these levels will fluctuate a great deal over a 24-hour period, which may necessitate rechecking six months later if low normal values are found. The autoantibodies, when elevated, are indicators that an immune mediated thyroid reaction is occurring or has recently occurred. If the panel is inconclusive, TSH is given to the dog and the thyroid is checked for response.

We like to get a baseline profile at one year of age and repeat the profile every two years thereafter. If at any time there is suspicion of hypothyroidism, check it out. In dogs less than two years of age, the values are expected to be at least in the normal mid-range or higher.

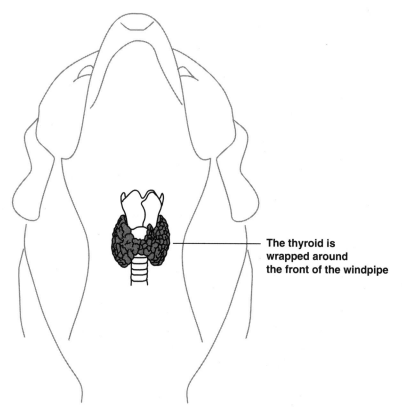

The thyroid is wrapped around the front of the windpipe

The thyroid gland.

HYPOTHYROIDISM

Thyroid dysfunction is the most *commonly* seen endocrine disorder in dogs. Hypothyroidism is a deficiency of the thyroid hormone. There are four hypothyroid syndromes. The two primary forms are lymphocytic thyroiditis and atrophic hypothyroidism, and the two secondary forms are pituitary-dependent hypothyroidism and euthyroid sick syndrome.

Lymphocytic thyroiditis is an immune-mediated disease in which the thyroid gland is infiltrated by lymphocytes. It is the most common cause of hypothyroidism, and may be initiated by the body's reaction to:

- medications

- vaccinations

- viral infections

- heavy metal toxicity from water or food supplies

This autoimmune response has been linked to a genetic predisposition. The primary indicator on the thyroid profile is elevation of the T_3 and/or T_4 autoantibodies.

Atrophic hypothyroidism results when the thyroid gland atrophies and glandular tissue is replaced with fat. The cause of this thyroid atrophy is unknown.

Pituitary-dependent hypothyroidism is caused by insufficient secretion of TSH by the pituitary gland. Drug reactions, illness or malnutrition may cause temporary suppression of TSH. Permanent deficiencies may be caused by congenital malformation, tumors, infections or hemorrhage involving the pituitary gland. Low levels of TSH on the function test, combined with low resting levels of TT_4 and FT_4 that are corrected by TSH stimulation, are the diagnostic for pituitary dependent hypothyroidism.

Euthyroid sick syndrome is where we must be careful. The TT_4 and FT_4 may decrease in many severe or chronic diseases as a compensation to conserve essential body tissue in the face of decreased caloric intake. Debilitating diseases, kidney failure, diabetes mellitus, and hyperadrenocorticism (Cushing's disease) may cause a decreased secretion of TSH and give a *false* indication of hypothyroidism. Correction or control of these diseases allows the thyroid to return to normal function.

The *clinical* signs associated with hypothyroidism can involve many body sys-tems, showing a multiplicity of signs. These signs usually become grossly evident after four to six years of age, and in the giant breeds as early as two to three years of age. Currently, hypothyroidism is found in increasing numbers in younger dogs. Most dogs will be hypothyroid for six months to one year before obvious clinical signs are evident. A change in *behavior,* often subtle, may be one of the first signs of hypothyroidism. However studies recently completed at the University of Southampton in England show that dogs who *suddenly* show aggressive behaviors can also be hypothyroid. The "text book" hypothyroid dog shows:

- Lethargy
- Infertility
- Weight gain
- Cold intolerance
- Exercise intolerance
- Dull, dry coat
- Slow hair growth
- Brachycardia (slow heart rate)
- Bilateral alopecia (hair loss of the trunk with the head and extremities spared)
- Hyperpigmentation, thickening (elephant hide) of the skin
- Behavior changes

A multiplicity of clinical signs can be seen in hypothyroidism. The following table lists clinical signs as related to individual systems.

SYSTEM-RELATED CLINICAL SIGNS OF HYPOTHYROIDISM

Alterations in Metabolism	Gastrointestinal
Lethargy	Constipation
Mental dullness	Vomiting
Exercise intolerance	Diarrhea
Weight gain	Change in appetite
Cold intolerance	

Reproduction—Male	Reproduction—Female
Lack of libido	Infertility
Testicular atrophy	Irregular estrus
Decreased sperm production	Weak, silent cycles
Infertility	Weak, dying, stillborn pups

Eyes	Heart
Corneal lipid deposits	Brachycardia (slow heart rate)
Uveitis	Cardiac arrhythmias
Dry eye (keratitis)	Cardiomyopathy

Skin	Neuromuscular
Dry, scaly skin	Weakness
Coarse, dull coat	Stiffness
Hair loss both sides of body	Knuckling, dragging feet
"Rat tail" (hairless tail)	Droopy eyelids
Soft, fuzzy, "puppy coat" in adult	Muscle wasting
Hyperpigmentation (black skin)	Megaesophogus
Seborrhea, oily skin and coat	Laryngeal/pharyngeal paralysis
Secondary pyoderma (skin infections)	Facial paralysis
	Head tilt

continues...

continued	
Blood Disorders	**Behavior and Other Disorders**
Poorly responding anemia	Separation anxiety
Bone marrow failure	Shying away from strangers
Low platelet count	Emotional instability/aggression
	Loss of sense of smell

The chemistry profile, CBC and thyroid function screening can diagnose early the nonclinical hypothyroid dog, as well as confirm hypothyroidism in those dogs demonstrating clinical signs.

BLOOD CHEMISTRY SCREEN AND CBC OF HYPOTHYROIDISM

Chemistry Screen	CBC
↑ Cholesterol	↓ RBC
↑ ALT	↓ PCV
↑ AP	↓ Reticulytes

The poorly responding anemia, as evidenced by the few numbers of reticulocytes, is a common CBC finding in hypothyroid dogs.

THYROID FUNCTION SCREEN

Test	Lymphocytic	Atropic Hypothyroid	Pituitary Dependent	Euthyroid Sick Syndrome
TT_4	Normal to Low	Low	Low	Low
FT_4	Normal to Low	Low	Low	Low
TSH	Normal to High	High	Low	Low
TSH response	Poor	Poor	Normal	Normal
Auto-antibodies	Increased	Normal	Normal	Normal

TREATMENT FOR HYPOTHYROIDISM

Treatment of hypothyroidism is very successful and gratifying. The medication Soloxine is used as a T_4 replacement. It is dosed twice daily. Over time, as regulation occurs, this dose may or may not be able to be reduced to once daily. Initially, thyroid response profiles are done at 10 week intervals until the TT_4 and FT_4 levels are stable in the mid-range levels. Once level, a yearly profile should suffice. Blood for testing will give the most accurate results if drawn four to six hours after the Soloxine is given.

In cases where liver disease or compromise occurs, conversion of T_4 to T_3 is often depressed or non-existent. Soloxine supplementation can raise TT_4 and FT_4 levels to normal or above normal but conversion does not occur. In this situation, T_3 supplementation may be necessary. This determination can only be reached by your veterinarian after definitive testing.

Acupuncture can be very helpful in the treatment of hypothyroidism. It will usually allow a noticeable reduction in the amount or frequency of Soloxine supplementation.

The use of the Natural Diet, together with a short course of glandulars, can also be an effective therapy in cases of hypothyroidism and sometimes brings the function of the thyroid back to normal. Occasionally, homeopathy has been used in the same way. If supplementation of Soloxine is still required, it is usually given at low dosage. Blood panels need to be drawn yearly.

EVO

A lovely Newfoundland, Evo, came to us when he was 10 months old. Rather withdrawn at first, he took a few months to really integrate himself into our family of dogs, all of whom were older than he.

When he was about 2 ½ years of age, we noticed that his joy for working was diminishing. He would rather hang out than run around the obedience ring or agility course. It seemed to require a great effort from him to be enthusiastic.

Prior to having him neutered when he was three, we took blood and did the routine testing which included a thyroid panel. It was sent to the University of Michigan and the results were a surprise. His autoantibodies were elevated and there was a slight change in his TT_4 showing autoimmune thyroiditis. The University asked if I was willing to place him in a study being done on this hereditary disease, to which I agreed. This meant that his blood had to be drawn every three months to see how the disease progressed.

We medicate Evo with Soloxine to regulate his behavior. His thyroid problems are the basis of the trouble.

During this period of time he was not to be medicated with Soloxine. But being the experimenter that I am, I thought it a wonderful chance to try the homeopathic Iodium to see if that would improve the thyroid function. The next test was done three months later, and it showed some change in the TT_4 and a slight lowering of the autoantibodies, but nothing significant. His behavior, however, was changing. He was becoming irritable with the other dogs, and growled at them on occasion. He also became extremely overheated when playing, and had to be put in a cool place to calm down, which took much longer than usual. He no longer greeted people with joy, but stayed in the background, allowing all the other dogs to take care of greeting behavior. Then, five months into the test, he had a fight with Manfred, one of our Dachshunds, over an old bone that Manfred happened to pick up in front of Evo. We were not happy.

Consulting with Sheila Hamilton-Andrews in England, who had just finished a study of aggression in the Bearded Collie and hypothyroidism, and talking it over with Kerry, we decided to try him on a low dose of Soloxine for a month to see if it brought about any behavior changes. After two doses, Evo's behavior normalized and he started to play again, he wanted to work, and he became his usual, happy and bouncy self. Needless to say, he'll be monitored carefully, but I suspect he'll be on Soloxine for the rest of his life.

CAUTION

Under normal circumstances, the readings on the thyroid panel would not have warranted putting Evo on medication. It was the change in his *behavior* that made me conduct this experiment. It could have easily, if given in too high a dose, sent him into hyperthyroidism and the behavior could have become much worse. That is why working with your veterinarian is so important in solving thyroid problems. Evo's blood levels are monitored on a regular basis to make sure that the dose of Soloxine is correct for him.

HYPERTHYROIDISM

Hyperthyroidism is unusual in dogs, and is most often associated with thyroid tumors. A firm mass in the area of the thyroid glands on the neck should be checked. Thyroid tests will indicate high T_4 levels and normal to high T_3 levels. Other clinical signs are an increase in thirst (polydipsia), hyperactivity, excessive panting, preference for a cool location, restlessness and fatigue. Treatment consists of surgical excision of the tumor. T_4 supplementation is needed if both lobes of the thyroid are removed. When the thyroid has been removed, there is a tendency for the body to store excess water, salt and protein, and the blood cholesterol levels rise. Nutritional support is crucial in both cases. The thyroid cannot function correctly without sufficient amino acids, carbohydrates, minerals, and vitamins in the diet.

SUMMARY OF THYROID FUNCTION

- Thyroid function should be evaluated periodically using the "premium" Michigan Thyroid Profile.

- Hypothyroidism can manifest as four syndromes: lymphocytic thyroiditis, atrophic hypothyroidism, secondary pituitary–dependent hypothyroidism and the euthyroid sick syndrome.

- Clinical signs involve multiple systems and often do not appear until six months to one year after hypothyroidism has started.

- A low thyroid test does not absolutely mean the thyroid is the problem (euthyroid sick syndrome).

- Treatment with Soloxine can be very rewarding.

- Acupuncture, diet and use of glandulars can be helpful and may allow a decrease in the amount of Soloxine needed.

- Hyperthyroidism is uncommon in dogs. Surgery is usually required.

THE ADRENAL GLANDS

The adrenal glands are a pair of small endocrine glands located at the anterior (front) pole of each kidney. These endocrine glands secrete glucocorticoids (cortisol), mineralocorticoids (aldosterone) and sex steroids (progesterone, estrogen and androgens). Simply put, they produce the sugar, salt and sex hormones. These hormones are metabolized and removed primarily by the liver.

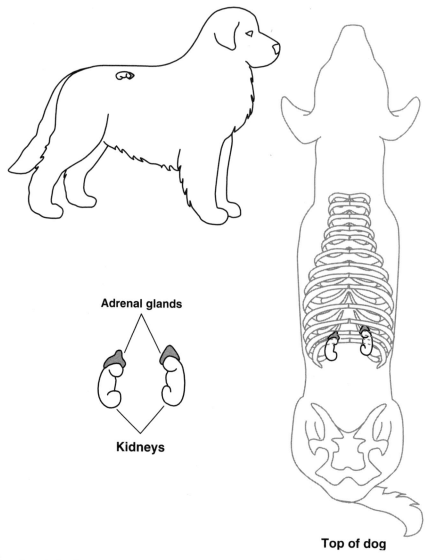

Adrenal glands

Kidneys

Top of dog

The adrenal glands.

Glucocorticoids (cortisol) are responsible for the intermediary metabolism of glucose. They also suppress both inflammatory and immunologic responses and exert a profound negative effect on wound healing. The secretion of ACTH by the anterior pituitary gland is the principle regulator of cortisol production by the adrenal glands.

Mineralocorticiod's (aldosterone) primary function is to control the levels of sodium and potassium. The renin-angoitension system of the kidney is the controlling factor for aldosterone production. These hormones are vital to the body's normal function.

CUSHING'S DISEASE

Over-secretion of glucocorticoids by the adrenal glands is termed hyperadrenocorticism or Cushing's disease. The most common cause of hyperadrenocorticicm is excessive secretion of ACTH from the pituitary gland (pituitary-dependent hyperadrenocorticism). This over-secretion may be caused by a pituitary tumor or a brain lesion of the hypothalamus, which causes the pituitary gland to excrete excess ACTH. Approximately 15% of the cases of Cushing's disease are caused by tumors of the adrenal gland (primary adrenal hyperadrenocorticism). These tumors secrete cortisol entirely independent of ACTH stimulation. Iatrogenic hyperadrenocorticism is a third form of the Cushing's disease. This is the result of prolonged use of oral, injectable or topical corticosteroids. These drugs cause atrophy of the adrenal gland cortex while producing clinical signs of excess cortisol.

Clinical signs: The clinical signs of Cushing's disease develop slowly. They are as follows:

- Polyuria (PU = increased urination)
- Polydipsia (PD = increased thirst)
- Pendulous abdomen
- Bilateral alopecia (hair loss over most of the body surface)
- Hyperpigmentation
- Thin, mineralized skin
- Lethargy and weakness

It is usually the increased thirst and urination, and the coat changes that draw our attention to this disorder. Diagnosis is based on a chemistry screen, CBC and urinalysis tests, and a cortisol evaluation.

CHEMISTRY SCREEN/CBC/URINALYSIS

Chemisty Screen	CBC	Urinalysis
Glucose—increase	WBC—increase	sg—low = 1.007
Cholesterol—increase	Neutrophils—increase	
Triglycerides—increase	Lymphocytes—decrease	
ALT—increase	Eosinophils—decrease	
GGT—increase		
Alk Phos—increase		

CORTISOL EVALUATION

Serum Cortisol Levels	Pituitary Dependent Hyperadrenocortism	Primary Adrenal Hyperadrenocortism	Iatronic Hyperadrenocortism
ACTH response			
pre	increase	increase	increase
post	increase = 3×	increase > 5× baseline	increase < 2×
Low Dex Suppression			
pre	increase	increase	increase
post	no suppression	no suppression	no suppression
High Dose Dex Suppression			
pre	increase	increase	increase
post	suppressed	no suppression	no suppression
Endogenous ACTH			
	increase	decrease	decrease
Urine Cortisol: Creatinine ratio			
	increase	increase	<20
Serum T$_4$			
		low but thyroid responds to ACTH	

Very often, we find infections difficult to control due to the glucocorticoid suppression of the immune response and the ability to respond to inflammation. We also find diabetes mellitus present due to the disruption of the normal glucose metabolism. Periodically we have cases where diabetes mellitus has been diagnosed, but is not controlled well with insulin therapy. Even though not indicated by other clinical signs and chemistry changes, cortisol evaluation confirms Cushing's disease. As the hyperadrenocorticism comes under control the diabetes clears and is no longer a problem.

Treatment of hyperadrenocorticism depends on the cause of the disease. With pituitary dependent hyperadrenocorticism (PDH) the treatment of choice is the oral medication Mitotane. Once maintenance levels of treatment are achieved, continuous monitoring is very important. An ACTH response test is performed every six months to confirm that the adrenal cortex is being kept in control. A general chemistry profile should be run at least once a year. In the case of an adrenal tumor, the tumor is confirmed and surgical excision is performed. Usually only one adrenal gland is involved. If tumors are present in both adrenal glands, follow up therapy with glococorticoids and DOCP will be required after surgery.

ADDISON'S DISEASE

Primary hypoadrenocorticism (Addison's disease) is a failure of the adrenal cortex to secrete glucocorticoids and mineralocorticoids. Immune mediated, infectious, vascular or chemical agents damage the adrenal cortex and damage the cells that produce cortisol and aldosterone. Addison's is most often a disease of young and middle-aged dogs. It often follows a waxing and waning course of illness. It is gradual and progressive as it develops, and is frequently misdiagnosed as a minor stomach or intestinal upset, allergy, or low-grade virus. The clinical signs for Addison's disease are often intermittent:

- Anorexia (loss of appetite)
- Diarrhea
- Vomiting
- Shaking/shivering
- Lethargy/depression
- Polyuria
- Weakness

- Waxing/waning course

- Weight loss

- Sensitive abdomen

The course of this disease can be slow and insidious or it may show up as apparent acute onset of coma and sudden death. I had a Standard Poodle suffer from the following symptoms on three occasions over a two-month period of time: anorexia, vomiting and lethargy. Each occasion seemed to clear with minimal treatment. The repeat of the symptoms suggested Addison's, and testing confirmed the diagnosis. Once treatment was started, the owner commented that his dog was acting like a puppy again, and that he had not been this active and vibrant for years. He had actually been coping with Addison's disease for several years.

The diagnosis for Addison's disease is made by chemistry screen, CBC and cortisol evaluation.

A serum (blood) sodium (Na) to potassium (K) ratio of less than 23 is very consistent with hypoadrenocorticism. The kidney function values (BUN and creatinine) rise due to low blood pressure and the resulting poor blood flow through the kidney.

CHEMISTRY SCREEN AND CBC (URINALYSIS—NORMAL)

Chemistry Screen		CBC	
BUN	increase	WBC	decrease
Creatinine	normal/increase	Neutrophils	decrease
Ca^{++}	increase	Lymphocytes	increase
Na	decrease	Eosinophils	increase
K^+	increase	RBC	increase
Albumin	increase	PCV	increase
Total Protein	increase		
Na : K ratio	<23		

CORTISOL EVALUATION
ACTH Stimulation Test
pre-cortisol—low post-cortisol < 2× baseline

Treatment is based on replacement therapy of glucocorticoids and mineralo-corticoids. Dogs that show signs of severe depression, dehydration and/or coma require emergency care and stabilization. This Addisonian crisis can result in sudden death if not treated as an emergency. Glucocorticoid treatment with Prednisone can quite often be discontinued after the disease is stabilized. Mineralocorticoids supplementation is a life long therapy. Recently, Novartis has developed DOCP (Desoxycorticosterone Pivolate) or *Percoten-V*. This is a very effective replacement therapy which results in the Na:K ratio returning to normal, usually within 25 days of the first injection. Therapy consists of an injection being given deep into the muscle once every 25 days. Evaluation of effectiveness is easily confirmed by checking the CBC and the Na:K ratio.

The recognition and diagnosis of early signs is very important. Observing your dog closely and knowing your dog well will allow you to pick up these early warning signs. Again, the significance of the yearly physical examination and chemistry screen cannot be over emphasized.

COCO—THE ADDISONIAN WHIPPET

As a young dog, CoCo was raised conventionally with all her vaccinations prior to 6 months of age when she was spayed. Ten days afterwards, she was given a rabies vaccine and during that same week her canine companion died. A very stressful situation for a young dog, especially since the rabies vaccine should not have been given until one month after the spaying, or one month after the other vaccines. One week later, the dog food that Debbie, her owner, was feeding her was found to be contaminated with toxins that made CoCo lethargic and withdrawn. Her eyes were vacant, and a physical examination and blood work revealed low sodium, high potassium levels, and an elevated BUN. Her weight dropped from 24 pounds to 16 pounds in seven days. She was diagnosed with Addison's disease.

CoCo was diagnosed with Addison's disease

For the first year after the diagnosis, CoCo was going into crisis. She was not eating or drinking and was suffering from a raised temperature, lethargy, weight loss and dehydration every four to six weeks. Debbie would just get her well again, have a couple of weeks of normalcy, and CoCo would crash again.

After putting CoCo onto the Natural Diet, a course of glandulars and homeopathics, CoCo has not crashed in almost three years. She is maintained on monthly injections of DOCP and prednisone to replace what is not being made naturally by her body. CoCo is enjoying her quality of life, and Debbie is less stressed!

SUMMARY OF ADRENAL GLAND FUNCTION

- Both hyper and hypo adrenal functions are serious and fairly common diseases.

- Routine yearly physical examinations and chemistry screens can provide early warnings of adrenal malfunction.

- Both diseases can be masked and mistaken for other more common problems.

- Both diseases can be treated effectively once the diagnosis is confirmed.

11 Kinesiology

"It's quackery, Wendy, don't even mention it!" This is what my staff told me in the early 1980's when I tried to introduce kinesiology into the nutrition and health curriculum at our training camps. But because I had had so much success in using it, I felt driven to teach it. If you believe in the concept that all matter has energy (Einstein's theory), sooner or later you will believe in kinesiology.

HISTORY

Kinesiology is the art and science of movement in the human body. It is also known as muscle response testing. It uses the muscle system of the body in the presence of a substance, as a source of information. A weakness of the muscle in the presence of that substance can show an allergy to it. The founder of this technique was Dr. George Goodheart, whose student, Dr. John Diamond, published "Your Body Doesn't Lie" (*see* Bibliography). This book is the basis for much of what follows.

Dr. Diamond taught that we can muscle-test anything we ingest to determine whether or not it agrees with us at the time of the test. For example, you can test the refined sugar you are about to put into your coffee to see if it's good for you. For most of us, the answer will be "no." The effect of a negative response of a given substance will range from sapping your energy to causing a violent allergic reaction, depending on the substance.

CASE HISTORY

At a recent seminar I was presented with a very thin Newfoundland named Becca. Becca was 14 months of age and had been a picky eater from the start. Her owner had brought her to the seminar in hopes of learning which kinds of food would be best for her. Diane, her owner, had given Becca as many different kinds of food as she could buy for her. Everything worked for a week or so, then Becca would stop eating again.

Becca was a picky eater until kinesiology and the Natural Diet changed her life.

We used Becca for our demonstration dog when I was teaching kinesiology. We found very quickly that Becca could only eat chicken. She tested very strong for the Natural Diet with chicken and chicken livers. She did not test for any other kind of meat protein. Nor did she test strong for any of the dog foods Diane had brought along. When I pointed out that on those packages, the animal protein listed usually consisted of a combination of chicken and lamb, or lamb with beef tallow for fat, Diane quickly understood why Becca was not eating. Becca instinctively knew that she couldn't digest these foods. Diane was much relieved to hear that the new dehydrated version of the Natural Diet was now available. Having a very demanding job, and traveling, she just didn't have time to make her own food.

Becca was put onto this food, and is still eating happily, and has not missed a meal since.

HOW TO USE KINESIOLOGY

Any muscle or set of muscles on a person can be used, but the deltoid muscle is the easiest to test since it "locks" into the shoulder joint. When the muscle is tested, the response—strong or weak—is immediately obvious to both the tester and the subject. A machine called a kinesiometer showed that the average healthy muscle can withstand around 40 pounds of pressure, versus a weak muscle which can only withstand 15 pounds of pressure, or less.

LEARNING TO TEST

Using kinesiology is not difficult and almost anyone can learn how to apply it. The potential benefit for your dog is enormous because you can monitor his or

her exact dietary needs on a daily basis—but first you have to lea
on yourself.

Choosing the Person to Work with You

Healthy skepticism when confronted with anything new is natural. Most people don't believe kinesiology can work until we show them, and then they are quite astonished. These people are skeptics with open minds. When you first get started, you will need to work with a partner. Do not try to work with someone who is a skeptic with a closed mind. Find someone who thinks it's fun to learn new things. If you have children, they are usually very good at kinesiology. You will also give them a tool that will last them a lifetime.

Initial Preparation

Items such as necklaces, earrings, watch straps, or anything that is metal and circles the body or part of it, interfere with the flow of energy and should be removed before testing.

Getting Started

1. Stand in an area with 16 inches of clear space around you (this is the combined measurement of both of your energy fields, about 6 to 8 inches around a person).

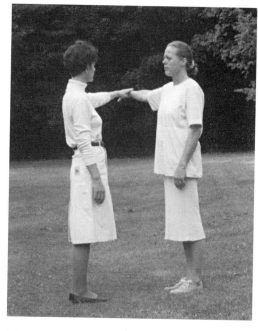

2. Stand away from the walls and furniture.

These two women are testing the strength of the deltoid muscle.

3. The subject has his or her left arm at their side and raises the right arm to shoulder height, parallel to the ground.

4. The tester faces the subject and places the right hand on the subject's left shoulder and two fingers of the left hand on the subject's right wrist.

5. The subject is instructed to "brace" and the tester firmly presses down *without jerking.*

6. A strong response is when the deltoid muscle of the subject will lock and it will be next to impossible for the tester to make the arm go down. Do not use so much force that it hurts the subject!

7. A weak response is when the subject's arm goes down.

Each person has differing strengths in the deltoid muscle, so some people may experience a little "give" in the muscle. This would be the norm for that person.

This photo illustrates a woman "testing weak" for a sample item.

HOW TO TEST FOOD

Prepare the items to be tested. Place a small amount of the product, approximately one tablespoon, into a plastic bag. For liquids use a small glass or plastic container without the lid. You can test vitamins or minerals with the capsule or tablet held in the left hand. Vegetables, fruit or other food can be tested by taking the whole item into your hand.

Line up the products. In order to "feel" the difference between those food items that test strong and those that test weak, include some refined white flour or white sugar (which test weak for almost everyone). You can also include a food to which you are allergic and one you don't like. Test these items first and then test a small amount of raw honey in a container. Honey tests strong for most people. You should feel the difference. You can also try a piece of natural whole wheat bread and then a piece of white bread.

1. Have the subject stand in the middle of the room with at least 16 inches of space around her.

2. The product to be tested goes into the left hand, which is placed into the solar plexus area. This area is a powerful center of the body's energy.

3. Have the subject hold up the right arm parallel to the ground.

4. The tester stands directly in front of the subject and places two fingers of the left hand on the subject's wrist.

5. The subject is instructed to brace against the tester, who presses down on the wrist.

The foods that test strong—the arm does not go down—are in harmony with your body. Foods that are not in harmony will cause weakness in the deltoid muscle and the arm will go down, thus decreasing your energy. You now have a wonderful tool with which to test the food you eat to see if it agrees with you.

While Dr. Diamond put food into the subject's mouth, we have learned that it is equally effective and less messy to put the food in the left hand and hold it in the solar plexus area.

All the foods you eat, as well as vitamin and mineral supplements, can be tested for compatibility. Moreover, the exact doses of supplements your body needs can be worked out. For example, have the

Testing an apple.

subject hold a 1-gram tablet of vitamin C in the left hand on the solar plexus and test. If you cannot overcome the muscle, add another tablet and test again. Keep adding tablets until the muscle tests weak, then take back one tablet and test again. This will tell you exactly how much vitamin C the subject's body needs *at that point in time*. You can do this with any supplements you take.

Kinesiology in some sense is like a blood test. It tells you the condition of the body at the time the test is done. In order to work out the correct doses of supplements needed on a daily basis, it is best to check several times during the day until a supplement program has been established. The same goes for those foods that that are not compatible with the body's energies. Check several times during the day and over several days to see if that food shows a strong or weak response. For example, if you are testing oranges just after drinking a glass of orange juice and your arm goes down, what your body is telling you is that it doesn't need oranges right now. Four hours later, you may get a different response. To get true results, test over several days and different times of the day for several days until you see a pattern that you can follow.

TESTING OUR DOGS

Dr. Goodheart's experiments showed that energy can be transferred from one person *through* another. He discovered that for an unconscious patient he could use the spouse or close friend or relative of that person as an energy conduit. It also worked with someone who was not associated with the patient, like his office nurse. Such a person is called the *surrogate tester*. The surrogate puts his or her hand on the body of the unconscious person, thereby transferring the patient's energy through his or her body.

The same technique has been adapted for our dogs, who, in a sense, are like the "unconscious" person.

SURROGATE TESTING

1. The dog is lying down by the owner's left side, with the owner sitting on the floor next to the dog. Take any metal collar off the dog.

2. Put a few kernels of the food the dog is currently being fed in either a plastic bag or glass jar and place on the dog's body—anywhere except the head area.

3. The owner's right arm is extended parallel to the ground.

4. The tester pushes down on the wrist of the owner.

You will immediately know the result. A strong response means the food is okay for your dog; a weak response means it is not the best choice. If you get a weak response, test several dog foods until you find one that tests strong.

There are over 3,000 brands of dog food available in this country. Dogs are all individuals with their own body chemistry and the chances are slim that one of these foods will test strong for all dogs.

HOW TO TEST YOUR DOG

The most accurate results are obtained when your dog is hungry. Prepare plastic bags that contain half a dozen kernels of different kinds of food—for example, a beef based, a chicken based, lamb based, a mixture of beef and chicken based, and fish-meal based food. Put into separate plastic bags all the supplements used with that dog. Also include any kind of medications, for example, heartworm tablets.

Sit the owner and the dog on the floor with the dog lying down on the left side of the owner. There should be a clear space around the handler and dog of about 16 inches, and the food to be tested should be several feet away. Have the owner hold a bag containing the dog food on the dog's body, then test. If the owner's arm registers a strong response by staying parallel to the ground, then that food would be compatible with the dog. Put those foods to one side and out of the 16-inch energy circle. Test all the foods and separate them out into groups of "strong" and "weak." Results will be more accurate if the owner doesn't know which foods are being tested.

Sometimes all of the foods show a weak response to varying degrees, that is, some will test weaker than others. The owner will feel that difference. If a food tests only slightly weak—the arm doesn't go all the way down—the dog can tolerate the food, but it will need to be supplemented.

When testing different products, make sure that the energy field around the dog and owner is clear. For example, many people put the

Now the two women test the food on the dog.

items to be tested on a chair or on the floor in front of them. These items are then in the same energy field as the dog and owner. To get a clear reading, they need to be kept at least 16 inches away.

Other animals or people need to be kept out of the 16-inch radius as well. I have observed that whenever I start to test, other animals in the household seem to appear out of nowhere. Perhaps they are just curious or are attracted by the energy field. Whatever the reason, remove other animals to another room while you are testing.

Nearly all dogs test strong for one or more of the following supplements:

- Vitamin C

- Vitamin B complex

- Vitamin E

- Digestive enzymes

- A multivitamin/mineral supplement

- An amino acid complex tablet

Put these supplements into separate plastic bags. Place the plastic bag containing the vitamin C—1 gram at a time, or 500 mg for small dogs—on the dog's body and have the tester press down on your arm. If the response is strong, add another tablet and check again. Continue adding more tablets until the arm goes weak. Take out the last tablet and check again.

When you are working with a large dog, and he tests strong for 4 grams of vitamin C, but weak for 5, it means that 5 grams are too much, and that 4 grams are what the dog needs.

Progress through all the supplements until you get the correct dosage for that dog. Then take the food that tested the strongest, add the vitamin/mineral supplements, combine them, and put the whole lot on the dog and check again. The arm of the owner should be strong as a rock. Remember that kinesiology is like a blood test. It is checking the body's needs at that moment in time. Those results will be different before and after meals.

Many vitamins are water-soluble and are washed through the body in a matter of a few hours, which means dosages need to be repeated in order to keep the levels constant in the body. This is the case with vitamins C and B, as well as the enzymes used to break down the food into digestible form.

Most dogs test for vitamins C, B complex, the vitamin/mineral mix and enzymes twice a day; and Vitamin E, and the amino acid complex once a day. Dogs are all individuals, and their environment affects their dietary needs. Longhaired dogs will have different needs than shorthaired dogs; and dogs living in hot climates will test differently than dogs of the same breed and age living in cold climates.

When you are working out your program it is best to test your dogs two different times in a day. After that, test again in a week.

BALANCING YOUR DOG

When you begin to supplement your dog's food, the dosages of whatever vitamins and minerals you are using may be quite high. Once the dog is in balance, the required dosages will decrease. So you need to retest about a month after you started supplementing. Frequently, the amount of vitamins C and B decreases, as well as the need for the other supplements, as the dog is brought into balance. If you are working with a very sick dog, you may have to test every week for several weeks until you find the maintenance diet for that dog.

In more complicated cases, follow up with diagnostic blood work.

ENVIRONMENTAL FACTORS

Other items to test that can affect your dog's health are the detergent you use to wash your dog's bedding, and your fabric softener. Also test the various cleansers you use in your house, as well as garden sprays, weed killers (and those your neighbor uses), the food dish (stainless steel or glass is best), and your water. Check the heartworm medication you use. There are many different brands on the market and you will find one that tests strong for your dog. The same goes for all medications. If your dog has a condition that requires antibiotics, test to see which brand is best for your dog. Your veterinarian will have two or three medications that he could use for any given condition and it is through his experience that he makes his choice. To take the guesswork out of this decision process, check with your dog to see which medication would be most effective. Put each of the products you want to test either in a small plastic bag or a clean glass container. If something tests weak, do not use it.

STRESS

The irony of knowing kinesiology is that when you need it the most—when your dog is sick, or there has been an accident—your stress levels may affect the outcome of any testing. If you are under stress for whatever reason and you feel agitated, have a friend hold the food or medication on the dog instead. Our own energies can affect the results.

YOUR DOG WILL TELL YOU

When you get comfortable with testing and have done it frequently, you will notice that the dog moves his or her body in a way that tells you what is in harmony with him and what is not. When you get close to the dog's body with a compatible product, he or she will be quiet, or curious to smell whatever it is that you are testing. He or she often rolls over and stretches out with tail wagging. When you enter the energy field with something incompatible, your dog may try to struggle away from you or actively get up and try to run away. You can also see from the expression on the face, such as mouth pulled back, ears and whiskers pulled back and wrinkles on the forehead, whether or not what you are testing is correct for him or her. They make it so easy for us!

HOW NUTRITION AFFECTS OUR DOGS

After teaching kinesiology for the last 20 years I have found it to be a simple and effective diagnostic tool in the field of nutrition. Many of the dogs that I see in a year—and I see hundreds—are not as energetic as they could be. They have dull eyes, poor coats and dry skin. Working and training dogs when they are not feeling up to par can be a frustrating experience. Many behavior problems, in particular aggression and the opposite, timidity, can be solved by feeding your dog the correct food.

Poor nutrition will affect a dog's ability to learn and to retain what is taught, resulting in a dog that cannot recall an exercise at the appropriate time. I often see this at dog shows, where the owner has no idea that the dog food he or she is feeding their dog does not supply sufficient nutrients to deal with the stress of the show. The dog is not only showing stress by not doing an exercise or behaving well, he or she is nutritionally deficient of nutrients at that time!

FOOD IS ETHNIC

I have also discovered through testing that food is ethnic. Many dogs that have been imported from Europe show allergies to corn, which up until fairly recently, has not been used in European dog food and is not indigenous to the heritage of the dog. Test a food that is oatmeal based on an imported Border Collie and it will test strong. The same applies to the Rottweilers and German Shepherds imported from Germany. My Newfoundlands and German Shepherds have been imported from Germany, and both breeds experienced digestive and skin problems using a dog food that was corn based. Using the rice-based foods created as many digestive difficulties for my dogs as did the corn-based products. On a diet of oats and buckwheat they thrived. I have also worked with many sporting, working and terrier breeds who test intolerant of corn and rice.

Using kinesiology enables you to find the right food for each of your dogs. You don't have to become a Ph.D. in nutrition to figure out what is best for your pet.

THE WRITTEN WORD

A more advanced way of doing kinesiology is by writing down the name of the food or supplement on a plain piece of paper and holding it on your dog's body. Incredibly, it works the same way as the actual product itself. While there is much speculation on how or why this works, it is another one of those mysteries that science as yet cannot explain. The fact is that it does work, and our philosophy has always been to use things that work, even if we don't understand them. You can try this technique after you feel comfortable with the first method of testing.

Take some dry dog food kernels and place them in a plastic bag and then put them on your dog. Have someone press down your arm and note the result. Then write down on a plain piece of paper the exact name of the food, for example, Brown's Mini-Chunks for Puppies, and hold that piece of paper on the dog and test. It will test the same. You now have an easy method of testing many foods and supplements without actually having them on hand.

Be specific when using the written word for testing. It is not enough to write down the name of a line of products, such as, Purina Dog Food, or Science Diet. It must be exact—Science Diet Adult Maintenance, or Purina Puppy Chow, for example. When choosing supplements for your dog, the exact name and form of

An alternative to testing with the actual food is using index cards labeled with foods. Here is a card file filled with such cards.

the supplement need to be used. For example, vitamin C comes in many forms, so you would write down 1 gram of vitamin C in the form of ascorbic acid, or 1 gram of vitamin C in the form of sodium ascorbate, etc.

When you have formulated the correct ingredients for your dog, including supplements, then take all of the separate pieces of paper and hold them together on the dog and test. The test will tell you whether or not the results are correct.

I have developed a card file for the different ingredients in dog food. The cards are separated into food groups—protein, fat, carbohydrates, vitamins, minerals, etc. I can then use these cards over and over again when working with a large number of dogs.

Using the written word is a good way to see if your kinesiology testing is working. If you experience differing results from the product to the written word, you may be out of balance. In the beginning, the results will be accurate if the surrogate does not look at the name of the food in the plastic bag, or the name written on the card.

ACCEPTING THE ANSWERS

One word of warning for all testing: If you start to test with preconceived ideas of what the answer will be, then kinesiology will not work for you. You have to be able to accept whatever answer you get, which is sometimes harder than it sounds. If you have been using a certain kind of food or medication for your dog and you are convinced it is correct, you will want the answer to be yes. If it is no, you won't believe it. Similarly, the answer may be yes, because you wanted it to be yes. When that happens it is better to have someone else test the product. Or, you can close your eyes, take a deep breath, relax for a moment and clear your mind, and then test again.

TIMES FOR TESTING

There is a time of the day when you feel more energetic than other times. Everyone experiences what we have learned to call biological downtimes. Find the time of the day when you feel most energetic and do the testing then. For example, if you are a morning person, do your testing in the morning.

Testing is tiring. It uses a lot of your energy. Do not try to do too much at one time. Testing more than two dogs in a row or for more than 20 minutes at a time without taking a break is not a good idea.

HOW TO ASK QUESTIONS

In order to diagnose any situation correctly, the questions asked the dog must be specific. Use the dog's name and ask a question that has a definite yes or no answer, or phrase your question in terms of a positive statement. For example, "Katharina, is there something in your food that is causing the red spots on your skin?" When the answer was yes, it was merely a process of elimination to find the offending ingredient.

Another way to get an answer is to make a positive statement, such as, "Fido, you are limping on your right front leg!" If the answer is yes, then say, "Fido, you are limping on your right front leg, because you fell when running after your ball this morning!"

Once you have diagnosed the problem, questions then can be directed toward the most effective treatment. For example:

- "Fido, the best way to treat the limp on your right front leg is to rest for four days."

- "Fido, the best way to treat the limp on your right front leg is to take you for an acupuncture treatment."

- "Fido, the best way to treat the limp on your right front leg is to get medication from the veterinarian," and so forth.

Make sure that the questions are specific. It is not good enough to say to your dog, "Do you need supplements in your dog food?" You would more correctly state, "You need digestive enzymes in your meal twice a day."

When testing for the correct medication for your dog, you can either hold the medication on your dog to see if he reacts positively, or write the name of the

The woman on the right demonstrates a strong response—the extended arm remains parallel to the ground.

Now the same woman demonstrates a weak response—her arm falls slightly and is no longer parallel to the ground.

medication on a piece of blank paper and hold it on your dog. If the medication tests strong, then you would write a question that for example might say, "Bean, you need 50 milligrams of this medication twice a day for two weeks," or "Bean, the bacterial infection you have will be cured by using 50 milligrams of XYZ antibiotic for two weeks," and so on.

Another use of kinesiology is when you take your dog for his annual physical examination, when vaccinations are normally given. You can ask your dog whether he needs the vaccination or if it is safe for him to have it at that time. This is very important with puppies who are in the vulnerable state of growth and teething. Some veterinarians give many vaccinations all at the same time, including rabies, and send their patients home with heartworm pills before the puppy is 6 months of age. Many young dogs never recover from such an assault to their immune system.

COMMON PROBLEMS IN TESTING

If you are experiencing difficulties when you test, and you feel you are not getting accurate readings, consider the following:

- Are you on medication of any kind? If you are, when do you take it? Kinesiology should be done when that medication peaks in your system.

If you take medication every 12 hours, test after it is in your body for six hours. Testing just before you need medication may give you inaccurate readings. Try testing at different times of the day, to find the correct time for you.

- Do you have scars on your body which cross the area of the solar plexus, where you are holding the ingredients? Scars disturb the energy flow. Look at the different energy centers on the map and put the item to be tested on a different energy field. I once had a lady in an audience that literally had scars all over her body from a car accident, and the only place left was on the top of her head. It provided great amusement to the rest of the audience when I put each item that was tested on her head, but it worked.

Like anything else, learning to do kinesiology is a skill. The more you practice, the better you get. It can be enormous fun, and even if it only works part of the time for you and your dog, you are that much better off than if you didn't use it at all.

SAMPLE QUESTIONS

Take a moment, sit down with some 3 × 5 index cards and write out the questions you need to ask your dog. You will need to have a protein, carbohydrate, fat, vitamin, mineral and water section. So you may have five cards with different proteins with the following question or statements:

- "Bear, is beef the correct protein for you?"
- "Bear, lamb is the correct protein for you.
- "Bear, chicken is the correct protein for you."
- "Bear, fish is the correct protein for you."
- "Bear, a combination of beef and turkey is the correct protein for you."

If you get a positive and strong response to one or more of the proteins, put those on one side of the table. Put the cards that test weak on the other side of the table. Do the same for your carbohydrates and other food groups. In the end you will have cards that may say beef, wheat, safflower oil, a particular brand of vitamin/mineral mix, vitamin C and digestive enzymes.

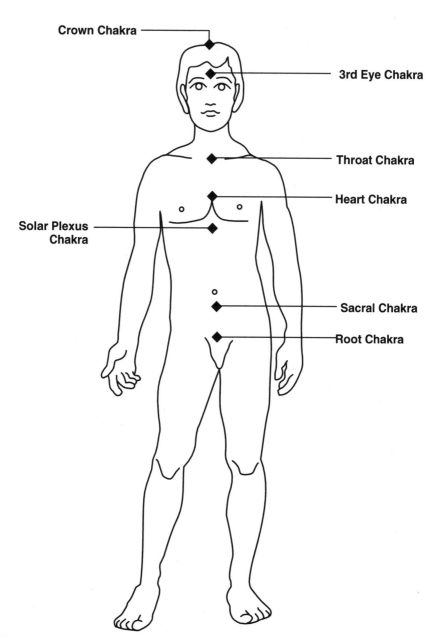

Crown Chakra

3rd Eye Chakra

Throat Chakra

Heart Chakra

Solar Plexus Chakra

Sacral Chakra

Root Chakra

Map of energy centers.

You can double-check this by actually putting those items in small amounts and in containers on your dog's body and test. Then take all of the cards containing the positive responses, and hold them on the dog at one time. This will ensure that there is no antagonistic response between the ingredients. Once you know the items for which your dog tests strongly, you will have to ascertain how much to use. The statements would then be:

- "Bear, your diet needs to contain 25% protein."

- "Bear, 10% fat in your diet is correct for you."

Look at the dog food packages to find a brand that comes the closest to the needs of *your* dog.

In ascertaining the health of your dog, you would phrase your questions or statements exactly the same way. If, for example, you suspected your dog may be harboring some sort of bacterial infection, your written question would be:

- "King, you have a bacterial infection," if yes, then move on to the following questions:

- "King, do you need an antibiotic?"—if yes, then you could visit your veterinarian and you could test the antibiotics to find out which one would be suitable for King. You could also ask how long King needs to take the medication:

- "King, you need to take ampicillin for two weeks"—if no,

- "King, you need to take ampicillin for three weeks."

Similarly, kinesiology can be used to test any form of medication, including the wormers you use.

If you suspect that your dog has a thyroid disorder, you would write your questions the same way:

- "Josie, your thyroid gland is not functioning correctly"—if yes, then write the question:

- "Josie, you need to have a thyroid medication"—if yes, then you would go to your veterinarian and request that he run a thyroid test on your dog.

There are many veterinarians using kinesiology routinely in their practices. The address for the American Holistic Veterinary Association which lists by state, veterinarians who have been holistically trained, is in Appendix II, "Sources of Ingredients & Products."

TESTING WITHOUT A SURROGATE

Once you have become proficient in the use of kinesiology, you will want to learn how to apply it without a surrogate. Unfortunately, that is beyond the scope of this book and you will need to consult a skilled practitioner, or come to a seminar or one of our Holistic Camps.

CONCLUSION

Ideally, all of your testing should be confirmed by blood tests, which is how we became convinced that kinesiology does in fact work. We diagnosed first by kinesiology, then did blood work to double-check our diagnoses. We did kinesiology again, formulated a diet with supplements, which the dog was fed for a month and then did more blood work. We did this for many dogs at different life stages and for different illnesses, and for us it has been enormously successful.

Kinesiology can't cure the dog that is dying. What it can do is to improve the quality of that dog's life, so that whatever he is eating, or medications he is taking, are correct at that time and not causing more harm than good.

SUMMARY

- Make sure that there is at least 16 inches of clear space around you and the dog when testing.

- Remove all metal articles such as jewelry from yourself and a chain collar from your dog when testing.

- Use either the product or the written word to test your dog.

- Be very specific in your questions if using the written word.

- Phrase your questions for a yes or no answer.

- If the answers are obviously not correct, check the balance of yourself and the person with whom you are working. Also recheck at another time of the day.

- Find the time of day that works best for you and do your testing then.

- When you are emotionally upset, have someone else do the testing for you. Your emotions can affect the outcome of the testing.

- Avoid putting test products on the areas of the body where there are scars.

- Follow up with blood tests.

12 Homeopathy

APIS FOR BEE STINGS

Obedience class was almost over, when I heard Bill yell from the other side of the room. He had been stung by a bee on his bottom eyelid and he was in agony. After pulling out the stinger, I gave him Apis, which I carry in my emergency first aid kit. Thirty minutes later, there was no swelling, there was no pain, and you couldn't even see that he had been stung at all. I called Bill the next day to see if there had been any bruising. He was feeling fine and had already forgotten about the incident.

WHAT IS HOMEOPATHY?

Homeopathy was discovered in 1790 by Dr. Samuel Hahnemann of Germany. A brilliant physician, he was dissatisfied with conventional medicine as it was then practiced and became a translator of medical texts. When translating a text by Cullen, a Scottish physician, he disagreed with Cullen's description of how Cinchona bark, the drug used to treat malaria, acted on the body. To explain the action of the bark more clearly, he took some himself, and he developed symptoms of malaria. After some time, the symptoms wore off and he was normal again. He tried it again, and reproduced the same symptoms.

Thus was born his new Natural Law of

similia similibus curentur

which means, let like be cured by like. Hahnemann wrote:

> *Every medicine which, among the symptoms it can cause in a*
> *healthy body, reproduces those most present in a given disease, is*
> *capable of curing the disease in the swiftest, most thorough and most*
> *enduring fashion.*

183

Hahnemann was a true scientist and over the next 20 years he tested his hypothesis using close to 70 natural substances on himself, his family, friends and medical school volunteers. Every symptom, however minute, was recorded and was compiled in what is called the *Materia Medica*. It was a documentation of the symptoms each substance (remedy) produced in a healthy person, which was then used to cure the same symptoms in a sick person.

Hahnemann had an abrasive personality and alienated his fellow physicians by writing articles about them and decrying conventional medicine. He could not, however, convince them that what he was doing was effective—that is until the war of 1812. Napoléon was marching across Europe and reached Leipzig, where Hahnemann lived. When typhus broke out, at that time a frequently fatal infectious disease, Hahnemann treated 180 cases and only 2 died. In 1831, a student of his treated 154 cases of Cholera and lost 6 (just under 4%), whereas conventional doctors treated 1500 cases and lost 821 patients (almost 55%).

Conventional medicine as we know it, uses drugs rather like magic bullets to target a part of the body where the disease has its hold. If the patient shows signs of liver, kidney or perhaps lung disease, drugs are used to target those specific areas of the body. Homeopathy looks at the whole patient, from how he behaves, how he looks, what he feels, past illnesses, plus the symptoms of the disease itself. The homeopathic physician looks up in his *Materia Medica* those symptoms, matching up the feelings, appearance, and behavior of his patient. When he comes up with an exact match, he then prescribes that remedy.

Christopher Day in his book *The Homeopathic Treatment of Small Animals* likens homeopathy to the art of judo. He says, "To apply a force opposite to the aggressor, if the aggressor is strong, will fail, whereas if only one applies a force in the same direction as the aggressor (the art of judo) a very powerful adversary can be defeated with small use of force. This superficially, is the strength of homeopathy."

Homeopathy, which fell out of favor once antibiotics entered the picture, is enjoying an enormous resurgence, and is used worldwide. In some European countries, veterinarians are trained in homeopathy, as well as allopathic medicine. In Britain, the royal family is one of homeopathy's greatest proponents.

HOW DOES HOMEOPATHY WORK?

How can homeopathic remedies work? Once you can think in terms of energy, you can see quite easily how it is possible for homeopathy to work. The dilutions contain the energy of the original product. Some scientists think that the alcohol or water with which the dilutions are made carry memory at an energetic level. They point out that once you stop thinking in terms of molecules and atoms and allow yourself to think of the energy fields of substances, for example, Einstein's theory of $E = Mc^2$, that this goes a long way to explain how homeopathy works. Those of us with sick dogs however, are glad that it does work.

HOMEOPATHY & OUR DOGS

The whole animal as a unique individual is taken into consideration when prescribing a remedy. The homeopathic practitioner takes into account the personality of the dog, the time of the year the symptoms are worse, the time of the day when the dog seems uncomfortable, the past illnesses the dog has had, what he eats, how he is housed, and perhaps most important, his relationship with his owner. This is called taking the symptoms and developing a drug picture or "repetoirizing." The owner becomes a part of the healing process.

In using conventional medicine with drugs to target a specific organ or disease, palliation or suppression of that disease has taken place, rarely a cure. The disease comes back. Skin conditions are a good example. Through antibiotics and steroids, it is fairly easy to suppress the symptoms of itching skin. While the drugs are being used, the dog is comfortable. As soon as the drugs are withdrawn and have worn off, the disease returns, usually worse than it was before. It has not been cured. With the proper use of the correct homeopathic remedy, the disease will not return.

POTENCIES

Hahnemann discovered—some think by accident—that by diluting his natural remedies they became more and more effective. The more the original substance is diluted, the more powerful it becomes. Through what is called "succussion" (banging and shaking the substances a certain number of times), the energy of that substance is released. The substance can then be diluted again, making it more powerful than the original.

Remedies are succussed either 10 times (x potency) or 100 times (c potency). An "x" potency is a substance that is diluted one in 10 times and a "c" potency is one diluted 100 times. So a 6x potency would be a remedy that is diluted one in ten, six times. Succussion is carried out at each stage and while making the substance more powerful, also removes the harmful toxins of the original substance. Thus all sorts of very poisonous substances are used—anything from deadly snake venom to poisonous plants. Since succussion removes the toxic effects, prescribing the wrong remedy can do no harm.

HOW TO USE HOMEOPATHY

There are two ways of using homeopathy.

- Classic homeopathy where one remedy is used, in a high potency, to cure a *chronic* illness. This is best left to the expert practitioner since taking the case history, and researching it (called repetoirizing) is an art in itself. If very high potencies are used without an underlying understanding of how the remedy works, aggravations of previous illnesses can appear and can be quite frightening and dangerous to an inexperienced person. The cure can also take a long time.

- Homeopathy can also be very effective for *acute* disorders with remedies in low potencies. The following is a list of remedies that I keep in my emergency kit (*see* Appendix II), and which I take with me when I travel. All of these remedies can be used by the layperson. They either work or they don't, and with low potencies, you can't do any harm.

HOW TO USE THE REMEDIES

The remedies come in different forms. Some are minute pellets, smaller than a pinhead. Some are the size of a pinhead, and some are small tablets. It depends upon the manufacturer and how he puts the energy of the substance into a pill form. My preference is the small pellets—they are easy to administer since they stick on the tongue and cannot be spit out.

Some remedies come in liquid form in a dropper bottle. These are also easy to use with dogs. By pulling out the flews on the dog's mouth, you just squeeze in a dose. Sometimes you will want to add the remedy to your dog's water bowl. Some remedies are for external use and come in creams, gels and oils.

When you give your dog a remedy in pellet form, avoid touching the pellets. Most of the pellets come in small bottles with either lids or attached stoppers that have been hollowed out, so you can count out the number of pellets you need into the stopper (anywhere from 1 to 5 pellets) and then drop them into your dog's mouth. If you feel more confident using the liquid form, you can crush the pellets and put them into a small amount of distilled water and use a dropper to dose your dog. The remedies should be stored in a cool and dark place, since they are affected by bright light.

DOSING

Using homeopathic remedies can be confusing at first. It's difficult to change one's thinking from giving drugs to giving remedies. But after a while I got used to it and came up with the following protocol for my family and my animals.

In treating acute problems—the bee sting, insect bites, poison ivy, a sprain, a pulled muscle, extreme stress, or whatever—I use one dose of the particular remedy and wait for five minutes. If it looks like it's working, I don't give another dose. If the symptoms are only a little better, then I will give another dose. I will continue this for 15 minutes, dosing every five minutes, which totals four doses. Then I wait 15 minutes, and if the symptoms are not greatly improved, I use it again. I wait for half an hour and use it again, then hourly as needed. I use remedies in the potencies from 6x to 30c, and occasionally 200c, but rarely higher. Using kinesiology also helps me determine the correct dosage for each situation, and how often to use it.

There are thousands of remedies from which to choose. Listed below are those that I have found most useful these last years in my kennel, at camp and in training classes. The list is not meant in any way to be complete. But rather it is meant as an introduction to get you started. You can make up your own kit or order the emergency kit I made up a few years ago which comes with its own first aid booklet. Remedies in the kit are supplied at a 30c potency (see Appendix II). I keep this kit in the car, in the house and in the kennel. This particular group of remedies allows me to deal with most emergency situations and buys me time for further study or, if I need to, getting help from a professional.

The following list is divided into parts. First, the remedies themselves, then a description of the scope of their use, and at the end, a visual guide for quick reference. Each remedy has multiple uses. If your dog has several of the described conditions, that would be the remedy to choose. No dog would have all the conditions listed. Go to the list in Appendix I, "A Brief Reference Guide," first, and find your dog's complaint. You will notice several remedies listed.

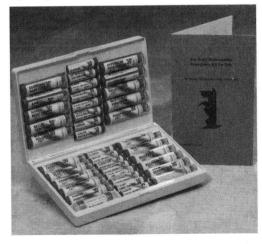

Homeopathic emergency kit.

Come back to this chapter, read through all of the remedies suggested, and choose which one comes closest to matching the problem with which you are dealing.

HOMEOPATHIC REMEDIES

Aconite Napellus   The first remedy to be used at the beginning of an acute disease state. Rarely used more than once. Sudden onset of high fever. Inflammations, red, hot swollen ears. Fright, anxiety and fear of thunderstorms, flying and traveling. Hoarse cough, tachycardia, full bounding pulse. Does not want to be touched. Eye inflammation.

Alumina   Abnormal cravings, eating strange things such as grass, leaves, dirt, rags, carpets, curtains, chalk. This behavior is called pica and can be a precursor to bloat. Sluggishness, prematurely old, staggering when walking. Nose cracked, inability to smell, thick yellow mucous. Pain in jaw when opening mouth. Constantly clears throat. Legs fall asleep and are numb. Pads tender and soft. Brittle nails, scratches skin until bleeds. Constipation.

Antimonium Tart   Respiratory diseases. Rattling of mucous in throat or lungs. Rapid, short breath, gasping for air. Especially effective with older dogs. Gapes, yawns and continuous coughing. Trembling in whole body with general weakness. Warts on penis in male dogs. Nausea and retching especially after eating. Uncomfortable except lying on right side. Vomiting which creates fear. Violent pains in lower back area. Twitching of muscles and limbs, worse at night.

Apis Mellifica   Bee stings, hives. Any swelling that is shiny in appearance, especially joint swelling. Allergic reactions, retention of fluids, inflamed eyelids. Swollen tongue, gums, mouth, uvula and tonsils. Sudden puffing up of whole body.

Arnica Montana   Sore bruised feeling, and any kind of muscle aches. Use immediately after any kind of injury to muscles from blows or falls. Muscular paralysis. Use after surgery, especially dental extraction. Fear of being touched. Strong antiseptic properties, use for septic conditions. Abscesses that do not mature. Agoraphobia (fear of leaving home). Blood in ears and in ear flaps (hematomas). Distaste for milk or meat, craves vinegar. Pain in left elbow. Symmetric spots on skin which are usually black. Involuntary stools when asleep.

Arsenicum Album Works on all organs and tissues. Use when there is weakness and exhaustion. Discharges from nose, eyes or mouth that cause skin irritation or ulceration. Wheezing respiration, bronchitis, kennel cough and allergic asthmatic conditions. Scaly or dry skin especially when it is cold and wet. Great thirst for small drinks of water. Eases all malignant conditions. Can't find a place to settle, constantly moving. Lupus. Cannot bear sight or smell of food. Liver and spleen enlarged. Abdomen swollen and painful. Ascites. Protrusion of rectum. Small, dark stools expelled with straining. Simultaneous vomiting and diarrhea. Diabetes, muscle cramps, swelling of feet. Ulcers on hock joint, paralysis of back legs. Skin ulcers with bad odor. Antidote to lead poisoning. *Do not multiple dose.*

Baryta Carb. Puppies and old dogs. Pups that do not grow well, runts, dwarfism. Swollen tonsils. Gums bleed easily. Old male dogs that suffer from heart problems or who have hardened testicles. Very averse to meeting strangers. Sudden lack of confidence. Hair falling out. Glands around ears painful and swollen. Dribbling of saliva. Spasms of esophagus when swallowing and refusal to eat even when hungry. Constipation with oozing at rectum. Fatty tumors around the neck. Weakness in the spine. Toes and pads sore and painful. Brain damage.

Belladonna Heatstroke, convulsions, hot red skin. Hot spots. Fevers of sudden onset. Epileptic spasms following by vomiting. Prevents airsickness. Sudden biting, rages with a desire to escape. Twitching facial muscles with swollen eyelids. Acute ear inflammations, Parotid glands swollen, sensitive to loud noises. Pupils are generally dilated with red conjunctiva. Bleeding nose, grinding teeth. Prolapsed anus, chalky stools, acute urinary infections, incontinence. Dry mouth with great thirst. Any condition that produces excess heat or red skin.

Bellis Perrenis Trauma of any kind to pelvic area. Use first when injury is deep in muscular tissues, especially after major surgery, spaying or neutering. Sprains and bruises, inability to walk during pregnancy. Sore, enlarged spleen. Yellow, painless, smelly diarrhea. Rumbling in bowels.

Berberis Vulg. Inflammation of the kidneys, sore back, very anxious. Urine that drips from male dogs instead of streams. Works on liver to produce more bile. Spinal irritation. Mucous in left nostril. Sunken face and eyes. Frothy, but little saliva. Fistulas in anus. Gray mucous and painful urinary symptoms in females, pain in testicles and scrotum of male. Intermittent incontinence. Use for conditions that get worse just before, during and just after a full moon.

Calc. Carb.   Eating dirt. Hot spots, eruptions behind and in ears. Pimples in whiskers. Interdigital cysts. Scratching of head upon awakening, itching of eyelids. Smelly dogs that like to stay inside. Pupil dilation, cataracts. Depraved appetites, swollen lymph nodes in throat, swelling of tonsils. Bone growth abnormalities, umbilical hernia. Prolapsed anus, warts on face and feet. Skin ulcerates but does not heal quickly. Good for pituitary and thyroid dysfunction. Seizures that occur during the full moon.

Calendula   Great antiseptic properties. Use when there has been any kind of injury. Aids in healing, especially after teeth extraction, or when there is pain out of proportion to injury. Use in cancer therapy. Injuries to eyes. Dogs that are easily frightened and always seem nervous. Green discharge from one nostril. Overeating.

Carbo Veg.   Gas pains in stomach, which causes bending over for relief. Hunched back with small steps. Stomach bloated. Any kind of gas. Dogs that never recover from a previous event—"never has been the same since." Moist flatulence or painful diarrhea in older dogs. Long coughing attacks, wheezing and rattling of mucous in chest. Joints weak, toes red and swollen. Moist skin, itching and hair that falls out in handfuls. Skin ulcers and gangrene. Useful in older dogs near death.

Chamomilla   Vomiting of yellow bile. Irritability in pups especially during teething. Swollen gums and abscessed teeth. Young dog remedy for diarrhea. Colic, swelling of lymph nodes. Painful nipples, false pregnancies. Stools green and watery. General whining and restlessness, especially during the night. Puppies under one year, especially Labradors that have seizures associated with teething or vaccines.

Cicuta Virosa   Epilepsy. Works on nervous system. Convulsions, hiccups, any violent spasm. Howling, head twisting to one side. Stares fixedly at objects. Yellow scabs on face or head, corners of the mouth and chin. Spasms of the esophagus and cannot swallow. Rumbling in stomach. Indigestion with frothing at the mouth. Eczema with no itching.

Cinchona Officinalis (*often referred to as Cina, pronounced China*)   Dog is debilitated from vomiting and diarrhea and loss of vital fluids. Use in Parvo cases. Vomits undigested food, slow digestion, belches bitter liquids. Stool is frothy and yellow with gas. Liver and spleen swollen under rib cage, and better when bending double. Suddenly roaching back. Gas after surgery. Dog is indifferent and disobedient. Skin sensitive to touch. Dizzy when walking, whites of eyes yellow, eyes look hollow. External ear sensitivity, ear flaps swollen and red.

Oversexed and excited male dogs. Heat cycles too frequently in females with bloody discharge in between seasons. Does not like to be outside.

Conium   Weakness and trembling in back legs. Helpful in paralysis of rear in older dogs. Mammary gland tumors, swelling of lymph nodes. Useful for any swelling of glands. Afraid of being alone. Pain under right side of ribs around the liver. Dribbling urine in old male dogs.

Ferrum Phosphate   Stops bleeding within 30 seconds. Nose bleeds, trauma and bleeding of any kind. Acute ear irritation (otitis), use for respiratory conditions especially when the tonsils are swollen. Vomiting of undigested food and fresh red blood. Use at first stage of heart disease.

Fragaria   Use for taking tartar off teeth. Prevents the formation of calculi. Use a 6x—30x potency. Give three times over a two-week period to remove existing tartar. Do not use during pregnancy or lactation, since it dries up milk supply. Not contained in emergency kit, and has to be bought separately.

Hepar Sulph.   Bacterial infections. Use when there is pus present. Good for hot spots that are oozing pus, skin ulcers and any skin condition that easily bleeds, is sensitive and stings. Middle ear infections, intense sensitivity to pain.

Hydrophobinum (*Lyssin*)   Homeopathic Rabies. Diseases of the nervous system. Should be given directly after the Rabies vaccine if any untoward reaction is seen. This reaction can occur up to 30 days afterwards, and at yearly intervals which coincide with the date of the previous year's shot. Frothing at the mouth, drooling, snapping in the air, sudden aggression, great weakness, collapse, convulsions and paralysis. Abnormal sexual desire. Worse around running water.

Hypericum   Takes pain away from injuries to nerves. Use in conjunction with Arnica for any injuries or trauma to the body. Useful in injuries to toes, nails and tails. Use for puncture wounds, lick granulomas. Multiple dose after surgery, if dog bites at stitches. Spinal and sciatic pain. Prevents lockjaw.

Ignatia   Stress, depression, sadness, grief, seizures and shock. Use when puppies are placed into new home, leaving their family behind. Use for mother dog who shows grief at losing puppies. Loss of loved ones. Useful for separation anxiety. Dogs that get agitated when shown and do not perform as well as they could. Breaking stays at shows.

Lachesis   Smelly wounds. Dogs that bite their feet, red in between the toes. Dogs that run away. Intense washing of sexual organs, constipation. Inflamed mammary glands. Black blood from uterus. Boils and carbuncles with purplish edges. Stiff neck, shortening of tendons. Do not repeat this remedy too often.

Ledum   Insect stings, spider bites, puncture wounds of any kind including those from vaccines or injections. Prevents tetanus from nails puncturing feet. Poison oak antidote. Anal fissures. Swollen hock joints. Arthritis in small joints and sensitivity of the right shoulder.

Lycopodium Clav.   For dogs that dislike being alone. Angry, aggressive dogs. Works on kidney, liver, digestive and respiratory systems. Appetite increased but quickly satisfied. Uric acid disorders. Blisters on the tongue. Small hard stool. Gives confidence when there is a fear of breaking down under stress. Very good for show dogs. Styes, ulceration and redness of eyelids. Herpes on face and corner of mouth. Brown spots on abdomen, hepatitis. Rattling of mucous in chest, aortic disease, cramps in legs. Skin ulcerations, abscesses under skin, chronic eczema. Skin that becomes thick. Graying prematurely.

Natrum Sulph.   Liver remedy. Use in head and neck injuries. Diarrhea with gas. Thick yellow discharge from nose and throat, green discharge from eyes and genitals. Brain damage. Vomiting yellow bile. Inflammation around the root of nails. Return of skin problems every spring.

Nux Vomica   Liver remedy. Poisoning, digestive system disorders. Use when dog has eaten something he should not have, or raided the garbage. Upset stomachs, hiccups, nausea and vomiting when there is a lot of retching. Sound-sensitive dogs, umbilical hernia in pups. After eating too much rich food, or when dog is exposed to any kinds of toxins, from flea and tick dips, anesthesia, heartworm medications and antibiotics. Use after any drugs are used. Aggressive and irritable dogs. Cracking of joints, dragging of feet. Great liver cleanser.

Phosphorus   Sound sensitivity to loud noises, gun shots, thunderstorms, fireworks. Old dogs, bone degeneration. Spinal paralysis. Sudden onset of disease state. Inflammation of respiratory tract. Paralytic symptoms. Starts suddenly. Loss of memory, restless and fidgety, temper flares easily, self-destructive behavior. Eats cat feces. Progressive Retinal Atrophy (PRA). Dandruff and hair that falls out in bunches. Cataracts. Bleeding, ulcerated gums. Food that is vomited back directly after eating. Hepatitis, pancreatic disorders, kidney disease. Large yellow spots on abdomen. Coughs that seem painful. Dogs that seek cold surfaces to lie down on when they are sick. Seeping blood from wounds. Stools that have small grainlike pieces in them.

Pulsatilla   Primarily a female remedy for shyness. A dog that gets discouraged easily. Highly emotional. External ear swollen. Yellow discharge from eyes, lids inflamed, acute conjunctivitis. Loss of smell. Loud rumbling in stomach.

Involuntary urinating at night. Usually little thirst. Yellow/green discharges from genitals. Male dogs that lift their legs in the house. Panosteitis, disrupted heats, false pregnancies and post-season pyometra. Usually happy dog but gets depressed or discouraged easily and even snappy at times. Use for side effects from Measles and Parvo vaccines. Dogs that sleep on their backs with their front legs stretched back over their heads as if they were stretching their chest and stomach. This is a Parvo vaccine reaction.

Rhus. Tox.   Poison ivy. Flea bite dermatitis. Lameness, rheumatism. Swollen, blotchy, red and intensely itchy skin with hot spots. Swollen joints, tendons and sheaths. Postoperative difficulties. Swollen, red eyes. Ulceration of cornea. Swelling of nose and face. Dislocation of jaw. Blisters around corner of mouth and on chin. Swollen glands in throat. Difficulty in getting up after sleeping, coughing at night.

Ruta Grav.   Ligament or tendon damage and sprains in general. Use if there are dislocations or lameness of joints. Legs that collapse under the dog. Sciatica.

Silicea   Splinters, or foreign bodies that lodge in the body—it pushes them out. Shyness or "lacking grit." Brittle nails. Inflammatory conditions. To get abscesses and boils to come to a head and discharge. Brittle bones, some epilepsy cases, side effects from vaccines. Use when there is pus. Skin eruptions and boils on the mouth, gums, lips or chin. Poor assimilation of food. Can effectively get scar tissue to break up. Swollen testicles, anal gland secretions that smell fishy. Nipples sore and ulcerated. Hard lumps in mammary glands. Deformed nails with white spots. Conditions worse around new moon.

Sulphur   Skin remedy, mange. Use for stubborn, irritable, smelly dogs, whose skin is dry, but red all over, causing hot spots. Dogs that look dirty even after a bath. Cleanses the system, and works for diarrhea and constipation. Red or brown spots over the chest. Mucous in urine, frequent colorless urine. Complete loss of, or excessive appetite. Dislikes heat, worse in hot weather and at night between 2 a.m. and 5 a.m. Use for flea bites.

Symphytum   Fractures or breaks in bones. Injuries to all joints plus sinews and tendons. Eye injuries. Internally good for ulcers. Use after amputations. Use with Arnica and Hypericum.

Thlapsi Bursa   Chronic cystitis. Inflammation of the urinary tract, anti-uric acid remedy. Often replaces the use of a catheter in obstructions in the urethra. Urine that drips from male dogs instead of coming out in a stream. Eyes and face puffy. Stops hemorrhaging.

Thuja Occidentalis   Reaction to vaccines and should be given immediately after each set of vaccinations. Acts on skin, blood, gastrointestinal tract, kidneys and brain. Spongy tumors, cauliflower-type warts and bleeding fungal growths. Has strong antibacterial action. Chronic otitis, ulceration inside nostrils. Teeth decayed next to gums and gums retracted. Complete loss of appetite, dislike of fresh meat. Rumbling in abdomen, flatulence. Anus painful and fissured, sometimes with warts. Thick green discharge from vulva. Chronic laryngitis. Heavy limbs, dragging feet, muscular twitches and trembling. Brittle nails, dry skin with brown spots.

Urtica Urens   Skin remedy, use when small red blotches appear. Symptoms that return at the same time every year. Bladder and spleen remedy, inability to urinate. Discharges from mucous surfaces. Rheumatism, flea bites, burns and scalds. Antidote to poisoning from seafood. Increases milk flow at 30c, decreases milk flow at 3x potency.

Veratrum Album   Use when there is a sudden collapse with coldness of the body. Postoperative shock. Violent retching and vomiting with leg cramps. Dysentery. Helps control dehydration. Eating of stools (coprophagia). Sits in a trance, staring. Aimless wandering. Neck too weak to hold head up. Constipation in puppies, with a lot of straining, then producing large stools. Hoarse, weak voice, chronic bronchitis in old dogs. Heart stimulant. Soreness and tenderness of joints, sciatica. Telescoping of organs. Skin that wrinkles on the paws.

BACH FLOWER REMEDIES

Bach Flower Remedies work primarily on an emotional level. Use for the timid dog or one that is easily frightened. To rehabilitate a rescue dog, the remedies can be invaluable. They come in liquid form, and can be either added to your dog's water bowl, or dropped directly into your dog's mouth. They can be used several times a day.

Rescue Remedy   A composite of five remedies:

Star of Bethlehem for shock

Rock Rose for terror and panic

Impatiens for mental stress and tension

Cherry plum for desperation

Clematis for disorientation

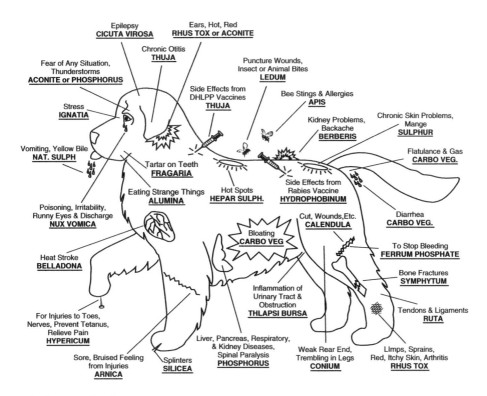

The homeopathic dog.

Use Rescue Remedy for shock, trauma, extreme stress, or unconsciousness and to heal wounds. It is one of the most valuable remedies to have. Put two drops into the mouth, or rub into the gums, nose or pads of feet. Put two drops into some distilled water and pour it onto wounds, or cuts. Good for soaking paws if cut or hurt. Use it several times a day. Keep with you at all times, and store in a cool, dark place.

Mimulus   Fear of being alone, fear of pain and of the dark. Afraid to use injured limb after it has healed.

Aspen   Inexplicable fear, fear of the unknown.

Red Chestnut   Anticipatory fear.

Cereato   Lack of confidence.

Gentian   For dogs who get discouraged easily.

Gorse   Hopelessness, giving up.

Clematis   Lethargy with no interest in anything.

Crab Apple   Cleansing and to help heal after illness.

Olive   For abused animals that lack strength to get well.

Chestnut Bud   For dogs that don't learn from experience.

Water Violet   For dogs that want to be left alone.

Impatiens   Lack of patience, act too quickly without thinking. Use for pain and anxiety after accident.

Heather   For dogs seeking company, that cannot bear to be left alone.

Agrimony   For happy dogs that get upset easily when there are arguments or fights. Use after injuries for pain.

Holly   For jealousy or anger with another dog.

Larch   For dogs, usually in multidog households, that don't try to do their best.

Sweet Chestnut   Overstressed dogs that can't take it any more. Self-destructive behavior.

Star of Bethlehem   Shock, fright following an accident or trauma.

Vervain   For an animal that tries to do too much after surgery or accident.

SUMMARY

Once you start to read about the possibilities of homeopathy and its enormous scope in treatment, you feel as if it is the absolute answer to everything that you may encounter with your dog. Don't succumb to this temptation. It takes many years to become proficient at using homeopathy properly. The ideal is to find a veterinarian trained in both conventional, and homeopathic medicine.

Be sensible, and get the blood and other diagnostic tests. There may be something going on you have missed that a good diagnostic workup will reveal. There is no substitute for a hands-on diagnostic workup.

All the modalities in this book can work together and can be complementary to each other. Look at all of your alternatives and then make an intelligent decision about what is right for your dog.

13 Complementary Therapies

In the complementary health care field there are many modalities that can be used together with more conventional therapies. What follows is a synopsis of some of the more common alternative therapies now being used.

CHIROPRACTIC— DIAGNOSES, PHYSICAL FINDINGS

A method of treatment based on the theory that disease causes interference to the nerve function of the body. By employing manipulation to the spine and joints, normal nerve function can be reestablished, and the body is put in a position of being able to heal itself.

DJ—THE UNPREDICTABLE BRIARD

DJ, my Briard, was responsible for my introduction to the power of chiropractic adjustments. DJ came to me when he was 11 weeks of age for socialization. At that time, he was showing apprehension around people and signs of mild aggression.

To socialize him, I took DJ everywhere—to classes, to the supermarket parking lot, to parks, to visit with friends. His behavior did not get better, and if anything, it got worse.

At camp one year, he was walking along by my side on leash, when a person with a video camera came toward me. DJ became uncontrollable, and hit the end of his leash trying to get to the person. He bounced off the end of the leash and in frustration, turned and bit me on the foot. Enough was enough.

DJ was put through every test known to veterinary medicine. Nothing could be found that even remotely indicated that something may be physically wrong with him. He was as healthy as the proverbial horse. But it was no fun traveling with him or taking him away from home. He is such a handsome dog and could

DJ is a dog whose bad behavior vanished with the help of a veterinary chiropractor.

have finished his championship, and he loved obedience training. But it was difficult to take him away from home.

It wasn't until he was 3 years old, that a friend told me about a visiting veterinary chiropractor who was coming to do a clinic in my area. I packed up DJ and off we went to meet Dr. Sue Ann Lesser.

By this time, DJ had decided that no one except me could touch his body. Anyone who came too close to him, he would try to bite. So how was I going to get this dog to accept being examined, much less adjusted, by Sue Ann? Sheer perseverance on Sue Ann's part— she talked to DJ calmly for quite some time, and ever so slowly, DJ moved closer and closer. Finally, he backed into her, and sat at her feet. After talking some more, he allowed Sue Ann to examine him. As it turned out, almost every vertebrae in DJ's body was out of alignment. The worst part was his neck and head. The cervical vertebrae control the nerve supply to the eyes, as well as many other organs. In DJ's case, those vertebrae were almost on their side, and Sue Ann told me, that for all intents and purposes, DJ was blind.

After Sue Ann adjusted him, DJ just lay down. He slept all the way home and all that day. The next day, I started the socialization again, taking him out into the car as often as possible. Today, DJ is 10 years old, and an absolute delight. He has become the favorite dog of everyone who visits.

WHAT IS CHIROPRACTIC?

The following information comes from Sue Ann Lesser, D.V.M., who was for many years the senior instructor for the American Veterinary Chiropractic Association.

Veterinary chiropractic in the dog is relatively new. It excels in the treatment of biomechanical problems thus minimizing, if not eliminating, objectionable gait deficits due to misalignments. Veterinary chiropractic can be used in conjunction with conventional veterinary medicine in the treatment of organic disorders. Members of the American Veterinary Chiropractic Association (AVCA) are currently reviewing the human chiropractic literature, as well as evaluating contemporary clinical studies in dogs, in order to develop a complete canine chart. The development of the human chart was based originally on research done with animals.

Without delving into neurophysiological chiropractic theory that is beyond the scope of this book, it is important to note that spinal misalignments can create disorders within the internal organs of the dog. Interruptions in the nervous system can occur and disorders of the internal organs through reflex neurologic pathways can create subluxations of the spine. Because of the difficulty of ascertaining which disorder came first, that of the internal organ or the spine, the AVCA recommends that the whole dog be adjusted so that balance is achieved between the sympathetic (thoracic-lumbar) and parasympathetic (cranial-sacral) nervous systems, both of which contribute to the function of the internal organs of the dog. It is this balancing of the autonomic nervous system that achieves the optimal clinical result when treating canine patients with internal disorders. Relieving musculoskeletal pain by correcting misalignments contributes to the dog's whole-body function. From the physiologic standpoint, it can be argued that pain is responsible for the initiation of the aberrant neurologic reflexes that contribute to both spinal subluxation and internal disorders. As a popular advertisement states, "It's all connected," and this principle is critical to remember when correlating spinal subluxations with internal disorders.

The following relationships between organic diseases and spinal subluxations can be made. The reader is advised that the disease entities listed below may also have causes beyond simple chiropractic subluxations, and that the dog under treatment be examined by a conventional veterinarian prior to referral to a veterinary chiropractor. A veterinary chiropractor will refer patients back to the primary care conventional veterinarian when certain disease entities, such as Lyme Disease, Hypothyroidism, or Cystitis, are suspected from the chiropractic examination.

Vertebrae	Areas	Effects
ATLAS / AXIS — CERVICAL SPINE — 1C	Blood supply to the head, pituitary gland, scalp, bones of the face, brain, inner and middle ear, sympathetic nervous system.	Headaches, nervousness, insomnia, high blood pressure, migraine headache, nervous breakdown, amnesia, chronic dizziness.
2C	Eyes, optic nerves, auditory nerves, sinuses, mastoid bones, tongue, forehead.	Sinus trouble, allergies, crossed eyes, eye troubles, earache, fainting spells, cases of blindness.
3C	Cheeks, outer ear, face bones, teeth, trifacial nerve.	Neuralgia, neuritis, acne or pimples.
4C	Nose, lips, mouth, eustachian tube.	Hay fever, catarrh, hearing loss.
5C	Vocal cords, neck glands, pharynx.	Laryngitis, hoarseness, throat conditions as sore throat or quinsy.
6C	Neck muscles, shoulders, tonsils.	Stiff neck, pain in upper arm, tonsillitis, whooping cough, croup.
7C	Thyroid gland, bursae in the shoulders, elbows.	Bursitis, colds, thyroid conditions.
1T	Arms from the elbows down, including hands, wrists, and fingers; esophagus and trachea.	Asthma, cough, difficult breathing, shortness of breath, pain in lower arms and hands.
2T	Heart, including its valves and covering; coronary arteries.	Functional heart conditions
3T	Lungs, bronchial tubes, pleura, chest, breast.	Bronchitis, pleurisy, pneumonia, colds and influenza.
4T	Gallbladder, common duct.	Gallbladder conditions, jaundice.
5T	Liver, solar plexus, blood.	Liver conditions: fevers, low blood anemia, poor circulation, arthritis.
6T	Stomach.	Stomach troubles, including nervous indigestion, heartburn, dyspepsia.
7T	Pancreas, duodenum.	Ulcers, gastritis.
8T	Spleen.	Lowered resistance.
9T	Adrenal and supra-renal glands.	Allergies, hives.
10T	Kidneys.	Kidney troubles, hardening of the arteries, chronic tiredness, nephritis, pyelitis.
11T	Kidneys, ureters.	Skin conditions such as acne, pimples or boils.
12T	Small intestines, lymph circulation.	Rheumatism, gas pains
1L	Large intestines, inguinal rings.	Constipation, colitis, dysentery, diarrhea ruptures or hernias.
2L	Appendix, abdomen, upper leg.	Cramps, difficult breathing, acidosis, varicose veins.
3L	Sex organs, uterus, bladder, knees.	Bladder troubles, menstrual troubles, painful or irregular periods, miscarriages, wetting, impotency, change of life syndrome, many knee pains.
4L	Prostate gland, muscles of the lower back, sciatic nerve.	Sciatica: lumbago: difficult, painful, frequent urination; backaches.
5L	Lower legs, ankles, feet.	Poor circulation in the legs, swollen and weak ankles and arches, cold feet, weakness in the legs, leg cramps.
SACRUM	Hip bones, buttocks.	Sacroiliac conditions, spinal curvature.
COCCYX	Rectum, anus.	Hemorrhoids (piles), pruritis (itching) end of spine on sitting.

Chart of the effects of spinal misalignment (human).

Cervical subluxations, especially of the atlas, occiput and axis, can be related to various behavioral abnormalities:

- The slow learner
- The hyperactive dog
- Attention deficit disorders
- Blurred vision, especially in certain types of fear-biters
- Sound sensitivity
- Recurrent ear infections
- Certain varieties of seizures
- Olfactory disorders

Mid- and lower-cervical subluxations can be related to:
- Motion sickness
- Certain anxiety states
- Lick granulomas
- Hypothyroidism

Subluxations in the thoracic region between the shoulder blades can be related to:

- Hypothyroidism
- Heart problems, especially mitral valve insufficiencies in older dogs
- Liver disorders
- Digestive disorders

In the horse, subluxations in the area of the withers are related to lung problems including allergic bronchitis, chronic obstructive pulmonary disease, and both inflammatory and infectious diseases of the respiratory tract. There is no reason to suspect that a similar situation does not also exist in the dog, but this has yet to be definitively demonstrated.

Thoraco-lumbar junction subluxations are the most common in the dog and can be related to both cystitis and diarrhea. Caudal lumbar subluxations combined with sacral rotations are related to acute onset incontinence and constipation. Subluxations of the thoraco-lumbar and cervical regions can also be manifested as incontinence. Back pain due to athletic overindulgence can also precipitate an incontinence episode. The chiropractic diagnosis of a dog with hypothyroidism depends on the number of subluxations found simultaneously, and then the condition is confirmed by a laboratory analysis.

The subluxation complex is profoundly affected by exercise, environmental conditions (ice, snow, slippery floors, playing hard with other dogs, etc.) emotional stresses (kenneling, etc.) and nutrition. Dogs that are fed properly do not exhibit the spinal abnormalities of a dog whose nutritional needs are not met. A change of diet to one with proper nutrition will improve the dog's chiropractic picture, and this has been demonstrated by the authors of this book.

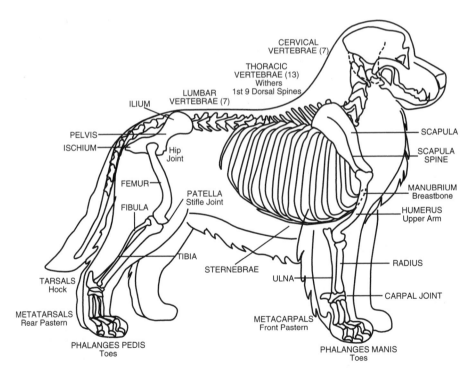

Skeletal Diagram.

HISTORY

While every dog is an individual, certain aspects of history and physical findings are consistent for the new canine chiropractic patient. The following are not in order of incidence, but dogs that have one or more of the examples listed should ideally be examined by an experienced, qualified animal chiropractor. Most dogs with a combination of these histories and physical signs have required adjustment. Other medical conditions can contribute to the physical signs listed. Veterinary chiropractic is an *addition to, not a replacement for* conventional veterinary care.

- Hit by a car.

- Playing, then becoming acutely lame. Lameness usually improves with minimal conventional treatment but the dog is never "quite right" afterwards.

- "Body Slamming"—patient is sideswiped by another dog while playing and gets rolled.

- Fell off the porch, deck, down some stairs, etc.

- Lost balance while running and hit wall, tree, door, etc.

- Any dog working in obedience, agility, schutzhund, etc.

- All German Shepherds over four years of age.

- Dogs that play Frisbee.

- Decreasing performance—especially show dogs that demonstrate inconsistent behavior and are not doing as well as they used to in either Breed, Agility or Obedience.

- Dogs that have been put under general anesthesia.

- Dog that cannot jump on couch, bed, etc., or won't go up and down stairs.

- Poor leash manners, straining from the neck, incorrect use of collars— number one cause of cervical subluxations.

PHYSICAL FINDINGS

- Personality change, not as active or happy. May start biting, or look as if they have a headache. Dogs that have faces that continuously look anxious.

- Tail cock—a tail that does not wag symmetrically.

- Stiff back, does not roll, or rolls and stops at one point.

- Lumpy/bumpy feeling through the spine, especially near back of the rib cage.

- Head tilt, or dog has problems in turning head in one direction.

- Scuffs one foot when gaiting.

- "Baby with wet diapers" look—gait in rear stilted. Sidewinding.

- Lack of symmetry limb to limb—catches or rattles through shoulder or hock.

- Tail clamped to body or under body. Tail held straight out, not relaxed.

- Dog wiggles skin on back or shakes when a particular point is touched.

- Hip Dysplasia: While chiropractic cannot cure the truly dysplastic dog, it can make the dog more comfortable and balanced.

- Aesthetics: Instead of seeing the whole dog, the eye is drawn to one part of the dog (back, pelvis, head, neck, etc.). Correct dogs have a certain presence about them, a sort of glow. If you have difficulty determining if the dog being examined is gaiting properly or not, he should have a chiropractic examination.

When we were training and showing our dogs on a regular basis, they went for adjustments every month to counteract the stresses of travel and work, especially jumping. Dogs that are regularly adjusted this way have longer show careers than those dogs that do not receive chiropractic care. Puppies that are examined and adjusted frequently in their first year of life when maximum growth occurs, have fewer orthopedic problems in maturity. If pups grow straight, they are inclined to stay that way.

Behavior problems that involve aggression or those that do not fit the norm should always be checked out by a competent veterinary chiropractor before any decision is made on how to treat the dog.

LASERS

Lasers use a powerful beam of light that can penetrate into body tissue. Used on acupuncture points and painful areas in the body, a simple laser can be quite effective in relieving pain and helping to heal many conditions. Light increases blood circulation to the area it penetrates, which in turn has a soothing effect on the painful area. This pain relief can last upwards of 12 hours.

While there are many powerful lasers on the market today, we use the pen-type laser that is commonly used for giving lectures. Found in Radio Shack or any good stationery store, they can be quite adequate to give some relief to painful areas. Best used directly on the acupuncture points, the hair can be parted to get to the exact treatment point. Rotate the laser in a clockwise direction for no more than 30 seconds on each point. Remember that the acupuncture points are located on each side of the body, so treat both.

We use this small laser for many conditions—limps, bangs, bumps and bruises, ear inflammations, and any kind of skin problem from cuts to hot spots. It is safe to use anywhere on your dog's body, except his eyes. The laser must be kept away from the eyes, and will cause blindness if the laser is pointed directly into them.

For more information and good maps of the acupuncture points, the best illustrations are found in the book, *Acupuncture Without Needles*, Dr. D.V. Carney, Parker Publishing, a division of Prentice Hall, 1997.

IRIDOLOGY

Iridology is another diagnostic tool to gauge the health of your pet. Based on the concept that the eyes mirror the health of the body, Iridology was pioneered by a Hungarian doctor, Ignatz von Peczeley, in the nineteenth century. As a young man he kept a pet owl. The owl broke its leg and Ignatz noticed a "hole" appear in the iris of both eyes. When the leg healed, the "holes" disappeared. This set him on a path of discovery and as a doctor in Budapest, he charted the eyes of all of his patients, recording the correlation between the spots in the eyes and the diseases presented to him. Iridology is practiced widely in Europe today and many medical doctors are trained in this accurate diagnostic approach.

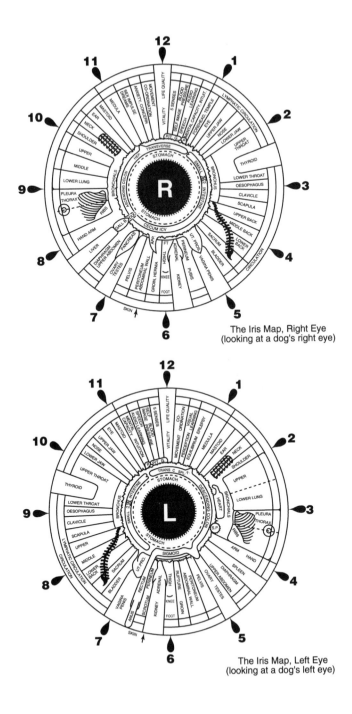

The Iris Map, Right Eye
(looking at a dog's right eye)

The Iris Map, Left Eye
(looking at a dog's left eye)

Iris Maps.

View the eye as a clock, each eye being a mirror image of the other. When Left or Right is mentioned, it refers to the dog himself, not the way you look at the eye. Not all disease states show up in both eyes. The eye needs to be observed in strong sunlight, or with a flashlight. If a flashlight is used, do not leave it on the eye for more than 10 seconds without removing it.

Think of the eye as a tunnel to the body. The outside rim of the iris represents the skin, the innermost part of the iris next to the pupil, the internal organs, such as the stomach and intestines. Any discolorations or markings mean something to an iridologist, who can predict disease states up to two years prior to clinical manifestation. It also reveals inherited disease states. For example, if you have a dog whose mother had heart disease, you may notice a black spot or "hole" between 2 and 3 o'clock on your dog's left eye. This does not necessarily mean that your dog has heart disease. What it is more likely to mean is that there is an inherited tendency toward weakness in the heart.

INFORMATION FOR BREEDERS

Iridology can be an invaluable tool for breeders since it can indicate possible genetic disorders in breeding animals. A simple understanding of iridology allows the breeder not to double up on breed-specific problems. Why, for example, double up on a dog with inherited heart weakness, if you have a choice of another dog that does not carry that weakness?

EYE COLOR

When we were breeding Newfoundlands, breeding stock was routinely selected for dark eyes. It was thought that dark brown, almost black, eyes denoted good overall pigmentation. Understanding iridology taught us that there are genetically dark brown eyes, and then there are eyes that appear dark brown because the body is toxic. The difference is that a healthy dog can bring genes for good pigmentation into a breeding program unlike an unhealthy dog that does not possess these genes.

Genetically dark brown eyes of a healthy dog have a sparkle and shine to them. The whites of the eye are clear with no bleeding out of the rim of the iris. The color of the iris, while being dark brown, is clear of markings. Toxic brown eyes, on the other hand, look as if there is a film of darkness over them—the eyes

Bean's eyes grew lighter as his health improved.

have many black markings on the iris and the outside of the iris bleeds into the white of the eye. This "bleeding" effect is a sign of toxins in the system and can be associated with chronic skin problems and more serious diseases. These eyes appear dull and without life.

We had an amusing incident with our Labrador, Bean, when studying this subject. When we got Bean, he was quite unhealthy and it took us several years to get him to the state of health that we felt was acceptable. When he arrived, he had the most beautiful dark, almost black eyes. As his healing progressed, his eyes got lighter, and when he was healthy, his eyes were a medium-to-light brown. His breeder was surprised and upset, until she learned the reason.

LIGHT

Light plays a important part in the health, growth, reproduction and behavior of animals. Dogs housed in an area that has improper light have been observed with chronic skin disease, an inability to reproduce, strange and neurotic behaviors and improper growth in puppies. Studies have also shown that there is a possible correlation between the rise in dental decay in dogs and the use of improper light.

Light controls the survival mechanisms of most species of animals. Young animals almost universally are brought into the world in the spring. This is when there is enough food for the young to eat. It would be nonadaptive behavior to have young in the fall or winter, when it is difficult to forage for food. Animals instinctively know, by the quality of light in which they find themselves, what time of the year it is. They must know this, if the species is to propagate. When light is controlled, or when it is of inferior quality, it gives false information to the brain of the animal, triggering inappropriate behavior.

FLUORESCENT LIGHT

What is improper light? It is light that is normally found in most light bulbs that are used in lighting fixtures plus fluorescent cool white lights that are found in hospitals, offices, homes and kennels. These lights do not contain the whole spectrum of light as it would come from the sun. Some parts are missing. Full spectrum lights contain all of the colors of the sun, and are a natural form of light.

Of the many articles written about the effect of light on the behavior of animals, one that caught our eye was from the *Journal of Optometry* in June 1979, which talked about experiments conducted on rats and breeding behaviors. Raised under normal fluorescent lighting, male rats had to be taken away from the female rat before she gave birth, due to a tendency of the males to eat the babies as they were born. Under the full spectrum lighting, their removal was no longer necessary, and the male rat showed good parental instincts and helped in the care of the young.

Other experiments were done on fish where it is normal to keep different species apart because of fighting and fin nipping. Under the full spectrum lights, it was possible to keep the fish together with no fighting behavior displayed. The improper light in these instances gave off false signals to the brains of these animals.

Experiments were conducted on mice that were divided into two groups. One group was exposed to daylight and the other group was exposed to pink fluorescent lights. The experiments were six months in length. These experiments were done by John Ott, head of the Environmental Health and Light Research Institute in Florida, who is the foremost authority on the effect of light on health. In six months, the mice under the pink lights had lost their tails. In another experiment, spontaneous tumors arose in those mice continually exposed to fluorescent light.

KIVA LIGHTS

Using full spectrum lighting with an extra amount of blue in it (Kiva lights) decreases bacteria and inhibits the spread of disease in an area where many dogs are housed. These lights are used in supermarkets to keep bacteria from growing on exposed meat and fish. They have been used to promote healing in hospitals. If put over counters and sinks, the light penetrates the water, which becomes softer.

COLOR & LIGHT

Many experiments have been conducted on the effect of color and light. People who wear tinted contact lenses or sunglasses have shown a marked decrease in muscle strength when natural light was not allowed to penetrate the eyes. Moods of tennis players and baseball players have been monitored by changing the color of the visors they wear to protect their eyes from the sun. Athletes who already exhibited temperamental behavior had their sunglasses, visors and uniform colors changed. Hyperaggressive, helmet-throwing athletes then became calm, relaxed and confident when the proper colors (blue and green, not red, orange, yellow or gray) were used.

CHOOSING LIGHTS FOR YOUR KENNEL ROOM

How does this information help us with our dogs? Dogs need to have time in their day when they are outside getting daylight. Even if they are in the shade of a tree, they are still getting adequate light. In bad weather, or long hard winters, they are denied that light. By using full spectrum lighting in a kennel, office, house or veterinary hospital, a calmer, more relaxed and healthier animal will emerge. Animals who are sick will heal faster and breeding cycles will become normalized.

If you are decorating a kennel, choose blue as your primary color as it is the most calming color, green for good overall health and white, which is neutral. Stay away from red, bright pink, orange and yellow, which can create aggression and sickness from prolonged exposure.

NAET

One of the newer techniques to appear in these last years, Dr. Nambudripad's Allergy Elimination Techniques or NAET for short, is a holistic, noninvasive treatment used in eliminating food and environmental allergies permanently, through the use of acupuncture, kinesiology, chiropractic and nutrition. The recognition of the systemic relationship between contact with an allergen and

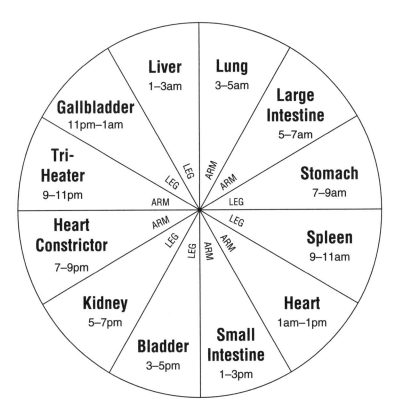

Daily Circle of Energy.

the resulting neuro-physiological effects produced in the body, resulted in Dr. Nambudripad discovering the key to the mystery of how the brain may be reprogrammed in its response to what it once took to be harmful or toxic.

Many doctors, and a few veterinarians, are trained in this exciting, new approach to illness that may prove to be the treatment of choice for many in the years to come.

CHRONOBIOLOGY

Chronobiology is a theory of time and rhythm, and studies the interaction of time among the nervous, hormonal and metabolic systems in the body. In essence, it means that at any given time of the day, the energy of the body in certain systems is either ebbing or flowing. If these times can be determined accurately, then using medication targeted at certain organs would be more effective. It also means that false/negative responses may be recorded if diagnostic procedures are carried out at the wrong time of the day. This concept has been effectively used in diagnosing heartworm.

It is interesting to note that the Chinese, in their Five-Element Theory, came to these same conclusions at least 2,000 years ago.

When diagnostic work is being done on a dog, draw blood and do other diagnostic testing at the time the energy is in the organ in question if at all possible. For example, if you want to accurately diagnose kidney disease, have your veterinarian draw blood between 5 and 7 p.m. in the evening. If kidney medication is indicated, it would make sense to give it to your dog at that time too. While Stanford University is doing a lot of work on people using the concepts of chronobiology, more work needs to be done on animals.

Part 3

The Five-Element Theory

14 A Short Course on the Five-Element Theory

Falcon was coming along in his training and almost ready to compete in the Obedience Open Class when one day he slipped while taking a jump, crashed into it and severely injured his shoulder. For all intents and purposes, his obedience career was over. Winner of a rare Dog World Award of Canine Distinction in Novice, Falcon was an exceptional dog. He was only three years old and had a terrific show career in front of him. After seeking opinions from numerous veterinarians and experts, including a teaching hospital, I was told that he would limp for the rest of his life. As time went on, the muscles of his leg atrophied from lack of use and just hung from the shoulder. He was miserable, and so was I.

At that point, the old saying, "When the student is ready, the teacher appears," took on new meaning for me. I had a call from a friend of mine in Boston, who told me that she had found a new veterinarian who also did acupuncture. Would I come to Boston—a seven-hour drive for me—and have him look at Falcon? She was sure he could help. Since I had tried everything else, I decided to go and that trip changed my life forever.

A year later, after acupuncture treatments and physical therapy, Falcon was able to compete again, and he earned his Companion Dog Excellent title, in both America and Canada.

Dr. Richard Kearns was one of the founding members of the American Holistic Veterinary Medical Association, which in the late 1970s was just getting off the ground. He was not only an expert in acupuncture, but also homeopathy, kinesiology, nutrition and other holistic approaches to healing. Dr. Kearns became my mentor, and for four years, I would make that long trip to Boston every two weeks. He would send me home with stacks of books, and quiz me on them on my next visit. He shared his knowledge with me, and inspired me to do the same with others

Acupuncture and physical therapy saved Falcon's show career.

What fascinated me the most, as a layperson, was the usefulness of the Five-Element Theory, to which Dr. Kearns introduced me, in diagnosing various disorders. The Five-Element Theory is an introduction to *preventative* medicine. In the treatment of our dogs, it covers all aspects of living and working with them.

THE FIVE-ELEMENT THEORY— WHAT IS IT?

The Five-Element Theory is an integral part of traditional Chinese medicine (TCM) and emphasizes balance and harmony. Yin and yang represent the opposing, yet complementary energies of the universe. Practiced by the Emperor Shen Nong, who lived around 3000 B.C., the theory of complementary opposites teaches that everything can be classified as yin and yang, and that health is influenced by their constant ebb and flow. Imbalances between yin and yang create disease.

The organs of the body are linked together, a yang organ paired to a yin organ. The yang organs are found on the exterior and back of the body, and the yin organs are found in the interior and front of the body. "Solid" organs are linked to "hollow" organs. For example, the liver (solid) is paired with the gallbladder (hollow), and the heart (solid) is paired with the small intestine (hollow).

Through centuries of observation, the Chinese learned that there was a direct correlation between the seasons and certain disease states. They studied the seasons and how they flowed into one another. They looked at the life cycles of plants and animals and compared them to their human counterparts. The natural elements, the seasons, and the human body became linked. The seasons were named after elements and the concept became known as the Five-Element Theory.

The theory maintains that if one set of organs malfunctions, it will not send the correct amount of energy to the next set of organs as the seasons progress. For example, if the liver is not functioning correctly, the first symptoms will manifest themselves at the end of liver season, or spring, and then in the stomach or spleen. If not corrected, symptoms continue to worsen and can manifest themselves early on in the summer, which is heart season. The practitioner traces the heart symptoms back to its origin and treats the liver, the stomach, as well as the system of the heart and small intestine.

THE FLOW OF ENERGY

Perhaps the main difference between western and Chinese medicine is something called Qi (pronounced Chi), which is considered the life force or energy of the body. Qi is "switched on" at birth, and extinguished at death. Qi travels around our bodies in a systematic way, stimulating and balancing each of the organ systems. Ill health is a sign that this life force is in need of treatment.

THE FIVE ELEMENTS

Each season is assigned an element:

Spring is wood, and Qi is in the liver and gallbladder.

Summer is fire, and Qi is in the heart and small intestine.

Fall is metal, and Qi is in the lungs and large intestine.

Winter is water, and Qi is in the kidneys and bladder.

The two weeks between the seasons are the element Earth, and Qi is in the stomach and spleen.

The Chinese found that when the energy of the prevailing season is in the corresponding organs, diseases of those organs are more prevalent. For example, more serious kidney diseases are diagnosed between the end of December and late February than at any other time of the year. Heart disease occurs more frequently in the summer months than at other times of the year. By treating a weak organ during the time when the Qi is in that organ, a cure can take place. Treatment any other time of the year achieves only palliation or relief.

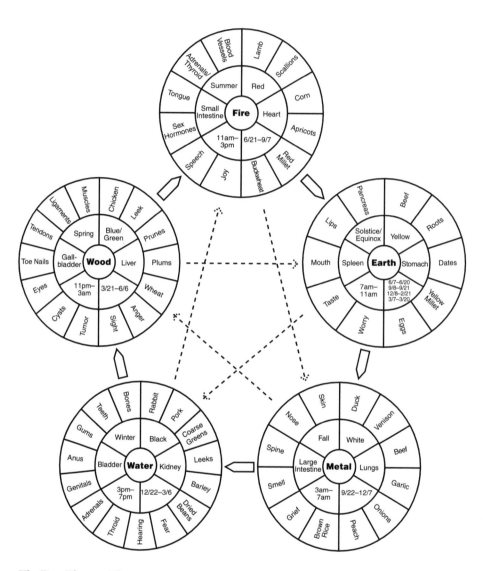

The Five-Element Theory.

MERIDIANS

Qi moves through the body using channels of energy called meridians. These meridians follow the energy flow from one organ to another and are linked just the same way as the five elements. The liver and gallbladder are linked together, and the heart and small intestine, and so on. Meridians are the connection between one set of organs and another. Think of them as an electrical wiring system, just below the surface of the skin. This system is the outward connection to the inner organs. A kink in one of the wires will interrupt the energy to that set of organs.

For example, the removal of a dog's front dewclaws leaves a small scar, which is a kink in the wiring system. This particular point is linked to the large intestine and is a major acupuncture point for relieving pain and for diseases of the sensory organs, face and skin. It follows that dogs who have front dewclaws removed are inclined to have more skin problems than those who do not.

Acupuncture treatments are beyond the scope of this book, but we will give you the points where you can use acupressure or a small laser to give your dog relief from certain symptoms until you can seek professional help.

For further reading, see *Four Paws, Five Directions* by Cheryl Schwartz, D.V.M. (Celestial Arts, California, 1996).

YOUR DOG WILL TELL YOU

Your dog does a wonderful job of diagnosing and treating himself. I am sure you have observed your dog scratching, nibbling, licking or biting at different parts of his body. Your dog is telling you something. Instinctively your dog knows how to treat himself.

If the behavior happens once or twice, there is no need for concern and you can forget about it. But if your dog repeatedly goes after the same spot, he is trying to stimulate the energy in a particular organ. For example, in the spring, you may see your dog nibble and lick his back feet and hock joints, sometimes until they are raw. When you locate the exact spot, it is nearly always either where the liver meridian starts or the stomach meridian ends. The dog is trying to stimulate his own liver and/or his stomach. How far out of balance those organs are, dictates the dog's own treatment. In the summer you may see your dog licking his front feet at the points where the small and large intestine meridians start. If you kept records on your dog, and you look back at the five-element dates, you will be astonished how accurate the theory is. By making adjustments to your dog's diet, plus doing some acupressure, you can provide symptom relief.

ACUPRESSURE

You can use the points on the charts to stimulate the organ systems, by either putting pressure on that point with your finger, or with the end of a pencil—the

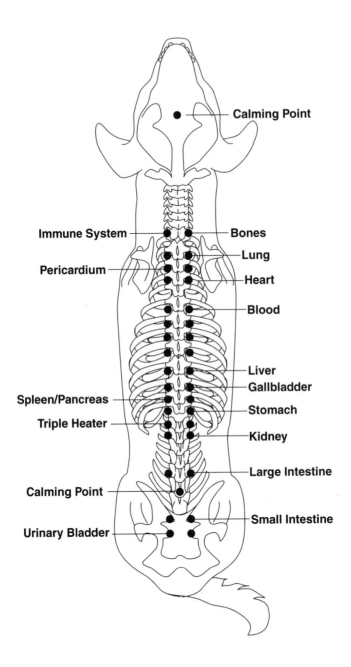

Association points.

kind that has an eraser on it. Apply pressure for one minute. Another way is to apply pressure while moving the skin around that point in a tiny clockwise circle for one minute. You can also use a small laser, moving it in a clockwise direction for 30 seconds on the acupressure point. While all the meridians start or end on the front or back feet of your dog, there are association points along the back of your dog that match up with the organ systems. By lightly stroking down the spine of your dog, his back will 'twitch' in those places where he needs treatment.

FOOD AS MEDICINE

Feeding your dog certain types of foods at specific times of the year will maintain balance and harmony in his body. These foods stimulate and provide energy to their respective organs.

Spring	wood	liver and gallbladder	sour-tasting-foods
Summer	fire	heart and small intestine	bitter foods
Fall	metal	lungs and large intestine	pungent foods
Winter	water	kidney and bladder	salty foods
Between seasons	earth	stomach and spleen	sweet foods

The relationship between the seasons and food, such as the source of animal protein, grains, herbs and vegetables, helps to maintain the balance between yin and yang in your dog. Using food as a support for the body is a kind and gentle way to better health. Waiting until there is sickness reminds me of the Chinese saying:

> *To take medicine only when you are sick is like digging a well when you are thirsty. Is it not already too late?*—The Yellow Emperor's Classic of Internal Medicine (2500 B.C.)

THE SEASONS & OTHER EXPRESSIONS OF YIN & YANG

EMOTIONS

Each season is associated with an emotion:

> Spring—anger
>
> Summer—joy
>
> Fall—depression
>
> Winter—anxiety
>
> Between the seasons—sensitivity, anxiousness to please

The Chinese practitioner might ask his patient whether he or she had angry outbursts in the spring, or, conversely, an inability to be angry. He looks for extremes, which will tell him about the energy of that organ and its associated emotion. For example, in the spring you may suddenly see aggression in your otherwise sweet dog, which may be an indication that his liver is not functioning correctly. To support the liver, feed the appropriate foods to calm and rebalance your dog.

COLOR

Colors are also an expression of ill health.

> Spring is blue/green.
>
> Summer is red.
>
> Fall is white.
>
> Winter is black.
>
> Between the seasons is yellow.

To use colors as a diagnostic tool, look for changes in the color of discharges or the skin. A yellow discharge from the eyes, or vomiting yellow bile, is a pretty good indicator that something is wrong with the dog's stomach. A blue/green discharge indicates something going on in his liver. A black discharge from the ears is a typical kidney expression.

EXPRESSIONS OF ORGAN IMBALANCE

When out of balance, each set of organs expresses itself in different parts of the body. For example, an imbalance in the lungs and large intestine may manifest itself in a drippy nose, a whitish discharge from the eyes, dry, brittle coat, dandruff and extreme shedding.

Each organ also affects the senses, for example, a dog who has skin problems could have a poor sense of smell.

The kidneys and bladder show their imbalances in the ears and bones. In the winter, you often see dogs that have a nasty black discharge from the ears, are slightly deaf, or even sound sensitive—the other extreme. The kidneys control the bones of the body, so in extreme cases you may get a broken bone. Both the kidney and bladder control "water" in the body and it is in winter when you may see excessive drooling or incontinence. Feeding your dog the foods that support both the kidney and bladder can help all of these conditions.

Look at the five-element chart for the relationship between the seasons and disease states.

DETOXIFICATION

The first step in rehabilitating a sick dog is to cleanse the systems of toxins, and through homeopathic remedies and diet, bring the body back into balance. The chapters that follow deal with detoxification and provide you with 21-Day Detoxification Diet charts by season to cleanse and support each set of organs. Although the information is general, it can be specifically tailored to the individual dog using kinesiology (*see* Chapter 11).

When detoxifying, it is advisable to support the body at the cellular level using the product Detoxification, as well as clearing the lymph system (the drains of the body), using Lymphatic Drainage. Both are liquids and are used together. After this first course of cleansing is finished, detoxification is stopped for one week to give the body a rest. The dog is then retested and the specific detoxifier for which the individual dog tests is used.

Put the liquid into the cap that comes with the bottle. A full capful for a medium to large dog, half a capful for a small dog. Open the flews (lips) of the dog at the side of his mouth, and gently pour in the liquid. Use for five days, then stop for two days and then continue until the bottle is finished. You can use these together if necessary putting first one capful and then the other into your dog's mouth. All homeopathic detoxifiers are available through Moss Nutrition.

If the process of detoxification goes too fast, you may see an aggravation of the symptoms of the disease you are trying to treat. For example, a skin problem may get worse. In that case, take a two-day break, and then continue following the above directions until the bottles are finished. Other detoxifiers are:

Environmental Detox—For chemical or environmental detoxification.

Heavy Metal Detox—To detoxify the liver and gallbladder from heavy metals and food additives.

Fungal-Yeast Detox—For chronic ear infections where yeast is present and candidiasis.

Bacteria Detox—For any suspected bacterial infection, especially those in the respiratory tract and after prolonged use of antibiotics.

Acute Stress Remedy—To counteract ongoing stress or stress that has occurred in the last few days (moving, loss of a loved one, etc).

Chronic Stress Remedy—To support the adrenal glands and to aid in the relief of emotional stress and those stresses from long-term sickness.

Detox Virus—For all suspected viral infections and the side effects from vaccines.

Parasite Detox—Supports the body following a parasitic infestation. Detoxifies the body from the waste produced by parasites.

Detoxification is a long and slow process—be patient.

SICK DOGS

It is possible that a dog that had mild untreated liver problems in the spring (wood), could show liver symptoms in the earth element (between the seasons) or even later in the fire element (summer). The energy from the liver was not as strong as it should have been going to the stomach/spleen organ system. It in turn could not generate enough energy to supply the heart/small intestine. A likely scenario could be a dog that has greenish discharge from his eyes (liver), throws up yellow bile (stomach/spleen), shows lack of appetite and loses weight, and has difficulty in urinating (heart, small intestine).

TREATMENT

These cases where symptoms from different seasons overlap are more complex and take more skill to treat. A working knowledge of kinesiology is helpful (*see* Chapter 11). The dog would need to have his liver supported and the correct diet for all three organ systems would have to be worked out. The easiest and quickest way to get these dogs in balance is to see a chiropractor to get the body in alignment, an acupuncturist to get the energy flowing to the organ systems, and to feed a tailored diet. In complex cases, an aggressive treatment protocol using all of the above will put the dog back in balance over a three-week period. *Note:* For the very sick dog, the vegetables and meat should be lightly cooked and fed together with a digestive enzyme. When you see improvement, reintroduce your dog to raw food.

THE CASE OF THE AGGRESSIVE NEWFOUNDLAND

The following case history is an example of how the Five-Element Theory was used to save a lovely Newfoundland from being put to sleep.

Beau, a 4-year-old Newfoundland, was put up for adoption by the local Newfoundland Rescue organization in October. His original owners had suddenly developed an allergy to him. A breeder of Newfoundlands who had bred these dogs for 25 years evaluated him at the rescue kennel. After bathing, grooming and clearing up

The Five-Element Theory saved Beau's life.

a nasty ear infection, the breeder found Beau to be a delightful, sweet and calm dog. After a month at the kennel, he was considered ready to be placed into the right home.

A young couple with children ages 5 and 7 adopted Beau in late November and they were very happy with him. He adapted well, and his new family loved him. Early in January, after coming home from a walk in the late afternoon with the children and the dog, the young mother, Ann, who was busy doing household chores, noticed that Beau was not around. She looked through the house and finally found him, head down, standing with his back toward her in the bathroom. Ann asked him in a good-natured tone what he was doing there. He did not respond. So she talked to him in a louder tone of voice. Beau's hackles rose all the way along his back and he growled, still with his head down. It was as if he didn't know who she was. Ann talked to him again in a normal tone of voice, reassured him that everything was okay and to come out. Beau backed up, shook himself vigorously, wagged his tail sheepishly and came out of the bathroom. The family forgot the incident.

In the middle of January, the family noticed a continuing and peculiar behavior. Every time a television show with a lot of noise and violence was on, Beau would growl at the TV set and his hackles would rise all the way up his back. It was difficult to get Beau away from the TV, and when they pulled on his collar, he growled at them. At this point, the family became afraid of Beau and he was returned to the rescue kennel. The family also complained of Beau's excessive shedding.

At this point that the rescue kennel called me. No matter what they did, the rescue people could not get Beau to exhibit any of the objectionable behaviors. The question was whether or not it would be safe to place Beau into another home with the knowledge that he had shown some aggressive behaviors in the past.

THE SOLUTION

Using the Five-Element Theory as a starting point, it was easy to diagnose Beau's problems. There were several clues in the original history that gave me the answer.

1. The time of the year the behavior occurred. Beau's behavior had been normal until late December and early January. In the two episodes of "aggression," Beau had put up his hackles all the way down his body from his neck to his tail. This hackle-raising behavior is called a pilo-erection, indicating fear and anxiety. True aggression will express itself

when the hackles only on the shoulders and neck are raised, making the dog look bigger. Frequently misdiagnosed as aggression, the piloerection indicated to me that Beau's kidneys were not in balance, as did the time of the day when the original behavior had surfaced in the bathroom. The time of the day when the body's energy is in the bladder and kidneys is 3 p.m to 7 p.m. He was expressing anxiety.

2. The other clue was that originally Beau had a nasty ear infection when first placed in the rescue kennel. When Beau was in front of the TV set and extra loud shows were on, he growled, indicating that the sound hurt his ears. Also, Beau's food had been changed in his new home to a popular brand bought in the supermarket, which no doubt did nothing to support his kidneys, thus the expression of fear and the "aggressive" behavior.

VETERINARY FOLLOW-UP

To see if Beau's problems were kidney or bladder related, he was sent to a veterinarian for a complete blood test and a urinalysis. His BUN (Blood Urea Nitrogen) levels were slightly elevated and the pH of his urine was too alkaline. His ear infection had also returned.

BEAU'S KIDNEY DIET

The Natural Diet would have been the best thing for Beau, but the rescue organization did not feel it could find anyone to take on that commitment for Beau. So we compromised and made up the next best diet for him, and one which provided adequate kidney support.

Beau was given a short course of detoxification and was put onto the Healthy Dog Diet (*see* Chapter 1).

From December until March, Beau got some herbs—parsley, dandelion leaves, nettles, corn silk and goldenrod—in his food to support his kidneys. All these are readily available through a health food store or a mail-order herb catalog. These were rotated through the winter months. Some winter vegetables, such as parsnips, carrots and beets, were added as well. Beau was a happy boy and has never shown the aggressive behaviors again.

Beau's new family had had dogs before and was willing to commit to his special needs. They were lucky to find a veterinary chiropractor in their area, who adjusted a very badly aligned spine, improving the nerve supply to all of Beau's organs. His head and first cervical vertebrae were out of alignment, thus the nerve supply to his ears had a "kink" in them, which made his ears sensitive to sound. With periodic adjustments, he has not had a recurrence of his ear infection.

CONCLUSION

It has been my experience that dogs are often misdiagnosed as aggressive, fear-biters, hyperactive or incorrigible, when in reality there is an underlying physical cause. For objectionable behaviors that are physical in nature, behavior modification approaches, such as obedience training or punishment, are not the answer. As in the case of Beau, the "aggressive" behavior disappeared through the application of the Five-Element Theory, and saved him from being euthanized. Dealing with dogs that show unusual behaviors requires playing detective and not giving up on them until a logical explanation for the behavior is found. Using the Five-Element Theory as a diagnostic tool can supply many of the answers that cannot be found elsewhere.

15 Spring & Summer

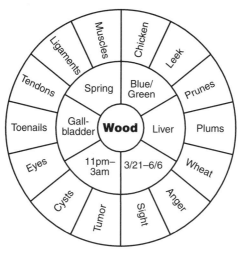

Wood.

MAX—THE LHASA APSO

A few years ago in the spring, a groomer friend called and she was very upset. A customer had brought in an old Lhasa Apso named Max to be bathed and groomed. Max was in bad shape—matted hair, long and brittle toenails, and green, gooey discharge from his eyes. He did not look healthy. Max had been rescued from the local humane society and my friend's customer had wanted to provide him with a comfortable home in his old age.

My friend bathed Max, cleaned his eyes, cut his nails, put him into a cage and turned the dryer on. She then made a brief phone call and when she returned and checked on Max, he was dead. She was frantic, not knowing what had happened.

EXPRESSIONS OF THE LIVER & GALLBLADDER

The element of spring is wood, the color is green, and the emotion is anger. It is also a time associated with a rancid smell and loud barking. The body's energy is in the liver and the gallbladder. Any weaknesses in these organs express themselves in the eyes and in the nails. Muscle weakness is also common, and tears in ligaments and tendons appear more often in the spring than any other time of the year. Some dogs experience violent headaches, and may rub their head on the carpet, against you, or against the wall. Aggression is more common in the spring than during other seasons. All these symptoms are exacerbated on a windy day.

INTERPRETATION

In the case of Max, his condition was made worse by wind, in the form of the dryer, with no way to escape. Obviously poor Max had liver degeneration, not uncommon in older dogs, which was evidenced by his eye discharge and his long, brittle nails. After sharing this information with my friend, she felt a little better, knowing that even without the bath and grooming, Max was a sick dog and did not have too long a life ahead of him.

CONDITIONS ASSOCIATED WITH THE LIVER & GALLBLADDER

- Irritability or aggression
- Pains in the upper back and hernias
- Tremors in the legs, paralysis, lumps and swellings
- Vomiting food
- Brittle nails
- Lick granulomas

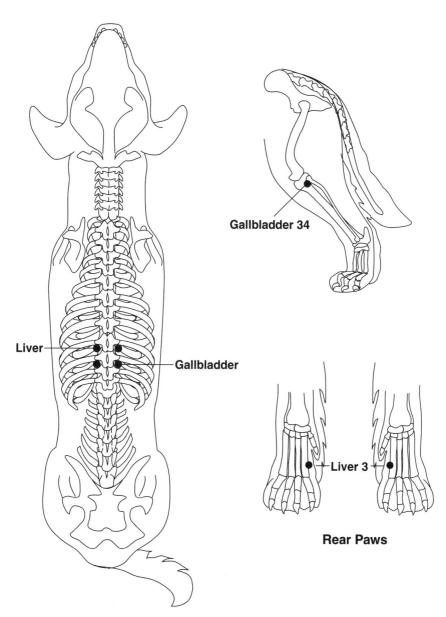

Liver

Gallbladder 34

Gallbladder

Liver 3

Rear Paws

Spring treatment points.

- Some forms of epilepsy

- Headaches, pain in the jaw or under the front legs, side of the chest and thigh

- Some problems with the back legs, including hip displaysia

- Greenish discharge from the eyes or genitals

Any tendon or ligament damage is associated with the gallbladder. Muscle damage is associated with the liver. Behavioral manifestations are irritability or aggression, frustration causing depression. The dog may also be sensitive to touch in the middle of the back or the rib cage.

LIVER & GALLBLADDER DETOXIFICATION— 21 DAYS

Dogs showing one or more of the listed symptoms will benefit from homeopathic support and cleansing.

> *1 capful Detoxification*
>
> *1 capful Lymphatic Drainage*
>
> Give in the morning, half an hour before food. If symptoms worsen during the detoxification process, stop for two days, let the situation calm down, then start again.

21–DAY LIVER & GALLBLADDER CLEANSING & BALANCING DIET FOR A 50-POUND DOG

Feed twice a day and adjust according to weight.

- **Proteins:** 25% of diet—Use one at a time—chicken, ground chicken gizzards, chicken mixed with chicken liver (75% : 25%), rabbit, eggs.

- **Grains:** 25% of diet—Use one at a time, rotating the grains or mix together—sweet brown rice, millet, quinoa, amaranth.

- **Vegetables:** 50% diet—Use one at a time rotating the vegetables or combine some together (lightly steam, or put through food processor)—beets, radishes, asparagus, kale, collard greens, leeks, carrots, romaine lettuce.

- **Herbs:** 2 teaspoons dried—Use two or three together and rotate—parsley, watercress, dandelion, milk thistle, peony root, powdered "green" drinks containing spirulina (Pro-Greens), pinch of ginger.

- **Fruit:** 1 tablespoon—Peaches, or plums, or raspberries, or blackberries.

- **Supplements:**

a.m. meal

1 gram (1,000 mg) vitamin C (calcium ascorbate)—start with 500 mg, then slowly increase to 1 gram

1 vitamin B complex

200 IU vitamin E

2 teaspoons lecithin granules

1 teaspoon blackstrap molasses

¼ teaspoon Wellness (vitamin/mineral mix)

⅛ teaspoon Unleash (digestive enzymes)

2 tablespoons Willard Water XXX

p.m. meal

1 gram (1,000 mg) vitamin C (calcium ascorbate)—start with 500 mg, then slowly increase to 1 gram

1 vitamin B complex

1 teaspoon apple cider vinegar

¼ teaspoon Wellness (vitamin/mineral mix)

⅛ teaspoon Unleash (digestive enzymes)

2 tablespoons Willard Water XXX

1 teaspoon raw honey

- **Glandulars:** Cytozyme LV (glandular)—1 tablet in p.m. meal (supports and rebuilds liver cells).

MAINTENANCE DIET

After the three-week cleansing diet, the dog can be switched over to the Natural Diet appropriate for his weight. Start on day five of the Transfer Diet (*see* Chapter 2), or day three of the Natural Diet Foundation (*see* Chapter 4). Use some milk thistle in your herbal mix to support the liver.

It is possible that a dog who has had liver problems one year, may show some or all of the symptoms again the following year, but less severely. This dog can be put back onto the cleansing diet, but for a much shorter time.

Liver problems can surface at any time of the year. A quick and easy solution is to cleanse the liver using the following flush:

---

¹/₄ cup of fresh lemon juice

1 cup of warm spring or Willard Water XXX

1 heaping teaspoon raw honey

With a turkey baster, give ¹/₂ cup in the evening before bedtime, and ¹/₂ cup upon arising in the morning. Put the baster between the dog's lips at the side of his mouth. Squeeze slowly to allow the dog to swallow. Keep his head parallel to the ground. Use for four days before feeding in the morning and before bedtime at night. Store what is not used in the refrigerator, and bring to room temperature before using again. Feed your dog normally during this flush.

WORKING WITH YOUR VETERINARIAN

Diseases of the liver and gallbladder need to be carefully monitored by your veterinarian with frequent blood tests.

SUMMER: JUNE 21 TO SEPTEMBER 9

HEART: 11:00 A.M. TO 1:00 P.M.

SMALL INTESTINE: 1:00 P.M. TO 3:00 P.M.

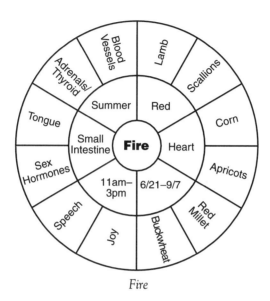

Fire

HARRY—THE UNHAPPY GOLDEN RETRIEVER

Sheila was the owner of several Golden Retrievers, all of whom were beloved pets. Every summer she took her dogs for a swim in the local lake. The dogs loved it. But it wasn't long before Harry, who was by far the liveliest of the bunch, broke out with hot spots around his neck and on his back close to his tail. That meant he had to be grounded until the hot spots cleared up. He was miserable. He became hyperactive and barked hysterically. There was no easy way for Sheila to provide an energy outlet for him, and playing retrieving games on dry land ended up with his having hot spots just the same. As the years went by, these hot spots got worse and started to appear at other places on his body. She had used sprays and cortisone treatments with some success, but when these failed to work, I got the call for help.

EXPRESSIONS OF THE HEART & SMALL INTESTINE

The element of summer is fire, the color is red, and the emotion is happiness. It is a time associated with a scorched smell and hyper-activity. The body's energy is in the heart and small intestine. Manifestations of malfunctioning of these organs express themselves in the circulation, heart, overheating, inability to cool the body by panting and digestive upsets. All are made worse by heat, so hot days can be miserable for these dogs.

Homeopathic treatment based on the Five-Element Theory combined with a change in diet cleared up Harry's stubborn hot spots.

INTERPRETATION

Sheila had a typical example of a dog "on fire." His body had huge, red hot spots, he had become hyperactive, which made his heart pound. His circulation was affected and in consequence his digestive abilities as well. Poor Harry was one unhappy dog.

I gave Sheila a homeopathic remedy to take care of Harry's hot spots while she was collecting together the ingredients for his new diet. She was also instructed to spray a mixture of $\frac{1}{2}$ apple cider vinegar and $\frac{1}{2}$ Willard Water XXX on Harry's hot spots. ACV changes the pH reading of the skin from alkaline to acid, inhibits hot spots from spreading and aids in healing. Harry was then put onto his new diet and everything cleared up.

I warned Sheila that while she was on the right track to curing Harry, his hot spots may recur the following year but with less severity. I advised her that Harry might have to go through the cleansing diet again for a short period of time.

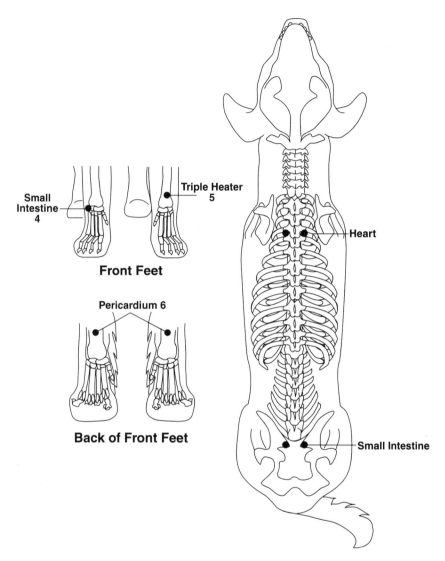

Triple Heater 5

Small Intestine 4

Front Feet

Pericardium 6

Back of Front Feet

Heart

Small Intestine

Summer treatment points.

CONDITIONS ASSOCIATED WITH THE HEART & SMALL INTESTINE

- Red, itchy skin with blotches all over the body, hot spots
- Panting and shallow breathing
- General weakness
- Pain in the pit of the stomach, or region of the heart
- Rapid heartbeat, insomnia
- Dryness in the throat, bleeding gums
- Pain along the middle of the front legs, with constant licking
- Difficulty in climbing stairs, limping
- Fluid retention
- Deafness
- Distention of the belly
- Painful places along the outside of the front leg and shoulder, limping in the front
- Difficulty in getting up after lying down for a while
- Excessive shedding
- Skin that turns black under the arms and belly
- Allergies that return at the same time every year

Behavioral manifestations are whining when moving, crying when climbing stairs, lack of interest in breeding, sudden limping on front or rear legs, occasional deafness, hyperactivity, excessive playing, or no play behavior at all.

HEART & SMALL INTESTINE DETOXIFICATION— 21 DAYS

Hot spots can be a manifestation of poisons coming out of the body, a circulatory problem, improper diet or a sign that the dog is overheating. Going on a 21-day detoxification program can only benefit the dog.

1 capful of Detoxification

1 capful of Lymphatic Drainage

Give in the morning, half an hour before food. If symptoms worsen during the detoxification process, stop for two days, let the situation calm down, then start again.

1 capful of Bacteria Detox can be given at bedtime if a secondary bacterial infection is present.

21–DAY HEART & SMALL INTESTINE CLEANSING & BALANCING DIET FOR A 50–POUND DOG

Feed your dog twice a day and adjust according to weight.

- **Protein**: 20% of diet—Use one at a time—white meat from chicken, lamb, mutton, cottage cheese, white fish slightly cooked, lamb and lamb liver mixed together, cooked pork and pork liver, mixed together. Use what your dog prefers.

- **Grains**: 40% of diet—Use one at a time, rotating the grains or mix together—millet, brown rice, oats and buckwheat.

- **Vegetables**: 40% of the diet—Use one at a time rotating the vegetables or combine some together (lightly steam, or put through food processor)—sweet potatoes, carrots, beets, celery, chard, asparagus, cauliflower, radishes, okra, broccoli and squash.

  Note: For the very sick dog, the vegetables and meat should be lightly cooked and fed together with a digestive enzyme. When you see improvement, reintroduce your dog to raw food.

- **Herbs**: 2 teaspoons dried—Use two or three together and rotate—garlic, savory, thyme, basil, sage, caraway, marjoram, chamomile, melissa, angelica, dill, parsley, peppermint, pinch of cayenne and/or ginger, hawthorn, licorice.

- **Fruits**: 1 tablespoon red grapes, or black currants, or blackberries, or shredded apples mixed with honey and goat's milk.

Supplements:

a.m. meal

1 gram (1,000 mg) vitamin C (calcium ascorbate)—start with 500 mg, then slowly increase to 1 gram

1 vitamin B complex

400 IU vitamin E

15 mg Co-enzyme Q-10

1 Amino acid complex tablet

1 capsule or 2 teaspoons lecithin

1 tablespoon honey

$^1/_4$ teaspoon Radiance (vitamin/mineral mix used for skin)

$^1/_4$ teaspoon Unleash (digestive enzyme)

p.m. meal

1 gram (1,000 mg) vitamin C (calcium ascorbate)—start with 500 mg, then slowly increase to 1 gram

1 vitamin B complex

1 tablespoon raw wheat germ

1 tablespoon honey

$^1/_4$ teaspoon Radiance (vitamin/mineral mix used for skin)

$^1/_4$ teaspoon Unleash (digestive enzyme)

Glandulars—Cytozme-H (neonatal heart) 1 tablet in the a.m.

This diet is lower in meat protein than the other cleansing diets and is used to calm down the small intestine.

MAINTENANCE DIET

After three weeks, return to either the Natural Diet or the Natural Diet Foundation (*see* Chapter 4). Any time hot spots reappear, do the cleansing diet again, but just for one week at a time, until the body has rebalanced.

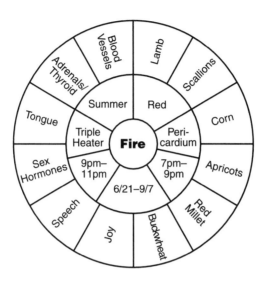

Fire—Part two.

CUBBY—THE LAME NEWFOUNDLAND

Early in May, Cubby's cruciate ligament was repaired. The operation went well, but the recovery period was going to be a long one, with no activity on Cubby's part. He had to have a sling put under his belly to help him up and to get him outside to relieve himself. Other than that, he was to have no activity. Terribly boring for a working dog, and also very debilitating. With no use of his muscles, they soon began to atrophy, which made getting up more and more difficult. Bethanne, Cubby's owner, also noticed that the skin on Cubby's belly and under his arms was getting black.

In July, Cubby was not able to urinate successfully. When he staggered outside, he was unable to have the proper "stream," and the urine just dribbled out, drop by drop. Bethanne was concerned and rightly so.

I explained to her that since Cubby had not been able to use his right rear leg, he put all the weight of his rather large Newfoundland body on his left front leg. And, in order to keep his balance, he had to hold his head at a strange angle.

My feeling was that he needed a visit to a chiropractor to get himself straightened out. Between the chiropractor and the homeopathic remedies specific to the bladder, we fixed the urination problem and within 24 hours Cubby was moving better. He was putting weight on his right back leg, his head came up, and the dribbling returned to a stream. The black skin under his arms and belly is the classic sign of hypothyroidism, and a blood test confirmed this diagnosis. I put Cubby on glandulars, which corrected that problem.

A veterinary chiropractor and homeopathic remedies helped Cubby recover from surgery and solved his bladder problem.

EXPRESSIONS OF THE TRIPLE HEATER & PERICARDIUM

During summer, the energy of the body is in two other organ systems, the triple heater and the pericardium. The triple heater is unique to traditional Chinese medicine. The Chinese divide the body into three parts. The upper body is called the upper heater, the middle body is called the middle heater, and the lower part of the body is called the lower heater. When a specific area of a dog's body is not functioning correctly, for example, the back legs, which would be in the lower heater, it puts the body out of balance and compensations have to be made in other parts of the body. Therefore, the triple heater has to be treated together with the other organ systems to regain balance.

The pericardium represents the sheath of tissue surrounding the heart and is considered its protector. Many emotional conditions manifesting themselves in odd behavior in our dogs can be treated using the pericardium acupuncture points.

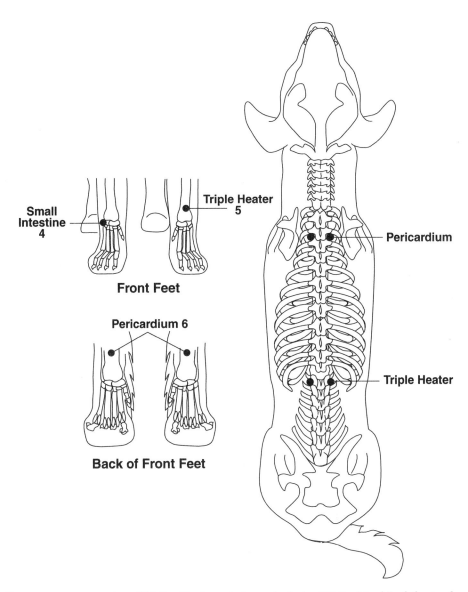

Summer treatment points. TH 5—Used to rebalance the body. PC 6—Used for behavioral abnormalities.

CONDITIONS ASSOCIATED WITH THE TRIPLE HEATER & PERICARDIUM

- Thyroid and adrenal malfunction
- Edema
- Difficulty in urination
- Limping and pain in front legs and shoulders
- Agitated and suspicious
- Running in circles, shaking, poor balance
- Head tilts, dizziness, staggering
- Swelling in armpits
- Biting feet from underneath
- Toenails that grow fast
- Lick granulomas in the middle of front leg
- Earaches, bleeding gums

Acupuncture and nutritional supplementation can do wonders in treating these conditions.

To calm a dog who hates having his nails clipped, use these points together.

Note: Where thyroid, adrenal, circulatory or heart conditions are suspected, a good working relationship with your veterinarian is a must. Continued monitoring through blood work, plus the use of medication, is often required for successful, long-term treatment.

DETOXIFICATION & DIET

Since these meridians and organs are energized at the same time of the year as the heart and small intestine, the detoxification and diet are the same.

MAINTENANCE DIET

After three weeks, return to either the Natural Diet or the Natural Diet Foundation (*see* Chapter 4). Any time symptoms reappear, go back and do the cleansing diet again, but for one week at a time, until the body has rebalanced.

16 Fall, Winter & In Between the Seasons

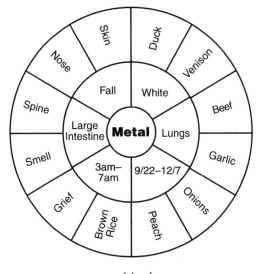

Metal.

SOLO—THE HYPERACTIVE COLLIE PUPPY

Solo was a cute 7-month-old Collie puppy who came to one of our training camps. Marcy, her owner, was a nervous wreck because she had never been able to sleep through a night since she had brought Solo home at 7 weeks of age. Every night, at about 3:30 a.m., Solo would snuffle, snort and sneeze, waking Marcy. Then, at 5:30 a.m., Solo had to go out and woke Marcy up again.

245

Fasting and a change of diet made Solo's hyperactivity disappear and helped her sleep through the night for the first time.

What I saw was a hyperactive puppy with hot spots and skin eruptions all over her little body. She just couldn't stay still and was in constant motion. She also had white discharge from her nose and eyes. Learning about Solo, I found out that she was born in July and before Marcy brought her home, Solo had:

• Had the dewclaws on her front legs removed.

• Had five sets of five-in-one inoculations, starting when she was 6 weeks old and continuing to 6 months of age.

• Had a rabies inoculation with the last set of five-in-one vaccines.

Following each set of vaccines, Solo had diarrhea, started to itch, her body became covered in hives and her eyes and nose had a whitish discharge. She was also running alive with fleas. Her veterinarian had prescribed steroids for the itching, stool hardeners and antibiotics for her diarrhea, and a flea and tick dip to be given every week. She was fed a dry commercial dog food with no supplements. This was one sick little puppy who needed immediate care.

EXPRESSIONS OF THE LUNGS & LARGE INTESTINE

September to December is the time of the year when the energy of the body is in the lungs and large intestine. This season corresponds to the metal element, the color white, the emotions of sadness and depression, a rank smell and the sound of whining and crying. The lungs and large intestine express themselves in the nose, skin and structure of the dog, as well as the elimination systems. These expressions worsen on dry days, when housed in a room with dry heat such as a wood-burning stove, or put under a hot hair dryer.

INTERPRETATION

The white discharge from Solo's nose and eyes told me that there was involvement with the metal element. The time she got Marcy up to go outside was also a clue because at 5:00 a.m. the energy of the body goes into the large intestine, responsible for elimination. The fact that she had had her dewclaws removed, leaving a tiny scar on a major large intestine acupuncture point, told me that the condition of her skin could be related to that too. But it wasn't that simple. The hot spots and hyperactivity showed me that there was a disruption in the energy to the heart and small intestine as well. Both systems were weak.

Solo was fasted for a day on goat's milk and honey, and for the first time since Marcy had owned Solo, they both slept through the night. An individual diet, combining both the lung and large intestine diet together with the heart and small intestine diet, was worked out for little Solo. She was cleared of the side effects of the vaccines by using homeopathic remedies. When Solo left camp, she was a quiet, calm, happy little soul and her skin was beginning to heal. The diarrhea had stopped and the discharge had almost cleared up. I told Marcy that I thought Solo should recover in about three weeks, but she was to keep her on the Natural Diet.

CONDITIONS ASSOCIATED WITH THE LUNGS & LARGE INTESTINE

- Skin conditions: hives, pimples, boils, abscesses, eczema appearing along the front legs, neck, shoulders or face

- Continuous itching with no fleas present

- White secretions from eyes or nose

- Structural abnormalities affecting the spine

- Inverted sneezing and hiccups

- Fusion of the spine or spinal degeneration found in aging dogs

- Difficulty in lying down, or circling for a long time before lying down

- Poor extension of a front leg, or pain and limping in the front legs

- Difficulty in getting up after lying down and not being able to lift head up higher than shoulder level

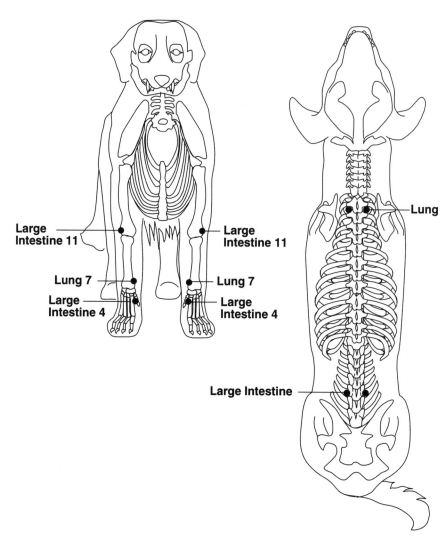

UFall treatment points. Use LU 7 for inverted sneezing and hiccups.

- Bloating in the large intestine
- Worms, constipation and diarrhea
- Dryness of the throat with a raspy bark
- Difficulty in breathing, or whining and crying
- Depression and sadness
- Inhalant allergies and nasal or sinus drips
- Lack of coat or one that is dull and dry

LUNGS & LARGE INTESTINE DETOXIFICATION— 21 DAYS

Dogs showing one or more of the listed symptoms will benefit from the following homeopathic support and cleansing.

> *1 capful Detoxification*
>
> *1 capful of Lymphatic Drainage*
>
> Give in the morning, half an hour before food. If symptoms worsen during the detoxification process, stop for two days, let the situation calm down, then start again.
>
> For skin conditions that have been treated unsuccessfully in the past, wait one week after the initial 21-day cleansing, then use Bacteria Detox together with more Detoxification, following the schedule above. If your dog needs to be cleansed from overuse of chemicals, heavy metals or environmental toxins, then use the appropriate Detox after the initial cleansing (*see* Chapter 11).

21–DAY LUNGS & LARGE INTESTINE CLEANSING & BALANCING DIET FOR A 50-POUND DOG

Feed twice a day and adjust according to weight.

- **Protein:** ¹/₃ diet—Use one at a time—raw beef, or raw beef mixed together with beef liver (75% beef, 25% liver), cottage cheese or yogurt.

- **Grains:** ¹/₃ diet—Use one at a time, rotating the grains or mix together—brown rice, oats or buckwheat.

- **Vegetables:** ¹/₃ diet—Use one at a time rotating the vegetables or combine some together (lightly steam, or put through food processor)—carrots, beets, celery, cucumber, parsnips, green or yellow beans, radishes and garlic.

- **Herbs:** 2 teaspoons dried—Use two or three together and rotate—comfrey leaves, fennel, burdock, aloe vera, strawberry leaves, mullein, ginseng, angelica, lobelia, fenugreek, golden seal.

- **Fruit:** 1 tablespoon—Black currants, or red grapes, or blueberries, or blackberries, or peaches.

- **Supplements: use in both a.m. and p.m. meals**

  1 gram (1,000 mg) vitamin C (calcium ascorbate)—start with 500 mg, then slowly increase to 1 gram

  1 Vitamin B complex

  2 Alfalfa tablets

  ¹/₄ teaspoon Wellness (vitamin/mineral mix)

  ¹/₈ teaspoon Unleash (digestive enzyme)

  1 capsule essential fatty acids

  ¹/₂ cup yogurt or kefir

  2 tablespoons Willard Water XXX

- **Glandulars:** Pneuma-zyme, 1 tablet in p.m. only—for three weeks

MAINTENANCE DIET

After three weeks of the cleansing diet and detoxification, your dog can be switched over to the Natural Diet or the Natural Diet Foundation. Start on day five of the Transfer Diet for the homemade food, or day three for the Natural Diet Foundation (*see* Chapter 4).

PARASITES—INTERNAL

Always check your dog for internal parasites especially during this time of the year. Worms live in the large intestine and if your dog has been infested and he has been wormed using a commercial product, the good bacteria present in the large intestine, necessary for normal stools, may have been killed off. Yogurt and/ or kefir will restore the good bacteria. Acidophilus capsules (the live bacteria contained in yogurt) can be bought at your nearby health food store. There are also many natural wormers such as Para-Yeast on the market (*see* Chapter 5) which can be used successfully.

PARASITES—EXTERNAL

Bathe your dog in a mild herbal shampoo, add some Neem oil and dilute with Willard Water XXX, 10 to 1 (*see* Chapter 3). Leave the shampoo on for about five minutes to kill any parasites on the skin. Rinse thoroughly with some apple cider vinegar, mixed half and half with warm water, and let the dog drip-dry. This changes the pH of the skin, kills parasites and helps the skin to heal.

After bathing your dog, let him drip-dry. Do not put him in front of a fan, or a blow dryer, since lung and large intestine symptoms are exacerbated by wind even from a blow dryer.

WORKING WITH YOUR VETERINARIAN

Diseases of the lungs and large intestine need to be monitored on a regular basis by your veterinarian. For your office visit, be sure to take a fecal specimen to check your dog for parasites. Blood work is always helpful in determining allergies and parasites.

WINTER: DECEMBER 22 TO MARCH 6

BLADDER: 3:00 P.M. TO 5:00 P.M.

KIDNEY: 5:00 P.M. TO 7:00 P.M.

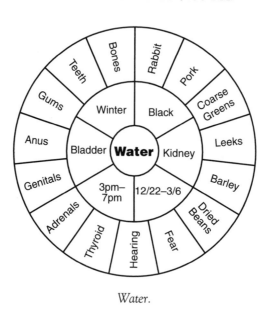

Water.

DEMI—THE WIREHAIRED DACHSHUND

Demi came to us when she was a year and a half old and a breed Champion. She was a pretty little girl, but showed some odd behaviors whose causes were difficult to pinpoint. When a stranger petted her, she could be sweet and affectionate one moment and then turn around and try to bite them the next. She was also difficult to housetrain, which we attributed to having been a kennel dog. At the annual Christmas party for our students, one of them bent over to pet Demi and she whipped around and bit. This time I saw what happened. The student had petted her on her lower back, behind the rib cage.

Off she went to the chiropractor, and sure enough her whole lumbar area was out of alignment. Since this area of the body controls the kidneys and the bladder, this misalignment of her spine disrupted the nerve pathways to those organs, causing pain in the area just below her rib cage. When touched there by a stranger, she would bite them. It also explained our difficulties in house-training her.

The lumbar region continued to be a weak area for Demi and she went regularly to the chiropractor. The biting behavior stopped and she became housetrained overnight. Training went well and she obtained her CDX in high style.

EXPRESSIONS OF THE KIDNEY & BLADDER

The element of winter is water, the color black, the emotions of fear and anxiety, a salty taste, a rotten smell and a groaning sound. The body's energy is in the bladder and kidneys. Malfunctioning of these organs will be expressed in the ears, the anus or urethra. The kidney and bladder control the bones of the body, the bone marrow and the

A veterinary chiropractor solved Demi's back problems and she no longer bites strangers.

brain. Their health is reflected in the hair on the head. The kidneys are responsible for growth, development of the skeleton, all reproductive functions and they control the fluids of the body.

INTERPRETATION

Trying to determine what caused Demi's behavior was not easy. It was obvious from the difficulty with housetraining that something was not right with her bladder, even though bladder infections had been ruled out. What was more difficult to perceive was that her back was hurting her. At the vertebrae above her tuck-up and also where her tail joined her body, there was a kink in her wiring. When someone other than ourselves petted her, she became anxious and fearful, and so she bit them. It was watching her emotions that gave us the first clue. The other clue was that the behavior occurred in the winter, and bladder and kidney conditions are made worse by the cold.

CONDITIONS ASSOCIATED WITH
THE KIDNEY & BLADDER

- Deafness or sound sensitivity

- Black discharges from the ears and eyes

- Anxiety, fear, can't stay still

- Too much or too little fluid in the following areas—lymph nodes, blood (anemia or hemorrhaging), saliva (drooling or dry mouth), reproductive disorders, too much or too little milk in lactating females, edema, and the inability to urinate or urinating too much

- Pain in the lower back, middle of thigh, weakness in the hind legs

- Diseases of the bone marrow

- Brittle bones, fractures, arthritis, aches and pains

- Chronic cystitis, bladder or kidney stones

- Incontinence, especially in old dogs

- Stomachaches, dryness and thirst, inability to digest food

- Conditions of the genitals, urethra and anus

- Bags under the eyes

- Diseases of the mouth, gums and teeth including crooked teeth, under- or overshot jaws, heavily tartared teeth

Behavioral manifestations can be anxiety and panic attacks, an inability to retain learning, shying away from hands close to the ears or lower back, shaking the head or rubbing the side of face on carpet, excessive rolling on back, scratching ears slowly with a lot of groaning, separation anxiety, aggression when touched on lower back and skin flinching on the lower back.

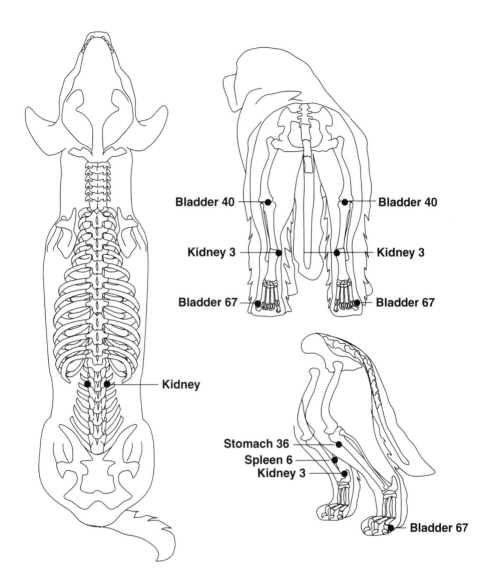

Kidney & bladder treatment points.

KIDNEY & BLADDER DETOXIFICATION—21 DAYS

Dogs showing one or more of the listed symptoms will benefit from homeo-pathic support and cleansing.

> *1 capful Detoxification*
>
> *1 capful of Lymphatic Drainage*
>
> Give in the morning, half an hour before food. If the symptoms worsen dur-ing the detoxification process, stop for two days, let the situation calm down, then start again.

21–DAY KIDNEY & BLADDER CLEANSING & BALANCING DIET FOR A 50-POUND DOG

Feed twice a day and adjust according to weight.

- **Protein:** $^1/_3$ diet—Use one at a time—beef, chicken, fish, lamb, cottage cheese, yogurt, or cooked five-minute eggs with shell.

- **Grains:** $^1/_3$ diet—Use oats singly, or combine half and half—$^1/_2$ oats with either brown rice, millet or buckwheat groats.

- **Vegetables:** $^1/_3$ diet—Use one at a time, rotating the vegetables, or com-bine some together (lightly steam, or put through food processor)—parsnips, beets, broccoli, leeks, kale, mustard greens, carrots, green beans, lettuce, radishes, celery, cucumbers.

- **Herbs:** 1 teaspoon dried—Use two or three together and rotate—goldenrod, nettles, parsley, uva ursi, dandelion, marshmallow.

- **Fruit:** $^1/_4$ to $^1/_2$ of a whole watermelon can be fed instead of one meal. Use skin and seeds, as well as fruit. Must be fed at least two hours before or after other food. Flushes and cleanses kidneys.

- **Supplements: Use in both a.m. and p.m. meals.**

  $^1/_2$ teaspoon Recover (vitamin/mineral mix with colostrum)

  $^1/_2$ teaspoon Unleash (digestive enzyme)

1 gram vitamin C (calcium ascorbate)—start with 500 mg, then slowly increase to 1 gram

1 B complex

2 tablespoons Willard Water XXX

200 IU vitamin E, in the a.m.

- **Glandulars:** Renal Plus. Use 1 tablet in the p.m. meal, and feed between 5:00 p.m. and 7:00 p.m.

MAINTENANCE DIET

After three weeks following this diet and detoxification program, your dog can be switched over to the Natural Diet, or the Natural Diet Foundation. Start on day five of the Transfer Diet for homemade food, or day three of the Natural Diet Foundation (*see* Chapter 4).

WORKING WITH YOUR VETERINARIAN

Kidney disease needs to be constantly monitored by your veterinarian. You will need to get a chemistry screen and a CBC. If the BUN and Creatinine levels remain elevated after your initial cleansing diet, our suggestion would be to follow it for another two to three weeks, and have the blood work done again. When the levels return to normal, go to the Natural Diet; either version will do.

Many undetected kidney disorders eventually lead to heart problems. The whole body is so interconnected that many diseases can result from poor kidney function. Have your veterinarian do a thorough yearly physical, including blood work.

IN BETWEEN THE SEASONS:
MARCH 7 TO 20

JUNE 7 TO 20

SEPTEMBER 8 TO 21

DECEMBER 8 TO 21

STOMACH: 7:00 A.M. TO 9:00 A.M.

SPLEEN/PANCREAS: 9:00 A.M. TO 11:00 A.M.

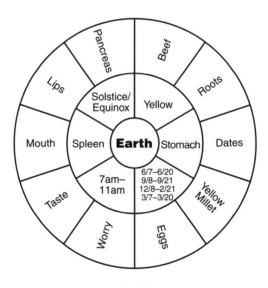

Earth.

SALLY—THE SHIH TZU

Ann was working with her Shih Tzu, Sally, in obedience classes and had great hopes of showing her. Sally had done well in the Novice classes and Ann was encouraged to go on and teach her the more advanced exercises of jumping and retrieving. At first, Sally's training came along well, but after a while the retrieving of the dumbbell was no longer fun for Sally. This puzzled Ann since Sally as a very young dog had always wanted something in her mouth and carried her toys everywhere she went.

After trying numerous ways to get Sally to retrieve, I got the call for help. In questioning Ann about when this first started, she mentioned that it had started in the spring, but became worse as the months went by.

Ann told me the following about Sally:

- Her breath smelled bad, and her doggie kisses were not as welcome as they used to be.

- She had started to eat her own stools.

- She was shedding excessively, with clumps of hair coming off of her body.

A change in diet, a homeopathic remedy and a thorough tooth cleaning put Sally back on track. She no longer refused to retrieve.

- She had brown tartar buildup on her teeth close to the gums and her gums looked very red and inflamed.

EXPRESSIONS OF THE STOMACH & SPLEEN

The earth element corresponds to late summer as well as the times between seasons, a damp climate, the color yellow, the emotions of sympathy and tolerance, a sickly sweet smell and a whining sound. The expression of the stomach and spleen is in conditions of the mouth, flesh and the limbs. All are made worse by moisture.

The spleen is the principal organ of digestion because it transports the nutrients and blood. It is responsible for turning food into nourishment and regulates the blood. The relationship between the stomach and spleen is that the stomach receives food and the spleen transports the nutrients.

When there is a weakness in the spleen, the body is unable to use the nourishment in the food which leads to lethargy. Weakness in the spleen is usually accompanied by diarrhea, limbs that are cold and pain in the region of the abdomen.

INTERPRETATION

The call to me came around the beginning of June when the energy of the body is in the stomach & spleen organ system, which expresses itself in the mouth. Tartar on the teeth pointed to an incorrect diet. With gums swollen and red, a collection of bacteria was present and making Sally's breath smelly. She was eating her stools in an effort to restore her enzyme balance. It was painful for Sally to pick anything up in her mouth and even though she was a happy little dog who would do anything for Ann, she simply couldn't pick up her dumbbell.

I suggested a visit to her veterinarian and a good teeth-cleaning. After that, a diet that was suitable for Sally was formulated and I told Ann about the homeopathic remedy Fragaria (*see* Chapter 12) for future tartar removal.

Not surprisingly, after a good teeth-cleaning, with gums in perfect health, Sally happily started to retrieve again.

I put Sally onto the cleansing diet for three weeks after the teeth-cleaning, and then she was fed the Natural Diet. She had no further problems with her teeth. Her breath smelled wonderful again, she was no longer eating her stools and her doggie kisses were once more welcome.

CONDITIONS ASSOCIATED WITH THE STOMACH & SPLEEN

- Burning sensation in the stomach and unusual hunger
- Bloat
- Bleeding from the gums, bad breath accompanied by constipation
- Abdominal distention, gastritis, edema
- Vomiting yellow bile (especially between 7:00 a.m. and 9:00 a.m.)
- Vomiting food immediately after eating
- Yellow discharge from the eyes or genitals
- Pain or limps in the hind legs
- Obesity/inability to put on weight
- Excessive bleeding, not coming into season, infertility

- A mournful expression

- Pain around the mouth and tongue, dirty teeth, foul-smelling breath, bleeding gums

- Hair that falls out in clumps

- Swallowing difficulties and gagging

- Too little or too much saliva producing excessive drooling, belching, a high-pitched bark and skin that smells sickly sweet

Behavioral manifestations are insecurity, loss of balance and nervousness, wanting attention, hyperactivity, aberrant eating—called pica, gobbling down of odd objects and a precursor to bloat, random snapping at other dogs, continuous whining or high-pitched barking, fixation on an object or another dog, constant swallowing, drooling, and the inability to take things in the mouth.

THE IMPORTANCE OF THE CHANGE IN SEASONS

Every three months, energy that has been in the major organ systems goes back through the earth element to be renewed and invigorated. Thus we find the energy of the body in the stomach and spleen as well as the pancreas more frequently than other organ systems. Physical manifestations of disorders in these organs are seen more frequently during these time frames than any others—the most common of which is vomiting yellow bile early in the morning, followed by bloat.

STOMACH & SPLEEN DETOXIFICATION—21 DAYS

1 capful Detoxification

Give in the morning, half an hour before food. If symptoms worsen during the detoxification process, stop for two days, let the situation calm down, then start again.

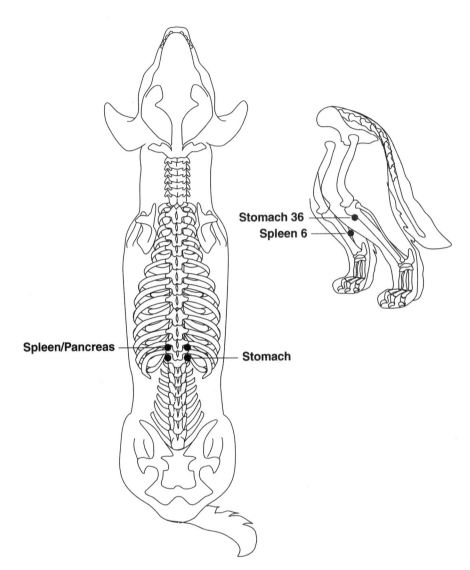

In between seasons treatment points. For a dog going into bloat, use acupressure on ST 36 and SP 6, the homeopathic remedies Alumina and Carbo Veg., while going to the veterinarian for help.

21–DAY STOMACH & SPLEEN CLEANSING & BALANCING DIET FOR A 50-POUND DOG

Feed twice a day and adjust according to weight.

- **Protein:** $1/3$ of diet—Use one at a time—beef and beef liver, chicken, turkey, lamb or slightly cooked whitefish.

- **Grains:** $1/3$ of diet —Use one at a time, rotating the grains or mix together—brown rice, spelt, millet or quinoa.

- **Vegetables:** $1/3$ of diet—Use one at a time rotating the vegetables or combine some together (lightly steam, or put through food processor)— sweet potatoes, yams, carrots, parsnips, cucumbers, squash, pumpkin, green or yellow beans.

- **Herbs:** 2 teaspoons dried—Use two or three together and rotate— peppermint, parsley, chamomile, catnip, comfrey root, golden rod, licorice, fennel, ginseng, kelp, blessed thistle.

- **Fruits:** 2 teaspoons fresh red grapes or apricots.

- **Supplements:** Use in both a.m. and p.m. meals

  1 tablet Hydrozyme (stomach enzyme)

  1 gram vitamin C (calcium ascorbate)—start with 500 mg, then slowly increase to 1 gram

  1 vitamin B complex

  1 teaspoon cold-pressed safflower oil

  1 teaspoon blackstrap molasses

  $1/4$ teaspoon Wellness (vitamin/mineral mix)—in a.m. only

  200 IU vitamin E in a.m. only

- **Glandulars**: 1 tablet Cytozyme SP—spleen glandular in a.m.

MAINTENANCE DIET

After three weeks following this diet and detoxification program, your dog can be switched over to the Natural Diet, or the Natural Diet Foundation. Start on day five of the Transfer Diet for homemade food, or day three for the Natural Diet Foundation (*see* Chapter 4).

COMMENTS

Dogs experiencing stomach upsets frequently benefit from their food being slightly cooked, or fed at room temperature. Avoid food that is straight out of the refrigerator. Feed in a peaceful environment and keep your dog quiet for at least an hour after meals.

Dogs that vomit yellow bile in the morning should have something in their stomach before they go to bed. Give a dog biscuit. Try feeding them before or after 7:00 a.m. to 9:00 a.m. If this condition continues, fast your dog for a day. A day without food, with plenty of fluids will help to rebalance the stomach and the spleen.

BLOAT

Most cases of bloat are diagnosed during stomach and spleen season. Bloat is a condition where the stomach expands and becomes full of gas or fluid. Once the stomach is distended it may twist either at the top or bottom. If it twists a full 180°, it is called torsion. The signs of bloat are excessive drooling or salivation, attempts to vomit, restlessness, pain in the stomach, stomach feels brick hard to the touch, and attempts to eat large quantities of dirt or leaves if outside, or fringes of carpets or curtains or piece of the couch, if inside. Torsion can occur by itself without the expansion of the stomach and is a life-and-death situation that calls for *immediate* veterinary care.

If you catch the symptoms, just as they start, you have a good chance of preventing severe shock syndrome that occurs with bloat and torsion (*see* illustration on p. 262).

Surgery is often required to correct a gastric torsion. The spleen, which can be severely damaged during the twisting of the stomach, may also be removed during this surgery, after which careful nutritional management is required.

Appendix I
A Brief Reference Guide

HOW TO USE THIS APPENDIX

This appendix is a partial guide to what can ail your dog. We list the treatment of our choice for each of the conditions. We often use more than one form of complementary treatment for an individual condition.

The easiest way to use this guide is with kinesiology to test which of the treatments would be the best for *your* dog. When homeopathic remedies are listed, more information can be obtained by reading about each remedy in the chapter on homeopathy (*see* Chapter 12). When we refer to diet, more information can be found in the chapters on the Natural Diet (*see* Chapters 2 and 4) and in the chapters on the Five-Element Theory (*see* Chapters 14 to 16). You can find even more information on products in Appendix II.

The following information is *not* a substitute for veterinary care. What it does provide is a "safety margin" in time, so that you can treat your dog, without doing harm, until you can get professional help.

CHART OF CANINE HEALTH CONDITIONS AND THEIR TREATMENTS

CONDITION	TREATMENT
Abscess	Arnica, Lycopodium, Silicea
Addison's disease	Licorice root, Natural Diet, kidney diet, baked cereals, DOCP, Florinef electrolytes, chiropractic, acupuncture
Aggression	Belladonna, Hydrophobinum, Nux Vomica, Rescue Remedy, Liver Diet + detox, PC6, exercise, training

continues

265

CONDITION	TREATMENT
Airsickness	Belladonna, Calm Stress, B complex
Allergies Tox.,	Apis, Arsenicum Alb., Ledum, Rhus Urtica Urens. Heart or Lung diet, Homeopathic or herbal Detox/Allergy blend, Histo-Plex
Amputations	Arnica, Hypericum, Bellis, Ledum, Symphytum, acupuncture, massage, chiropractic
Anal glands, secretions	Silicea, Natural Diet, wash with Willard Water XXX
Anaphylactic shock	Aconite, Arnica, Rescue Remedy, raw honey
Anemia	Arsenicum Alb., Silicea, Raw Liver Natural Diet
Anesthesia antidote to use after	Nux Vomica Arnica
Antibacterial	Thuja, garlic, goldenseal, echinacea, Willard Water XXX
Antiseptic	Calendula, Arnica, garlic, goldenseal/echinacea formula
Anus fissures fistulas prolapsed protruding	Ledum, Thuja Berberis vul. Belladonna, Calc. Carb. Arsenicum Alb., acupuncture, chiropractic, Natural Diet
Anxiety	Aconite, Ignatia, Nux Vomica, Rescue Remedy, Kidney Diet, Willard Water XXX, Tranquility Blend, Calm Stress, acupuncture/chiropractic, lavender pillow

CONDITION	TREATMENT
Appetite	
depraved	Alumina, Calc. Carb., Cicuta Vir., Phosphorus, get help, this is a sign of bloat. Arsenicum Alb.
diminished	Calc. Carb., Calendula, Sulphur
excessive	Baryta Carb., Nux Vomica, Sulphur
loss of	Thuja
Arthritis	Arnica, Rhus Tox., Ruta Grav, Lycopodium, Silicea. Miristin, Miristaid (CM), Liver or Kidney Diet, Alfalfa/Yucca herbal formula, acupuncture/chiropractic
Assimilation (poor)	Phosphorus, Silicea, Digestive enzymes
Bacterial infections	Hepar Sulph, Willard Water XXX, Golden Seal/Echinacea formula
Barking, hysterical	Belladonna, Ignatia, Calm Stress, Lavender Oil, Lavender pillows in crate, Heart Diet, Valerian Root capsules. Homeopathic Detox, PC 6, TH 5, chiropractic, exercise, training
Bee stings	Apis
Behavior problems	Rescue Remedy, Natural Diet, glandulars, chiropractic, PC6, TH5 (calming), training and exercise
Bites—any kind	Hypericum, Arnica, Ledum, wash with Willard Water XXX, Calendula cream, use laser to relieve pain
Biting	see aggression

continues

CONDITION	TREATMENT
Bladder	
inflammation	Urtica Urens, Cranberry capsules, Recover
stones	Tinkle Tonic (Urinary Formula), Calc. Carb, Berberis, Thlapsi bursa, Lycopodium, Kidney diet, glandulars, acupuncture, chiropractic
incontinence	Conium, Belladonna, Berberis, Pulsatilla. Kidney/Liver diet, acupuncture, chiropractic, Recover, glandulars
Bleeding	Ferrum Phos., Phosphorus, Thuja, Calendular lotion
Bloat	
eating strange objects	Alumina
distended stomach	Carbo Veg., Lycopodium, ST 36, SP 6, Stomach/Spleen Diet
torsion	Nux Vomica, Get to veterinarian immediately, this is an emergency
Boils	Silicea, Natural Diet, Homeopathic Detox
Bones	
brittle	Silicea, Natural Diet
degeneration	Phosphorus, Natural Diet
dislocations	Ruta Grav, chiropractic, acupuncture
fractures	Symphytum, Arnica, chiropractic
growth abnormalities	Calc. Carb.
injuries	Symphytum, Ruta, Arnica, Laser, chiropractic, acupuncture
Bowel rumbling	Bellis Perrenis
Brain	
general	Thuja, Nat Sulph., Baryta Carb.
swelling	Apis, Cytozyme B

CONDITION	TREATMENT
Bronchitis	Arsenicum Alb., Carbo Veg., Veratrum Alb., chiropractic, acupuncture, Coltsfoot/Wild Cherry formula
Bruising	Arnica, Bellis Perrenis
Burns, scalds	Urtica Urens, Aloe Vera, Calendula, Arsenicum Alb., Vitamin E with honey on burn, Willard Water XXX spray
Cancer	Cancer program & diet
Caesarian, postoperative	Arnica, Bellis Perrenis, Willard Water XXX on surgical site, decrease scar with Vitamin E. Recover
Cataracts	Calc. Carb., Phosphorus, Silicea, Bl. 18, L9, Liv 3, Liver Diet
Circulation	Ferrum Phos., CM, Co-Enzyme Q-10, Heart diet, Cytozyme H
Coldness of body	China, Veratrum Alb., Honey
Colic	Aconite, Carbo Veg., Chamomilla, Nux Vomica
Collapse	Hydrophobinum, Veratrum Alb., Rescue Remedy, GV 26, KI 1, get veterinary help
Concussion, all-head trauma	Aconite + Arnica + Hypericum
Conjunctivitis	Ledum, chamomile, Similsan eyedrops, Euphrasia
Constipation	Alumina, Baryta Carb, Arsenicum, Alb., Lachesis, Lycopodium, Nux Vomica, Sulphur, Veratrum Alb., Natural Diet, LI 4, Bl 28, chiropractor, Para-Yeast supplement

continues

CONDITION	TREATMENT
Convulsions	Rescue Remedy
seizures	Belladonna
pupils dilated	Nux Vomica, Liver Diet
after eating garbage	Circuta Vir., Natural Diet
epilepsy	Homeopathic Detox, Melatonin, Cytozyme B, Liver or Cancer diet
rabies vaccine	Hydrophobinum, Natural Diet
vaccines	Thuja, Homeopathic Detox, Natural Diet
Labradors	Thuja, Chamomilla, Natural Diet
grief, stress	Ignatia, Lung Diet
Coprophagy (stool eating)	Veratrum Alb. Digestive enzymes
in winter	Papaya enzymes, with Vitamin B_6 + Complex, green leafy vegetables
Cornea	Ledum
Coughs	Aconite, Antimonium Tart, Arsenicum Alb., Carbo Veg., China, Phosphorus, Rhus Tox., Lung Diet
Cystitis	Berberis, Urtica Urens, Thlapsi Bursa, Kidney Diet, Cranberry Juice capsules
Cysts	
between toes	Calc. Carb., Silicea, Hepar Sulph., Lachesis, Liver or Heart diet
on body	Silicea, Natural Diet
Dehydration	Arsenicum Alb., China, Veratrum
Dental surgery	Arnica, Hypericum, Chamomilla
Depression	Ignatia, Lachesis, Pulsatilla, Lung Diet
Dermatitis	see Skin.
Diarrhea	Diarrhea Relief, Arsenicum Alb., Bellis Per., Carbo Veg., Chamomila, China, Nat Sulph., sulphur, Veratrum, canned pumpkin, slippery elm bark acidophilus, yogurt, kefir, see veterinarian if diarrhea continues

CONDITION	TREATMENT
Digestive system upsets	Carbo Veg., China, Lycopodium, Nux Vomica, Hydrozyme, Unleash, Natural Diet
Dirt eating	Calc. Carb., Silicea, check for worms
Discharges	Arsenium Alb., China, Lachesis, Nat Sulph., Pulsatilla, Thuja, Urtica Urens
Dog bite	Ledum, Arnica, Hypericum., wash out with Willard Water XXX, Calendula cream. Laser, check to see dog has had rabies vaccination
Dribbling of urine	Thlapsi Bursa, Pericardium diet, seek veterinary help
Dripping nose	Nat Mur., Allium Cepa, Lung diet
Drooling	Hydrophobinum, Kidney Diet
Dry coat	Essential EFAs, parasite detox, Natural or Kidney Diet, Thyroid/Adrenal
Dwarfism—runts	Baryta Carb.
Ears	
mites	Sulphur, Conium, clean with garlic oil mixed with a little olive oil, 5 drops 3 times per day; increase garlic in diet, Sulphur, Conium
yeast infection	Para-Yeast capsules, Conium
discharges	Aconite, Belladonna, amino acids
general	Thuja, Aconite, Arnica, Baryta Carb., Belladonna, Calc. Carb., China, Ferrum Phos., Hepar Sulph., Pulsatilla, IAG, Silicea, Kidney Diet, chiropractic, acupuncture
deafness	Conium, Aconite, Rhus Tox., chiropractic
loss of balance	acupuncture

continues

CONDITION	TREATMENT
Ear flaps	
hot, swollen	Belladonna
hematoma	Arnica 1M + 30c used together, once a week or as needed
red, dry, itchy	Sulphur
deafness, old age	Silicea
E. coli	killed by cinnamon
Eczema	Arsenicum Alb., Rhus Tox., Cicuta Vir., Lycopodium
Edema	Apis
Epilepsy	see Convulsions
Esophagus	
spasms	Baryta Carb., Cicuta Vir.
with breathing difficulties	Antimonium Tart., Lu 2. Feed in elevated dishes.
Eyelids	
inflamed	Pulsatilla
itching	Calc. Carb
styes, ulcerations, swollen	Lycopodium, Belladonna, Rhus Tox.
Eyes	Similisan Eyedrops, Ledum, Aconite, Apis, Arsenicum Alb., Calendula, China, Pulsatilla, Rhus Tox., Symphytum, Thalpsi Bursa, Liver Diet
False Pregnancy	Chamomilla, Pulsatilla, slightly increase calcium levels
Fear	Aconite, Arnica, Phosphorus, Rescue Remedy, Kidney Diet
Feet	Chiropractic, acupuncture
biting at	Lachesis
dragging	Nux Vomica
painful/sore toes/pads	Baryta Carb.
soles of pads raw	Calc. Carb., Willard Water XXX soaks, New Skin to cover cracks

CONDITION	TREATMENT
swollen	Arsenicum Alb.
toes red and swollen	Carbo. Veg.
toes/nails injured	Hypericum, Silicea, Calc. Carb., Thuja
Fever	Aconite, Arsenicum Alb., Belladonna, China, Pulsatilla, Sulphur, Echinacea/Goldenseal blend
Fistulas	Silicea, Thuja
Flatulence/farting	Carbo Veg., Thuja, digestive enzymes, Natural Diet
Flea bite dermatitis	Rhus Tox., Sulphur, Urtica Urens, Scratch Free homeopathic blend, Natural Diet Detox/Allergy herbal blend
Fluid—retention	Apis, increase B complex, Vitamin C
Foaming at mouth	Hydrophobinum
Fractures	Arnica, Symphytum, Laser
Gangrene	Carbo Veg., Lachesis
Gasping for air	Antimonium Tart., Rescue Remedy, chiropractic, acupuncture, Lung Diet
Gastrointestinal	Nux Vomica, Pulsatilla, Thuja., LI4, ST 36, chiropractic
Glands	Calc. Carb., Silicea, Baryta Carb., Belladonna, Conium, Lachesis, Rhus Tox., Sulphur, Glandulars
Glaucoma	Phosphorus
Gout	China, Natural Diet
Gums	Apis, Baryta Carb., Chamomilla, Phosphorus, Silicea, Thuja
Grief	Ignatia, Rescue Remedy
Hair loss	Sulphur, Silicea, Carbo Veg., Baryta Carb., Phosphorus, Natural or Kidney Diet, Amino acid complex

continues

CONDITION	TREATMENT
Head & neck injuries	Cicuta Vir., Lachesis, Natrum Sulph., chiropractic, acupuncture
Heart	Baryta Carb., Ferrum Phos., Lycopodium, Veratrum Alb.
strokes	Conium, Arnica, Lachesis (left side) Kidney or Heart diet, Cytozyme H
Heat	Rescue Remedy
collapse from	Belladonna, GV 26, KI
shock	Aconite
swelling that is hot & shiny	Apis
Heatstrokes	Belladonna
Hematomas (blood blisters)	Arnica
in ears	Arnica 1M + 30c once a week
Hemorrhage	
internal	Arnica, China, Ferrum Phos., Thlaspi Bursa, get veterinary help
external	Crush Ferrum Phos. and put directly on wound
Hepatitis	Lycopodium, Liver diet
Herpes	Rhus Tox., Silicea, Herpes Nosode, Acidophilus, Amino Acid Compled + L-Lysine
Hormonal	check thyroid, adrenal, pituitary
male	Cytozyme M
female	Cytozyme F, Cytozyme O
Hot spots	Calc. Carb., Calendula, Hepar Sulph., Rhus Tox., Sulphur, Urtica Urens, Heart diet, check thyroid/adrenals, ACV, Willard Water XXX
Hypersexuality	China, Hydrophobinum, Natural Diet, Thyroid/Adrenal/Pituitary glandulars
Hypothermia	Aconite and Arnica together

CONDITION	TREATMENT
Hysteria	Belladonna, Rescue Remedy
Immune system	IAG, Cytozyme THY, Cytozyme SP, Golden Seal/Echinacea Blend, get titers on dog before revaccinating, Natural Diet
Incontinence	Conium, Belladonna, Berberis Vulg., Pulsatilla, Equisetum 6c, acupuncture BL 40, KI 3, BL 23, Kidney Diet, chiropractic
Indigestion	Carbo Veg., Cicuta Vir., Hydrozyme
Infections	
bacterial	Bacterial Detox, Cytozyme THY, antibiotics
viral	Viral Detox, Cytozyme THY
Injury	Arnica, Bellis Per., Calendula, Hypericum, Natrum Sulph., Rescue Remedy
Insect bites	Apis (if allergic reaction and swelling), Ledum, Laser, Willard Water XXX
Irritability	Chamomilla, Nux Vom., Sulphur, Arnica, Liver Diet + detox, Rescue Remedy
Jaw dislocation	Rhus Tox., chiropractic
Joints	Apis, Calc. Carb., Carbo Veg., China, Ledum, Nux Vom., Pulsatilla, Rhus Tox., Ruta Grav., Symphytum, Veratrum Alb., CM, Kidney Diet, Alfalfa/Yucca herbal blend
Kennel cough	Arsenicum Alb., Kennel cough nosode
Kidney	Berberis Vulg., Lycopodium, Phosphorus, Thuja, Kidney Diet, Cytozyme KD
Lameness	Rhus Tox., Ruta Grav.

continues

CONDITION	TREATMENT
Laryngitis, chronic	Thuja
Lead poisoning	Arsenicum Alb.
Lick granulomas	Hypericum, Liver diet, acupuncture around lesion, chiropractic
Licking at	
feet and paws	Lachesis, read Five-Element chapters
stiches after surgery	Hypericum
genitals	Lachesis
Ligament	Ruta Grav, Liver Diet, Cytozyme AD
Limping	Conium, Rhus Tox., Ruta Grav.
front end	chiropractic, acupuncture, LI 4, SI 11
rear end	chiropractic, acupuncture, ST 36, GB 34
Liver	Arsenicum Alb., Berberis Vulg., China, Lycopodium, Natrum Sulph., Phosphorus, Sulphur, Liver Diet, Cytozyme LV, acupuncture, chiropractic
Lockjaw	Hypericum and Ledum used together
Lungs	Antimonium Tart., Carbo Veg., Lycopodium, Lung Diet
congestion	Apis, Carbo Veg., Ferrum Phos., Phosphorus, acupuncture, chiropractic
Lymph nodes	
swollen	Calc. Carb., Chamomilla, Conium
tumors	Conium, Lymph Detox, Cytozyme TH
Mammary glands	
inflamed, purplish	Lachesis, antibiotics, go to vet
lumps, hard	Silicea
tumors or swelling	Conium
Mange	Sulphur, Neem products, Ivermectin, Natural Diet, Cytozyme THY
Mastitis	Apis, Belladonna, hot pack, express milk by hand, antibiotics, get to vet.

CONDITION	TREATMENT
Memory loss	Phosphorus, Cytozyme B, DHEA
Mouth	Alumina, Arsenicum Alb., Lycopodium, Rhus Tox., Silicea, Stomach Diet
Mucus, chest, lungs or throat	Antimonium Tart., Carbo Veg., Lycopodium
Muscle twitching	Antimonium Tart., Thuja, Liver Diet, massage, acupuncture, chiropractic
Nails	Silicea, Ledum, Hypericum, Natrum Sulph., Thuja, Liver Diet
Nausea	Antimonium Tart., Nux Vom., Seacure capsules
Neck	chiropractic for all conditions
fatty tumors in	Baryta Carb.
injuries	Natrum Sulph.
stiff	Calc. Carb., Lachesis
too weak to hold up	Veratrum Alb.
Nerve damage	Hypericum
Nervous	Aconite, Calendula, Phosphorus, Ignatia, Rescue Remedy
Nervous system	Cicuta Vir., Hydrophobinum
Nipples	
painful	Chamomilla
sore, ulcerated	Silicea
Nose	Alumina, Arsenicum Alb., Belladonna, Berberis Vulg., Calendula, Natrum Sulph., Pulsatilla, Rhus Tox., Thuja
Older dogs	Baryta Carb., Carbo Veg., Conium, Phosphorus, Veratrum Alb.
Overeating, rich food	Nux Vomica
Pain	Arnica, China, Hypericum
intense sensitivity to	Calendula, Hepar Sulf., Rescue Remedy

continues

CONDITION	TREATMENT
Pancreatitis	Phosphorus, Stomach Diet, Enzymes, Cytozyme PAN
Panosteitis	Pulsatilla, Vitamin C, B complex, Natural Diet, Alfalfa/Yucca Herbal Blend
Panting	Belladonna, Antimonium Tart.
Paralysis	Acupuncture, chiropractic, Natural Diet
general	Hydrophobinum, Phosphorus
back legs	Conium
muscular	Arnica
spinal	Phosphorus, get titers on dog before revaccinating
Parasites	Para-Yeast capsules, Goldenseal/ Echinacea herbal blend, Silicea, Bromelain Plus CLA
Parvo	China, Parvo nosode, fluids, Transfer Diet
Pelvic injury	Bellis Per.
Penis	
discharge	Natrum Sulph, Liver/Kidney Diet
swollen	Rhus Tox.
warts	Antimonium Tart.
Pituitary	Calc. Carb. Cytozyme PT/HPT, Cytozyme B
Pneumonia	Aconite, Arsenicum Alb., Lycopodium, Phosphorus
Poison ivy	Rhus Tox., Willard Water XXX spray
Poison oak	Ledum, Willard Water XXX spray
Poisoning	Arsenicum Alb., Nux Vomica
Postpartum	Acupuncture, chiropractic
traumatic delivery—mother	Bellis Per., Rescue Remedy
difficulty urinating	Apis
hemorrhage	Aconite, Lachesis, Thlapsi Bursa
mismothering	Lachesis, Pulsatilla, Rescue Remedy

Condition	Treatment
retained afterbirth	Pulsatilla
traumatic delivery—puppies	Arnica, Baryta Carb., Rescue Remedy
PRA (progressive retinal atrophy)	Phosphorus, Liver Diet
Pregnancy, inability to walk	Bellis Per.
Pulse	
full bounding	Aconite
thready and weak	China
weak	Lachesis
Puncture wounds	Hypericum, Ledum, Laser
Pupil dilation	Belladonna, Calc. Carb.
Puppy	Rescue Remedy
cold and collapsed	Carbo Veg.
constipation	Veratrum Alb.
diarrhea	Chamomilla, Diarrhea Relief
slow growth, runt	Baryta Carb.
teething	Chamomilla
umbilical hernia	Nux Vomica
Pus	Hepar Sulphur, Silicea
Pyometra	Pulsatilla
Rage	Belladonna, Hydrophobinum, Rescue Remedy, Liver Diet, Amino acid complex
Respiratory	Antimonium Tart., Arsenicum Alb., Carbo Veg., China, Ferrum Phos., Lycopodium, Phosphorus, Colts Foot/ Wild Cherry herbal formula, chiropractic
Restlessness	Arsenicum Alb., Chamomilla, Rescue Remedy, Phosphorus, Kidney Diet
Rotten food	Arsenicum Alb., Nux Vomica, Veratrum Alb.
Runt of litter	Baryta Carb.

continues

CONDITION	TREATMENT
Salivation	Baryta Carb., Berberis Vulg., Cicuta Vir., Hydrophobinum, check pH of diet
Scars	Silicea, Vitamin E on scar, acupuncture around scar
Scratching	see Skin.
Seizures	see Convulsions.
Separation anxiety	Ignatia, Rescue Remedy, Lavender pillows, Lavender spray, Cytozyme AD, check thyroid/adrenal/pituitary
Shock	Aconite, Arnica, Carbo Veg., Ignatia, Veratrum Alb., Rescue Remedy
Shyness	Pulsatilla, Silicea, Lavender pillow, exercise, Cytozyme PT/HPT, Kidney Diet. Check thyroid/adrenal, Rescue Remedy
Sinus	Silicea, Neutrophil Plus, IAG, Bacteria Detox
Skin	Alumina, Apis, Arnica, Arsenicum Alb., Calc. Carb., Carbo Veg., Cicuta Vir., Hepar Sulphur, Lachesis, Lycopodium, Natrum Sulph., Phosphorus, Rhus Tox., Silicea, Sulphur, Thuja, Urtica Urens., Veratrum Alb., Heart or Lung Diet, Detox, ACV, Willard Water XXX, titer dog before vaccinating again, acupuncture, chiropractic
Sound sensitivity	Aconite, Belladonna, China, Nux Vomica, Phosphorus, Kidney Diet, chiropractic
Spinal injuries	Conium, Hypericum, Ruta Grav., Rescue Remedy, acupuncture, chiropractic

CONDITION	TREATMENT
Spleen	Arsenicum Alb., Bellis Per., Urtica Urens, China, Stomach Diet, acupuncture, chiropractic
Splinters	Silicea
Sprains	Arnica, Bellis Per., Rhus Tox., Ruta Grav., Laser
Staggering	Alumina, Rescue Remedy
Staring at objects	Cicuta Vir., Veratrum Alb.
Stings	Apis, Ledum, Laser, Willard Water XXX
Stomach rumbling	Cicuta Vir., Pulsatilla, Thuja
Stool eating	Veratrum Alb., Natural diet, digestive enzymes, fresh herbs or greens in food
Stools	Chiropractic or acupuncture
chalky	Belladonna
contain grain-like pieces	Phosphorus
green and watery	Chamomilla
involuntary	Arnica
small, dark	Arsenicum Alb.
small, hard	Lycopodium
yellow, frothy	China
yellow, smelly	Bellis Per.
Stress	Ignatia, Lycopodium, Rescue Remedy, Calm Stress, Tranquility Herbal Blend, Acute or Chronic Stress Homeopathic blend, Valerian Root capsules
Surgery	Arnica, Bellis Per., Calendula, China, Hypericum, Rhus Tox., Veratrum Alb., Feverfew/Skullcap
Sweating	China, Belladonna, Thyroid
Swelling	Apis, Conium, Rhus Tox.
Tail injury	Hypericum

continues

CONDITION	TREATMENT
Teeth	
abscessed	Chamomilla
extraction	Arnica, Calendula, Hypericum
retained puppy	Silicea, Calc. Carb.
tartar	Fragaria, Natural Diet
Teething—pain & irritability	Chamomilla
Telescoping of organs	Veratrum Alb.
Tendons	Rhus Tox., Ruta Grav., Arnica, Hypericum, Lachesis, Symphytum, CM, balance board
Testicles	
hardened	Baryta Carb.
pain in	Berberis Vulg.
swollen	Silicea
Tetanus	Ledum
Thirst	
increased	Aconite, Arsenicum Alb., Belladonna, Calc. Carb., Chamomilla, Lycopodium, Rhus Tox., Veratrum Alb., Kidney Diet
decreased	Apis, Carbo Veg., Ignatia, Pulsatilla
Thunderstorms	Aconite, Phosphorus, Borax, Rhododendrum, Rescue Remedy
Thyroid	Calc. Carb. Iodum, GTA, Medastim, Heart Diet, Seloxine, chiropractic, acupuncture
Tongue, blister on	Lycopodium
Tonsils	Apis, Baryta Carb., Belladonna, Calc. Carb., Chamomilla, Ferrum Phos., Rhus Tox.
Toxin exposure	Nux Vomica

CONDITION	TREATMENT
Trembling	Antimonium Tart., Conium, Thuja
Tremors & twitching of	
muscles	Antimonium Tart., Belladonna, Thuja, Liver Diet
Tumors	Arsenicum Alb., Calc. Carb., Conium, Thuja, Natural Diet
Ulcers	Arsenicum Alb., Calc. Carb., Carbo Veg., Hepar Sulph., Lachesis, Lycopodium, Phosphorus, Nat. Diet, Symphytum, Thuja, Silicea
Umbilical hernias	Calc. Carb., Nux Vomica
Urinary	Kidney diet, parsley, cranberries
acute infection	Belladonna
calculi	Calc. Carb., Lycopodium, Berberis Vulg., Thlapsi Bursa
inflammation of tract	Thlapsi Bursa, Urtica Urens
obstruction	Apis
retention	
Urine	Kidney diet, acpuncture, chiropractic
dribbling, males	Conium
drips instead of stream	Berberis Vulg., Thlapsi Bursa
involuntary	Pusatilla
with gray mucus	Berberis Vulg.
with mucus, frequent,	
colorless	Sulphur
with sediment	Lycopodium
Vaccines	Thuja, Silicea, Pulsatilla, Ledum, Nosodes, Detox Virus
rabies vaccine	Hydrophobinum, use if dog has never been the same since vaccine

continues

CONDITION	TREATMENT
Vomiting	
yellow bile	Natrum Sulph., Chamomilla, small meals, often. Stomach Diet, feed before 7:00 a.m. or after 9:00 a.m.
in general	Antimonium Tart., Arsenicum Alb., Belladonna, China, Ferrum Phos., Nux Vomica, Phosphorus, Veratrum Alb.
Warts	Antimonium Tart., Calc. Carb., Thuja, Silicea
Weakness	Rescue Remedy
overall	Arsenicum Alb., Lachesis
back legs	Conium
in general	Antimonium Tart., Hypericum
Wounds	Calendula, Arnica, Ferrum Phos., Hypericum, Lachesis, Ledum, Phosphorus, Laser, acupuncture, Willard Water XXX, Rescue Remedy
Yeast infections	Para-Yeast capsules, Fungal/Yeast Detox, Colostrum, Vitamin E

Appendix II
Sources of Ingredients
& Products

The sources of the products listed below are those that are referred to in the text, as well as others that we use. Each of the products are used for a very specific reason, and in some instances companies have worked with us to make available what we needed. While other products can be substituted, we have not tried these.

Some of the suppliers have changed from the first edition of this book. For example, the PHD Company now carries the "Quality of Life" products. The names may have changed, but the products are still the same ones we used in our original testing. The product line has even expanded in the last few years. There are several other companies that have copied these formulas, but again, we have not tried these products.

DOG & CAT FOOD, NATURAL DIET FOUNDATION, VITAMIN & MINERAL MIXES, HOMEOPATHIC EMERGENCY KIT

PHD Products
P.O. Box 8313
White Plains, NY 10602
1-800-743-1502
Web page: phdproducts.com

Dog and cat food, dog biscuits; Natural Diet Foundation; Colostrum; Comfort; Homeopathic Emergency Kit; Para-Yeast Control; Radiance— Skin & Coat; Recover; Soothe— herbal oils for skin; Unleash— Enzymes; vitamin C and B complex; Wellness—Vitamin/Mineral Mix

Nature's Most
60 Trigo Drive
Middletown, CT 06457
1-800-234-2112

DHEA, amino acid complex, Kyolic garlic, pancreatic enzymes, melatonin, vitamin E

Bronson Pharmaceuticals
1945 Craig Road,
P.O. Box 46903
St. Louis, MO 63146-6903
1-800-235-3200

Deodorized garlic tablets, garlic capsules, vitamin E

L & H Vitamins
37-10 Crescent Street
Long Island City, NY 11101
1-800-221-1152

Similasan homeopathic eyedrops, Bach Flower Remedies, Willard Water, kefir starter

ORGANICALLY GROWN GRAINS & INGREDIENTS FOR THE NATURAL DIET

Many quality ingredients can be bought through your local health food store. The following companies will deliver directly to your door.

Walnut Acres
Penns Creek, PA 17862
1-800-433-3998

Organic grains

Frontier Natural Products
Norway, IA 52318-0299
1-800-669-3275

Kelp, nutritional yeast, raw wheat germ

HERBS

Most health food stores and some supermarkets stock herbs that you can buy in small amounts. Store tightly sealed, in a cool, dry place or in the freezer.

Blessed Herbs
109 Barre Plains Rd.
Oakham, MA 01068
1-800-489-HERBS
Fax: 508-882-3839

Organically grown herbs

Mountain Rose Herbs
20818 High Street
North San Juan, CA 95960
e-mail: http://botanical.com/mtrose

Organic herbs sold in small quantities. Also stock Greg & Mary Wulff-Tilford's herbal compounds. Write or call 1-800-879-3337 for catalog.

Seeds of Change
P.O. Box 15700
Sante Fe, MN 875-6
1-888-762-7333

Organic seeds to grow your own

Horizon Herbs
P.O. Box 69
Williams, OR 97544-0069
Phone: 541-845-6704
Fax: 541-846-6233

Nonprofit organization, member of Plant Savers

BONE MEAL & COD-LIVER OIL

UPCO
3705 Pear Street
Box 969
St. Joseph, MO 64502
1-800 254-8726

Cod-liver oil is called "Codivet,"
Bone Meal

NATURAL PET PRODUCTS

Bearpath Pet Products
139 Jewel Road
Canajoharie, NY 13317
518-673-5047
e-mail: bearpath@capital.net

Nature's Most products, PHD Products, Nature's Sunshine Herbal capsules

Naturmix, US., Inc.
P.O. Box 682
Cummings, GA 30128
1-800-825-1669

Neem flea and tick products, Specialized enzymes, Natural treats

HOMEOPATHICS

Newton Labs 1-800-448-7256	Homeopathic remedies in bulk. Save your bottles from the emergency kit, and refill from these bottles.

HOMEOPATHIC DETOXIFIERS

GLANDULARS, SPECIALIZED PRODUCTS

Moss Nutrition 2 Bay Road, Suite 102 Hadley, MA 01035 1-800-851-5444	Cytozyme Glandulars, Seacure, Mixed EFAs, specialized Chinese and Ayurvedic herbs. Hydrozyme, Homeopathic cleansers for detox from: vaccines, allergies, chemicals, heavy metals, worms, tick-borne diseases, viruses and bacteria. Bromelain Plus, Pro-Green—herbal powder. All Biotics Research products. Five-Element Herbal Teas

Mentioned in Appendix IV, "Interpretation of Blood Work & Urinalysis," and throughout the text, these products should be used under the guidance of your veterinarian or health care professional. Dogs can be tested with kinesiology to determine exact dosages and the length or treatment, which in most cases is short.

Homeovetix P.O. Box 8243 Naples, FL 1-800-677-4439	Homeopathics used with puppies, Supportasode, Viratox

INDIVIDUAL REPLACEMENT HOMEOPATHIC REMEDIES FOR EMERGENCY KIT (BOIRON)

Bigelow Chemists
1-800-793-5433

HOMEOPATHIC NOSODES

Hahnemann Laboratories
1940 Fourth St.
San Rafael, CA 94901
415-451-6978
Fax: 415-451-6981
1-888-427-6422

Homeopathic Mixtures
Very Healthy Enterprises
Dr. Goodpet products
1-800-222-9932

Calm Stress, Diarrhea Relief, Scratch
Free, Flea Relief, Digestive Enzymes

ARTHRITIS

EHP Company
P.O. Box 1306
Ashland, KY 41105-1306
1-888-EHP 0100

CM (Cetyl Myristoleate), Salmon Oil

HOMEMADE DOG BISCUITS

Best Bones
P.O. Box 502
Cambridge, NY 12816
518-677-3564

Our dogs' favorite biscuits. Many
hypoallergenic recipes.

BOOKS

DogWise
8 Summercreek Place
P.O. Box 3073
Wenatchee, WA 98807
1-800-776-2665

Handles all our books and videos,
plus a wonderful selection of books
on pet-related subjects.

Dr. Sue Ann Lesser, D.V.M., CAC
20 Burgess Ave.,
S. Huntington, NY 11746
Fax: 516-549-7760
Hearts, Hands and Hounds, Sue Ann
Lesser, DVM, CAC 1997

Canine bodywork and massage. Send
check or money order: $12 plus $3.50
postage and handling.

Redwing Book Company
44 Linden Street
Brookline, MA 02146
617-738-4664

A good source for alternative modality books. Write for catalog.

B. Jain Publishers Overseas
1920 Chuna Mandi, Street 10th
Pahraganj, Post Box 5775
New Delhi—110055
India
Fax: 91-11-7510471

This company carries many inexpen-
sive homeopathic and medical texts
that are printed on thin paper. Write
for a catalog.

Bowtie Press
1-800-426-2516
*All You Ever Wanted to Know About
Herbs for Your Pet.* Mary Wulff-
Tilford and Greg Tilford, Bowtie
Press.

Catherine O'Driscoll
http://www.ourpets.com/books/
vacbook.html
*What Vets Don't Tell You About
Vaccines*, 2nd edition. Catherine
O'Driscoll, Abbeywood Publishing,
England, 1998.

HERBAL & DECORATIVE COLLARS, LAVENDER PILLOWS

Barking Bear
http://www.barkingbear.com

LIGHTS

KIVA LIGHTS

Kimo International Vitalized Association, Inc.
912 Broadway NE
Albuquerque, NM 87102
505-242-5200

(Full spectrum plus blue). These lights keep down the bacterial count in the environment. Place over counters and sinks. Excellent for use in kennels, veterinary hospitals, etc.

FULL SPECTRUM LIGHTS

Use anywhere dogs are housed, also in kitchen, offices, etc. Can be found at most good lighting stores.

PH STRIPS, NEW SKIN

Available through drugstores, L & H Vitamins or your veterinarian.

ASSOCIATIONS—WRITE FOR PRACTITIONERS IN YOUR AREA

American Holistic Veterinary Medical Association
2218 Old Emmorton Road
Bel Air, MD 21015
410-569-0795

Directory of practicing veterinarians who offer holistic services, including acupuncture, homeopathy and chiropractic. This Association puts out an excellent magazine that anyone can buy. Membership is open to everyone. Write the Association for more details.

American Veterinary Chiropractic Association
623 Main St.
Hillsdale, IL 61257
309-658-2920

ANIMAL POISON CONTROL CENTER

1-900-680-0000
Web page:
http://www.napcc.aspca.org

If for any reason your dog gets into something toxic, here is the phone number of the Animal Poison Control Center. It costs $45 for a consultation. Available 24 hours.

Appendix III
Vitamins & Minerals

Vitamins				
Nutrient	**Found In**	**Nutritional Function**	**Works With**	**Deficiency Signs— Shows Up In**
Vitamin A	Liver, eggs, yogurt, kefir, carrots, yellow fruit, green leafy vegetables	Eyes, mucous membranes, gums, skin, teeth, bone & hair growth, resistance to infections, antioxidant, immune booster	Vitamins B complex, choline, C, D, E & F, zinc	Eye diseases, dry skin & coat, nerve damage, susceptibility to infection, allergies and fatigue. Too much Vitamin A can be toxic.
B complex, B1, 2, 3, 5, 6, 9, 12, 13, 15, 17 with Folic Acid, Biotin, Choline, Inositol and PABA	Liver, milk, eggs, brewer's yeast, wheat bran and germ, kelp, molasses, kidney & heart NOTE: Made up of many individual parts, this vitamin should be fed in the complex form. If one of the parts is isolated it should be fed with the complex and not more than 30 days without checking to see if it is still needed.	Promotes growth and healing after surgery, fights motion sickness, stress, cracks around the mouth, many skin conditions. Needed in the correct utilization of protein and functioning of digestive tract. Prevents hyperactivity, herpes, stool eating, dry flaking skin, doggy drool, birth defects. Needed by adrenal glands. Promotes good pigmentation & antibody response. Prevents graying, cholesterol buildup, hemorrhage, allergies and deficiencies caused by vegetarian diets.	All other vitamins and minerals	Poor pigmentation, constipation, skin conditions, neuritis, hair loss and early graying, weakness of back legs, loss of appetite, stool eating, poor immune system, attracting fleas, ticks, worms and parasites. Lack of ability to deal with stress, poor reaction to vaccines, inability to digest and utilize protein.
Vitamin C	Fruits, vegetables, parsley, watercress, melons, grasses and weeds. Needs to be supplemented daily in your dog's diet. Use calcium ascorbate which is buffered.	Protects against allergies, viral diseases. Antioxidant, needed for hair, skin, blood vessels, bones, collagen production, gums and teeth. Promotes wound healing, needed by females in season, older dogs and puppies. Counteracts side effects from drugs.	All other vitamins and minerals	Urinary tract and skin infections, bladder stones, poor immune or musculoskeletal system. Can only work with correct protein in each meal.

293

Vitamins

Nutrient	Found In	Nutritional Function	Works With	Deficiency Signs— Shows Up In
Vitamin D	Yogurt, kefir, fish. Small amounts found in dark, green leafy vegetables	Calcium and phosphorus absorption, proper bone growth. Acts as a hormone and works with the parathyroid to regulate calcium.	Calcium and phosphorus, vitamins A, C, F & choline	Rickets, bone growth abnormalities, heart disease, strokes, blood vessel disorders
Vitamin E	Whole wheat, wheat germ, safflower oil, green leafy vegetables, lettuce, alfalfa	Circulation, antioxidant, health of skin, hair and reproductive organs— pregnancy, sperm count	Selenium, Manganese, vitamins B complex, A, C	Reproductive disorders, destruction of red blood cells, heart and circulatory problems, elevated creatinine levels, retinal degeneration
Vitamin F	Cold-pressed safflower oil, nuts oils, flax seed oil, evening primrose and black currant oils, fish oils	To provide enough linoleic acid to the system to maintain health of mucous membranes, healthy skin and coat. Lowers triglycerides and cholesterol levels and reduces risks of heart attacks and strokes.	Phosphorus, vitamins A, C, D, & E	Diseases of bones, teeth. High fat levels in blood, poor skin and hair coat, dandruff, some forms of T-cell immune mediated diseases, such as arthritis of all kinds, some gastrointestinal disorders & lupus.

Minerals

Nutrient	Found In	Nutritional Function	Works With	Deficiency Signs—Shows Up In
Calcium	Goat's milk, egg shells, yogurt, kefir, green leafy vegetables	Bones, teeth, iron stores, heart function, blood clotting, ability to relax	A, C, D, F, sodium magnesium, iron, phosphorus, potassium	Bones, teeth, sore muscles, nerves, palpitations, parathyroid problems
Chlorine	Vit/min mix, cabbage, parsnips	Digestion of protein, acid/alkaline balance, liver detox, antiparasitic	Sodium, potassium	Tooth and hair loss, digestive and muscle disorders, Cushing's disease, obesity
Chromium	Liver, chicken, brewer's yeast, brown rice	Insulin regulator, circulatory system, carbohydrate metabolism, thyroid & adrenal glands	Insulin	Carboydrate metabolism disorders, heart problems
Copper	Liver, raisins, green leafy vegetables	Enzyme activity, hair, skin and cell growth, iron absorption, healing, formation of adrenal hormones	Zinc, Iron	Retarded growth, skin & respiratory problems, loss of pigmentation, premature graying, poor thyroid/adrenal function
Iodine	Egg yolks, vit/min mix, swiss chard, turnip greens, watercress	Rate of metabolism	Protein, carbohydrates, tyrosine (amino acid)	Thyroid problems, black skin, symmetrical bilateral hair loss, sluggishness, overweight
Iron	Liver, vit/min mix, brewer's yeast, raisins, eggs, dark green leafy vegetables	Oxygen to muscles, hemoglobin, iron stores in cells	C, B complex, calcium, copper	Anemia, fatigue, infertility, brittle nails, legs twitching
Magnesium	Vit/min mix, apples, safflower oil, green leafy vegetables	Calcium & vitamin C absorption, strong nerves, bones, muscles, teeth, heart, needed for sodium and potassium transport	C, D, B6, D, Calcium, Phosphorus, Protein	Poor appetite, aggression, nervousness, heart disease, rage syndromes, seizures, cancer, muscle twitching
Manganese	Whole grain cereals, eggs, green leafy vegetables, peas, beets	Anti-inflammatory, counteracts fatigue, irritability, dizziness, poor memory, activates enzymes, used in bone production	B vitamins, calcium, phosphorus, not usually isolated	Glandular dysfunctions, thyroid disorders, disc degeneration, seizures, poor muscle coordination, aggression
Phosphorus	Milk products, eggs, beef, chicken, fish, turkey, whole grains, brewer's yeast, wheat germ and bran	Cell, bone & hair growth. Carbohydrate metabolism, brain function, formation of tooth enamel	Calcium, A, D, F, iron and proteins	Bone & teeth disorders, weakness, poor nervous system, excessive shedding

Minerals (cont.)

Nutrient	Found In	Nutritional Function	Works With	Deficiency Signs—Shows Up In
Potassium	Bananas, potatoes, green leafy vegetables, bee pollen, alfalfa, parsley, brown rice, sea salt, dried apricots and dates	Balance of body fluids, regulates acid/alkaline base, muscle and nerve impulses	Sodium, vitamin B	Kidney & heart problems, muscle weakness in right rear, paralysis of neck and forelegs, water retention, Cushing's disease
Selenium	Organic grains, brewer's yeast, wheat bran, broccoli, tuna, vit/min mix	Antioxidant, fertility–female, sperm production, tissue elasticity	Vitamin E	Premature aging, male sexual dysfunction, heart, cancer, liver and muscle diseases
Silicon	Stems of grasses and weeds, Boston lettuce, parsnips, buckwheat, millet, oats, cucumber rind peel, carrots, dirt	Wound healing, nails, skin disorders, pushes pus out of body. Helps to bring abscesses, boils and pustules to a head.	N/A	Epilepsy, worms, poor hair coat, crooked poorly formed teeth & brittle nails. Dogs that eat dirt are often deficient in silicon
Sodium	Vit/min mix, table salt, celery, carrots, beets, cucumbers, zucchini, apples, asparagus	Enzyme activity, adrenal glands, iron absorption, healing process, skin, hair and cell growth	Zinc, iron, potassium, chloride	Improper fluid levels, Addison's disease, retarded growth, respiratory, dry skin and hair loss
Zinc	Beef, liver, fish, whole grains, carrots, beets, cabbage	B complex and insulin activity, skin healing, DNA & RNA synthesis	Copper, calcium, phosphorus, vitamin A	Browning out of coat color, skin lesions, dry eye, poor wound healing, allergies, senility and fatigue

Appendix IV
Interpretation of Blood Work & Urinalysis

The following is based on established normal laboratory analysis of blood work and urinalysis for dogs by Antech Diagnostics and Vet Research Labs.

The interpretation of the blood work is based on our own work, plus the research of Harry Eidenier, Ph.D., on over 50,000 humans. The suggested products, all of which we have used successfully, are made by Biotics Research in Texas, available through Moss Nutrition 1-800-851-5444.

These products are a starting point for kinesiology testing to determine your dog's needs. Normally, one product will test more strongly than others. Using more than one product at a time is unusual, and nearly all of them are used only for short time frames.

When looking at blood work, do not rely on one test being out of the normal range to determine a diseased state. Compare the test results and look for patterns. Work closely with your veterinarian to get a true diagnosis.

COMPLETE BLOOD COUNT (CBC)

Test	Range	Increased In	Decreased In	Supplemental Support If Increased	Supplemental Support If Decreased
Total WBC (white blood cells)	4.0–15.5	Leukocytosis. Active bacterial infections. Blood disorders. Overactive adrenals.	Leukopenia. Chronic bacterial/viral infections. Toxicities. Metabolic disorders. Underactive adrenals.	Bio-Immunozyme Forte. Dismuzyme Granules. Cytozyme-THY. IGA. ADP. Bacteria or Virus Homeopathic.	Same as Increased.
Neutrophils	3.0–11.4	Stress. Inflammation. Bacterial infections. Tissue necrosis. Overactive adrenals.	Toxemia. Viral infections. Bone marrow depression. Overwhelming bacterial infection. Underactive adrenals.	Same as WBC.	Same as WBC.
Neutrophil Bands	0–3.0	Active infection.	Not applicable	Same as WBC >. Increase Cytozyme-THY and IGA while Bands are >.	Not applicable
Lymphocytes	690–4500	Chronic inflammation/ infection. Recovery from acute infection. Leukemia. Underactive adenals.	Stress. Steroid or chemotherapy treatment. Overactive adrenals.	Same as WBC.	Same as WBC >. see Albumin <.
Eosinophils	0–1200	Allergic/sensitivity reactions. Parasites. Eosinophillic inflammation. Underactive adrenals.	Stress. Steroid treatment. Overactive adrenals.	Parasites A.D.P. Bromelain Plus. CLA. Herbal Support. HCL Plus. Methionine-200. Allergy/Sensitivity Bio-AE Mulsion Forte. Bio-Immunozyme Forte. HCL Plus. Ara-6.	Not applicable

COMPLETE BLOOD COUNT (CBC)

Test	Range	Increased In	Decreased In	Supplemental Support If Increased	Supplemental Support If Decreased
Monocytes	0–150	In stress. Granulomas. Tissue necrosis. Chronic inflammation. Steroid treatment.		Infection *see* WBC >. Parasites *see* Eosinophils >.	Not applicable
Basophils	0.0–0.1 x 10.3	Heartworm disease. Hyperlipidermia. Overactive adrenals.	Not applicable	Parasites *see* Eosinophils >.	Not applicable
Platelets	2.0–6.0 x 10.5 (listed as normal to low)	Free radical damage. Bone marrow overproduction (cancer).	Immune dysfunction. Lupus. Hemolytic anemia. Severe hemorrhage-intravascular coagulation.	Polycythemia Super Phosphozyme. Intenzyme Forte. Neonatal Multi-Gland. Livotrit-Plus. Beta-TCP.	*see* Gamma Globulin <.
RBC Red Blood Cell Count	4.8–9.3	Dehydration. Too many red blood cells. Polycythemia.	Anemia.	Polycythemia *see* Platelets increased. Dehydration. Increase water intake. Eliminate dairy, grains. Emphysema *see* Alpha 1 Globulin <.	*see* Serum Iron <, change to check.
Hematocrit or Packed Cell Volume (PCV)	36.8–54	Dehydration. Overproduction of red blood cells.	Reduced bone marrow production. Hemorrhage. Autoimmune hemolytic anemia. Vitamin B12. Iron deficiencies. Parasites.	*see* RBC >. HCL Plus. Ara-6.	*see* Serum Iron <, change to check.
Reticulocytes	0–1.5%	Chronic hemorrhage. Chronic hemolytic anemia.	Chronic anemia. Bone marrow not producing red blood cells.	FE-Zyme. Bio MultiPlus.	Not applicable

CHEMISTRY SCREEN

Test	Range	Increased In	Decreased In	Supplemental Support If Increased	Supplemental Support If Decreased
Glucose	70–138	Diabetes mellitus. Thiamine need. Overactive adrenals. Excess progesterone. Stress.	Hypoglycemia. Glycogen storage disease. Pancreatic tumors. Underactive adrenals. Chronic liver disease. Excessive exercise. Long-term starvation.	Glucobalance. Mixed EFAs. Bio-38-G.	Bio-Glycozyme Forte. Bio-38-G. Aminogen.
Blood, Urea, Nitrogen (BUN) Kidney	6–25	Acute/chronic renal failure. Heart disease. Underactive adrenal. Shock. Aging, postrenal obstruction.	Liver disease. Low protein diet. Steroid use.	Renal-Plus. Argizme.	Protein Need. Hydrozyme. Aminogen. Gamoctapro. Pregnancy see Calcium >.
Creatinine (Kidney)	0.5–1.6	Renal dysfunction as BUN.	Pregnancy. Bone growth. Rarely seen.	Renal Dysfunction see Bun >.	Not applicable
Total Protein	5.0–7.4	Dehydration. Cancer of lymph nodes. Cancer of bone marrow.	Kidney disease. Liver disease. Malabsorption syndrome. Starvation.	Hydrozme. Aminogen.	Hydrozyme. Aminogen. Gamoclapro.
Albumin	2.7–4.4	Dehydration. Liver dysfunction.	Chronic liver or pancreatic disease. Hemorrhage. Kidney disease. Burns. Need for vitamin C.	Increase water ingestion. Livotrit.	IAG. Bio-C Plus 1000. Bio-Immunozyme Forte. Dismuzyme Granules. Livtrit-Plus. Cytozyme-THY. Bioprotect. Retenzyme.
Globulin	1.6–3.6	Chronic infection/ inflammation. Multiple myeloma. Lymphosarcoma. Parasites. Liver disease.	Immunodeficiency. Intestinal inflammation. Hemorrhage.	Hydrozyme.	Gastrazyme for 30 days then Hydrozyme.
Alkaline Phosphatase	5–131 Can be higher during growth	Obstructive/ congestive liver disease. Overactive adrenals. Steroid/ anticonvulsant medications. Pre-cancer state.	Lack of zinc.	Bone Loss see Calcium >. Liver Dysfunction see SGPT >.	ZN-Zyme Forte. Bio-Glycozyme Forte.

CHEMISTRY SCREEN

Test	Range	Increased In	Decreased In	Supplemental Support If Increased	Supplemental Support If Decreased
ALT (SGPT)	12-118	Liver cell damage (Necrosis). Acute Pancreatitis.	Vitamin B6 deficiency.	Livotrit-Plus. Cytozyme-LV. Beta-Plus or Beta-TCP.	B6 Phosphate.
AST (SGOT)	15–66	Liver damage. Heart muscle damage. Skeletal muscle injury.	Vitamin B6 deficiency.	Cardiac Stress Bio-Cardiozyme Forte. COQ Zyme 30. Bioprotect. Muscle damage Chondroplus. Bio-CMP. Bioprotect. Liver Dysfunction see SGPT >.	B6 Phosphate. Bio-B 100.
Total Bilirubin	0.1–0.3	Bile duct obstruction. Fatty liver. Biliary stasis destruction of red blood cells. Spleen dysfunction.	Not significant	Livotrit-Plus. Cytozyme-SP. beta-TCP. Intenzyme Forte.	Not applicable
GGT	1–12	Bile duct obstruction. Pancreatitis.	Vitamin B6 deficiency.	Vitamin B-6. MG-ZYME. Bio-C Plus. Cytozyme-PAN.	Not applicable
Cholesterol	92–324	Hypothyroid. Overactive adrenals. Bile duct obstructions.	Glandular hyperfunction. Vegetarian diets. Free radical pathology.	Same as Triglycerides >.	see Albumin <.
Triglycerides	29–291	Diabetes mellitus. Underactive adrenals. Hypothyroid. Diets too high in carbohydrates.	Not applicable	Dysinsulinism. Glucobalance. Mixed EFAs. Gamoctapro.	see Albumin <.
Amylase	290–1125	Pancreatitis. Bile duct obstruction. Salivary gland disease. Stomach problems. Obstruction in intestines.	Not applicable	Reduce carbohydrates. Unleash. Digestive enzymes.	Add grains or starch-producing vegetables.

CHEMISTRY SCREEN *(cont.)*

Test	Range	Increased In	Decreased In	Supplemental Support If Increased	Supplemental Support If Decreased
Lipase	77–695	Acute pancreatitis. Upper intestinal inflammation.	Not applicable	Unleash. Digestive enzymes.	Not applicable
Creatinine Phospho-kinase (CPK/CK)	59–895 Normally lower in females May be higher during growth	Heart muscle damage. Skeletal muscle damage. Brain damage.	Not applicable	Cardiac Damage see SGOT >. Muscle Damage see SGOT >. Brain/Nerve Damage Cytozyme-B. Phosphatidy-choline. Aminogen. MG-Zyme. Nucleozyme Forte.	Not applicable
Calcium	8.9–11.4 May be higher during growth	Bone tumors. Kidney failure. Underactive adrenals. Thyroid/Parathy-roid dysfunction. Vitamin D toxicity. Early signs of cancer in lymph glands.	Acute pancreatitis. Hypothyroid. Hypoparathyroidism. Uremia/kidney failure. Pregnancy.	CA-MG Plus. Super Phosphozyme. MG-Zyme. Check TSH to determine further support.	CA/MG Plus. Thyroid Dysfunction. see T-3 Uptake.
Phosphorus	2.5–6.0 May be higher during growth	Kidney failure. Overactive thyroid. Underactive parathyroid. Vitamin D toxicosis. Bone growth or repair.	Diabetic ketoacidosis. Primary hyperparathyroidism. Malnutrition. Malabsorption. Need for amino acids.	see BUN >.	Hydrozyme. Super Phosphozyme. Aminogen.
Sodium	139–154	Dehydration. Salt poisoning. Use of water softeners.	Underactive adrenals. Kidney disease. Liver dysfunction. Diabetes mellitus. Pancreatitis. Vomiting/diarrhea. Low salt diet.	Increase water ingestion. Support as indicated under BUN >.	see Potassium >.
Potassium	3.6–5.5	Kidney disease. Urethral blockage. Dehydration. Underactive adrenals. Acidosis. Tissue destruction.	Prolonged vomiting/diarrhea. Diabetes mellitus. Acute kidney failure. Use of diuretics. Overactive adrenals.	Adrenal Hypo-Function. Cytozyme-AD. Bio-Glycozyme Forte. Renal Dysfunction.	Adrenal Hyper-Function Cytozyme PT/HPT. ADHS. Bio-CMP.

URINALYSIS

Test	Range	Increased In	Decreased In
WBC	0–few seen	Inflammation of genitourinary tract. Kidney infection.	
pH	6.0–7.0 (lower in a.m. higher in p.m.)	Alkaline urine. Cystitis. Diet high in carbohydrates.	Acidosis. High meat diet. Values should not be taken alone to determine acid/alkaline balance.
Protein (Albumin)	0–4+	Extreme exercise. Excessive dietary protein. Urinary tract hemorrhage. Kidney failure.	Dilute urine. Chronic kidney disease. Infection. Inflammation or tumors in lower urinary tract.
Glucose		Hyperglycemia. Stress. Diabetes mellitus. Malnutrition. Steroid therapy. Overactive adrenals.	
Ketones		Diabetes. High fat diet. Starvation.	Not applicable
Bilirubin		Liver disease. Bile duct obstruction. Reflux. Cancer.	Not applicable
RBC		Hemorrhage in genitourinary tract. Inflammation. Trauma.	Not applicable
Specific Gravity (concentration)	1.030 to 1.050	Dehydration. Diabetes mellitus. Severe vomiting/diarrhea. Severe hemorrhage.	Diabetes insipidus. Overactive adrenals. Pyometra. Steroid therapy. Extreme thirst.

Bibliography

Balch, James F., and Phyllis A. Balch. *Prescription for Nutritional Healing.* 2nd ed.. Garden City Park: New York: Avery Publishing, 1993, 2nd edition 1997.

Belfield, Wendell O., and Zucker, Martin. *How To Have a Healthier Dog.* New YorkGarden City, NY: Doubleday & Co.Inc., 1981.

Chaitow, Leon. *Thorsons Guide to Amino Acids.* London: Harper Collins, 1991.

Day, Christopher. *The Homeopathic Treatment of Small Animals.* Saffron Walden, England: C.W. Daniel Co.Ltd., 1992.

Diamond, John. *Your Body Doesn't Lie.* New York: Harper and Row, 1979.

Dodds, W.J. "Autoimmune Thyroid Disease." *Dog World,* 77 no. 4 (1992): 36–40.

Gerber, Richard. *Vibrational Medicine: New Choices of Healing Ourselves.* Santa Fe, NM: Bear and Company, 1988.

Haas, Elson. *Staying Healthy with Nutrition.* Berkeley, CA: Celestial Arts, 1992.

Hall, Dorothy. *Iridology: How the Eyes Reveal Your Health and Your Personality.* New Canaan, CT: Keats Publishing, 1981.

Jarvis, D.C. *Folk Medicine.* New York: Fawcett Books, 1988.

Levy, Juliette de Bairacli. *Common Herbs for Natural Health.* New York: Schocken Books, 1974.

Levy, Juliette de Bairacli. *The Complete Herbal Book for the Dog and Cat.* 6th ed. Winchester: Faber & Faber, Ltd., 1991.

Macleod, G. *A Veterinary Materia Medica and Clinical Repertory with a Materia Medica of the Nosodes.* Saffron Walden,: England.: C.W. Daniel Co. Ltd., 1983.

National Research Council Study on Dog Nutrition. *Nutrient Requirement of Dogs.* Rev. ed. Washington, DC: National Academy Press, 1985.

O'Driscoll, C. *What Vets Don't Tell You About Vaccines.* Longor, England: Abbeywood Publishing (Vaccines) Ltd., 1998.

Ott, John N. *Health & Light: The Effects of Natural and Artificial Light on Man and Other Living Things.* Greenwich, CT:: CT. Devin-Adair Publishers, 1973.

Pitchford, P. *Healing with Whole Foods: Oriental Traditions and Modern Nutrition.* Berkeley, CA: North Atlantic Books, 1993.

Plechner, Alfred and Zucker, Martin. *Pet Allergies: Remedies for an Epidemic.* Inglewood,: CA.: Very Healthy Enterprises, 1986.

Schwartz, C., D.V.M. *Four Paws, Five Directions.* Berkeley, CA: Celestial Arts, 1996.

Tizard, Ian. "Risks Associated with the Use of Live Vaccines." *Journal of American Veterinary Medical Association*, 196, no. 11 (1990): 1851–1858.

Tizard, Ian. *Veterinary Immunology: An Introduction.* 4th ed. Philadelphia: W.B. Saunders Co., 1992, p. 498.

Volhard, Wendy and Brown, Kerry, D.V.M. *The Holistic Guide for a Healthy Dog.* 1st ed. New York: Howell Book House, 1995.

Werbach, Melvyn R. and Moss, Jeffrey. *Textbook of Nutritional Medicine.* Tarzana, CA: Third Line Press, Inc.,1999.

Williams, Sue Rodwell. *Nutrition Diet Therapy.* 6th ed. St. Louis: C.V. Mosby, 1989.

Index